I0340951

Don Garlits
The Enigmatic Hero

WARREN MILLS

COVENTRY PRESS

Published in Australia by
Coventry Press
www.coventrypress.com.au
33 Scoresby Road Bayswater VIC 3153

ISBN 9780648804420

© Warren Mills 2020

All rights reserved. Other than for the purposes and subject to the conditions prescribed under the *Copyright Act*, no part of this publication may be reproduced, stored in a retrieval system, or transmitted in any form or by any means, electronic, mechanical, photocopying, recording or otherwise, without the prior permission of the publisher.

Catalogue-in-Publication entry is available from the National Library of Australia
http://catologue.nla.gov.au

All efforts have been made by the publisher to credit images correctly. Please contact the publishers directly if you feel there is an incorrect crediting.

Printed in Australia by Brougham Press

Prologue		5
1	Beyond Thunderdome	11
2	Tampa, Florida	29
3	The Rat Gets the Cheese	49
4	Safety Fast	75
5	Top Fuel	91
6	Don Garlits Meets "Big Daddy"	117
7	The Making of Don Garlits' Strong Soul	129
8	Godspeed	143
9	Team Garlits	171
10	The Swamp Rat Dynasty	195
11	Persistence Wins	205
12	Alter Ego	219
13	The Final Chapter	241
Epilogue		261

Don Garlits. The Enigmatic Hero

Can a Drag Strip Hero Become a Hero of Faith?

Don Garlits is a motor racing champion of more than 60 years. From pioneer of the sport, to elder statesman "Big Daddy" of drag racing, he is idolized by millions of motorheads. One such hero-worshiping motorhead is Warren Mills, who, in this book entitled: *Don Garlits. The Enigmatic Hero,* asks the question: Can a secular hero also become a hero of faith?

The question of mixing sports with religion is vexed with paradox, if not contradiction. Garlits will unlikely fit your preconceived ideas of religion or spirituality. He is an enigmatic hero whose success is largely due to his Christian wife, Pat, whose encouragement and restraint enabled him to bridge the divide of the profane and Divine. Garlits is not the only contradiction in this story. There is another man who heroically merged the divide. Christian faith is about this God-become-man, friend of outcasts, Lord of the Cosmos who gave himself to save us, who cannot save ourselves.

And because life itself is a paradox, this story is overlaid with yet another enigmatic voice. We hear the timeless wisdom of King Solomon and The Teacher of Ecclesiastes who grapple with the same confusion of issues we face today.

With these three heroes in mind, the author tells Garlits' intriguing story, measuring the effect on his own life. And why? because he and maybe you, and many others, follow in the footsteps of unlikely heroes, inspired to combined faith with passion to become more human.

Acknowledgements

Thanks to the many who have encouraged and guided me, especially Sarah Raiter, Michael Murphy, Nicci Douglas, Paul Vander Klay, Eugene Kneebone, Larry O'Toole, David Wraight and Phil Munday.

To Elaine, my wife and best mate, for all we have done together.

Prologue

The Bitter Taste of Despair

Crushing, remorseless despair overwhelmed him. Garlits had experienced its bitter taste previously when the sport he loved dealt him a cruel hand. But nothing prepared him for this. In the instant that it takes for an explosion to wreak havoc, Garlits went from being the most successful professional dragster in the history of the sport, to facing life as a "cripple", or so he thought. His achievements flashed before him—the wins, the hard work, the money and fame. His successes were replaced with a new reality. The picture in his mind was now his wife Patricia. He had seen her tears before and that thought only compounded the grief.

Don Garlits had worked his way through the field. It was March, 1970, the Grand American Top Fuel Championship event at Long Beach, California. Full of confidence from a series of wins in major events, he was on his way to an end-of-season, Championship prize of $20,000 (with an advantage over his young rival in the next lane, Richard Tharp). Recent improvements with the M+H Racemaster slicks allowed the track to take a lot more power. This in turn enabled Garlits to develop an experimental two-speed transmission (exploiting the extra traction without over-speeding the engine). What he thought to be an advantage was, however, the cause of an horrendous, unprecedented accident. Minutes earlier, his crew was under pressure to get the long, black dragster to the starting line for the last run of the day. In haste, the transmission was not completely filled with oil. This omission was responsible for a massive over-speed of the planetary drum. Like a hand grenade tossed into the confines between Garlits' feet, it disintegrated.

Don Garlits. The Enigmatic Hero

1970 Lions Dragstrip transmission explosion, cutting the car in half at the start line (PHOTOGRAPHY BY STEVE REYES).

Garlits' first thought was confusion. He imagined he was running through the lights at 200 mph against Tharp, for the Top Eliminator prize. Where were the timing lights at the end of the drag strip? All he could see was blue sky, and all he could hear was silence. No noise, no speed, and no vibration. That is when the face of his crew chief, TC Lemons, unexpectedly appeared above him. Suddenly, the confusion cleared. "I'm hurt real bad, Tommy. Please help me. Get me out."

"Please Help Me, Tommy"

Lemons' face was soon joined by Larry Sutton, (who had started the race just seconds before), and Mickey Thompson, the drag strip promoter. "Mickey, I'm so... I'm so cold. I think I'm going into shock." While Mickey fumbled with the seat belts Don realised Thompson was trying to shield his gaze. With blood-stained goggles and helmet still in place Garlits could see that his right boot was ripped away. The grisly remainder was left hanging while the boot was pumping blood. No one could have guessed that the new transmission would cause such an explosion. In the time-honoured, hot-rod tradition of cut-and-try, there is no telling what can happen when the full force of a nitro-methane-burning, Chrysler Hemi engine is concentrated on the one, unknown, weak link. But now they knew. Not only had the quarter-inch-steel scattershield ruptured like a sardine tin, but the chassis was cut in two by the force of the explosion. The back half of the car, with Garlits still strapped in the protective cage, was facing skyward. Mercifully, the front half had come to rest a few feet further down the track. But the worst was not over. When he was finally extracted from the car and lifted into the ambulance, what remained of his foot was caught in the door when it slammed shut. Thankfully, only Garlits and a young spectator were injured. It could have been much worse.

"I Lied to Her"

When they arrived at the hospital Garlits, could only think to call Patricia. As he had done previously, when he was burned at Chester, South Carolina, he lied to her. "I think they're gonna be able to put everything back together okay. I'm hurt pretty bad... No, no burns... just my foot.... Yeah, it's gonna be okay... They're gonna save it." Doctor Larson, the specialist surgeon (that Mickey Thompson had flown in by helicopter) had already told Garlits that there was no possibility of saving his foot. But, if Garlits accepted, he could re-attach the hand of the young spectator, Tim Ditt, by taking him into surgery first. Don agreed just before the morphine was administered. The next morning Don awoke to find Pat beside him. He was overwhelmed with regret and compassion to see her. She was the one for whom he had given up drag racing. She was also the constant source of intuition and inspiration that encouraged her restless husband to return to the dangerous sport after only a few months of wedded bliss. Any thoughts of winning against Richard Tharp (who had also crashed but was not seriously injured), were distant. Any notions of dragster performance, competitive advantage, prize money, success and adulation of the crowds were dissipated by his pain and his new reality. Filled with sorrow, he could contemplate only the devastating handicap of having one foot—unable to work or to care for his wife and family. When he was previously burned, Garlits' first thought was that he was going to die. As long as the pain stopped he didn't care. He was conscious enough on that occasion to know that he was shielded from the worst of the fire by the new leather jacket that Pat had given him. She had stayed at home pregnant with their first child. He rang her before the drugs took effect. "I had to talk to her—to lie to her." Everything would be alright if she could just fly up to be with him for a few days while he recovered.

His Father's Harsh Discipline

Pat was his antidote. (Not that she was happy to be in this nursing role through yet another racing accident.) This was the hand she was dealt and she must play out. Pat would encourage her husband with the will to live, to recover from his injuries and to regain the energetic lust for life that she found so attractive. She had sublimated her anxiety toward his profession during Don's almost 15 years at the top of the sport. Now she must provide the resolve and strength that was usually Don's role. Pat hoped this time might have a different outcome. This time Don might abandon his fatal attraction to the fire-breathing, death-dealing monsters that Top Fuel dragsters had become. She visited him daily to pray for him, to comfort, encourage and reassure him—not to beg or demand, as she knew this would only work against her. From her reading of Scripture Pat would have known that a father's discipline may appear to be harsh, but it builds character and a strong soul. "Therefore, strengthen the hands that are weak and the knees that are feeble, and make straight paths for your feet, so that the limb which is lame may not be put out of joint, but rather be healed."[1] Whatever the source of her inspiration, it was Pat who had the resources that enabled Don to become an exemplar for millions of young men.

"Take Your Medicine, Mr Garlits"

Incredibly, Garlits immediately resolved to take no more painkillers. His previous experience of recovery from burns (after weeks of therapy and codeine treatment), had left him with one nightmare replacing another. Unable to sleep, he would lie awake at night staring at the ceiling. Eventually he would resort to walking the streets until he was exhausted, only to spend the day as a Zombie. To add insult to injury, Brock Yates, (a prominent journalist that Don trusted as a friend), mis-represented his condition, implying that Garlits had become a drug-addled wreck. So, to refuse opiates was a new measure of his resolve and determination. The nursing staff remained sceptical by refusing to change his bed-sheets, wet with perspiration. "Good night, Mr Garlits. Your medicine is there when you're ready to take it", was their parting gesture.

"Father, Help Me"

Predictably, on the third night of his hospitalisation in Long Beach, the pain became unbearable. But the resolve remained. In his anguish, and having exhausted all other options Garlits played

---

[1] Hebrews 12:12-13.

his one remaining card. He called out to the God of his youth and of his wife. "Father, help me!" The response was immediate. Garlits recalls a sense of the very presence of God entering his room. The pain left him never to return (except for when Dr Larson removed the stainless-steel staples with Dykes pliers). His rehabilitation was momentarily delayed only when it was discovered that his left leg was also broken in five places. Don Garlits, the tough, drag-racing competitor, discovered what it took the wise King of Israel a lifetime to discover. *We need to make our souls accountable to the one who made us.* When we do that, we can progress on the journey of life with renewed purpose, less susceptible to despair, and with hope to overcome the many obstacles along the way—whether a King of Israel, or a King of the dragsters.

A New Beginning

As the record of his life shows, this episode was not the end of Don Garlits' career. Less well-known is Garlits' new beginning. In this season God played a more prominent role, and to him a tribute was emblazoned on Garlits' dragster. Whether he knew it or not, Garlits was being prepared by his Father for life as a tough competitor with a strong soul in the gritty sport of drag racing, not because God loves cars, but because God loves people, who love cars. This commenced a period of innovation in the sport when speed, popularity and safety improved as never before, and this, largely attributed to what Big Daddy, Don Garlits, learned during his "dark night of the soul".

Chapter 1 Beyond Thunderdome

"There is a time for everything, and a season for every activity under the heavens."
– Eccles 3:1

Don Garlits' "Rat Roast"

Three hundred guests are elbowing into a boisterous, hotel ballroom on a balmy, February evening. It is Pomona, California, 2012. The event, known as the "Rat Roast", is to recognize the life of a living legend and an American nation builder. A buxom blonde is crooning a Marilyn Monroe-esque "Happy birthday to you...", because friends, competitors and those who may have been enemies are here to celebrate his 80th birthday. The hero? Champion drag racer, Don Garlits. Journalist David Freiburger, of *Hot Rod* magazine sums up the man of the night: "Don Garlits is the 'Big Daddy' of drag racing, not just for his accomplishments in the sport, but because at 80 years of age, he still enjoys the respect of everyone who knows him, for his accomplishments and role as the spokesman for the sport, and for his human decency".

Among the "roasters", who need little encouragement from MC Bob Frey, is the pantheon of drag racers, suppliers, engineers, commentators, officials and others who helped create the sport. They include retired racers Don "The Snake" Prudhomme, "TV" Tommy Ivo, Jerry "The King" Ruth, "Fast Jack" Beckman, and contemporary Funny Car Champion, John Force. Suppliers include nonagenarian, camshaft grinder Ed "Isky" Iskenderian, engineers

Don Garlits. The Enigmatic Hero

Ed Pink and Sid Waterman, artist Kenny Youngblood, veteran broadcaster and announcer, Dave McClelland. And drag racing, beauty queen Linda Vaughn, (as much a sensation at the roast as she was at the races), is the charmer singing happy birthday to the star of the show. The speeches, enjoyment and emotions of the night are summed up by McClelland when he poignantly demonstrates his love for Garlits with a kiss to the forehead.

Although Garlits has been much lauded, this event is perhaps the highest honor ever bestowed upon the motor racing champion, whose list of awards over almost 40 years, read like what you might expect of a war hero who performed some memorable deed every day he got out of bed. But to say these things of a drag racer is unprecedented. Perhaps it could be expected of a revered figure like Enzo Ferrari, whose scarlet cars greatly impacted the post-war resurgence of motor racing in Europe and its relationship to the rebuilding of the war-torn continent. Or perhaps multiple World Champion Formula 1 racer, Manuel Fangio, who came from Argentina as a humble, amateur driver/mechanic to dominate the best Europe had to offer. Perhaps even the driver/constructer/engineer from Australia, Jack Brabham, who also beat Europe's best, in self-built, Formula 1 cars. It is likely that an all-American, Indy star like AJ Foyt, or NASCAR legend Richard Petty or an all-rounder like Dan Gurney might be celebrated in this way. But a hot-rodder from Florida? Could this man be so dominating and good at his craft to be considered Big Daddy, the greatest racer of all?

Who is the Greatest Racer Ever?

Drag racing is the purest form of motor sport, according to British motor racing journalist Simon Taylor. In an interview with John Force, multiple Funny Car champion Taylor, elucidates the sport to be awesome, frightening, and an exciting contest of car against car and driver against driver.[2] Recognizing Simon Taylor's high estimation of drag racing and the years of Garlits' competition at its top level (including the number of championships and major events won, his speed and safety innovations, and the records set as a designer, constructor, driver and elder statesman of the sport), Don Garlits is indeed accepted to be drag racing's (and therefore one of motor racing's) greatest competitors. But what has "human decency" got to do with being a champion in the selfish sport of motor racing?

"Don Garbage"

Labelling Garlits "decent" is unlikely. Not only was he a shade-tree car designer, engineer, mechanic and driver. The social status of drag racing was regarded as just a step above criminal intent—performed illicitly on city streets where innocent lives were at risk. This man was not only a clandestine street racer, he came from the backwaters of Florida running a car made from junk. His origins earned him the title "Swamp Rat", which, true to his nature, he wore as a badge of honor by painting it on the side of his dragster. But Don "Garbage", or "Tampa Dan", as he was first named by his detractors, commenced a transformation when, in 1962, drag-race announcer, Bernie Partridge or 'Dave McClelland, (who gave Garlits the name "Big Daddy"). Initially, this was just spruiker's banter, but the title followed him throughout the rest of his career when he became Big Daddy not just in name, but also in nature.

Don Garlits' story is worth telling for its rich insights: making sense of life's contradictions when living at full throttle and the great satisfaction of doing that well. Garlits' name is known by millions from his era, but many of his fans have no idea of his life

---

[2] "Lunch with John Force", *Motor Sport* Magazine, Volume 90, Number 6.

story because it is obscured by celebrity and sporting accomplishments. Indeed, even some of his friends may not have unpacked the complexity of this man to see the simplicity of his impactful story. Don's transformation from a hotrodder into a strong soul who has experienced an "abundant" life, has potential to inspire and encouraged many to consider new ways of thinking, doing and achieving.

"Links in a Supernatural Chain"

This is not your usual tale of *poor boy makes good* or *champion achieves career goals*. Rather, it is a journey of discovery; a journey of unexpected dimensions and relationships; the persistent seeking of an elusive goal while dealing with hardship and the vagaries of life. These discoveries are made despite, or perhaps because of, imperfections of the human soul—imperfections perhaps unknown or unknowable even to the possessor except by insights of unexpected revelation. Referring to his experiences of discovery Don Garlits calls these, "links in a supernatural chain". One makes sense of these links through an external source of goodness.

Garlits is an unusual man of many facets whose actions speak louder than the basso profundo of his Swamp Rat dragster. Certainly, he is an inspiring model to the few who know his story. Somehow, he managed to achieve the unlikely transformation from the illicit pastime of street racing into the ultra-competitive sport of professional drag racing. This vocation, in turn, became a life of faith in God and according to Garlits, a Divine calling. To accomplish this transformation Garlits combined his many instinctive drives for hard work, frugal, self-reliance and unrelenting competitiveness. Compounding these qualities were courage, fear, loneliness, desperate survival, clever innovation, dogged persistence, passionate love, simple faith and lasting hope. He drew inspiration from an equally-diverse range of sources amongst whom were his father, mother, step-father, wife, daughters, Jesus of Nazareth, extra-terrestrials, Albert Einstein, Richard Nixon and Star Trek.

Three-dimensional Lives

I am attracted to the idea that our lives are a rich tapestry: full of color, useful purpose and different materials, made at different times and influenced by different people. But this image lacks depth because a tapestry is essentially flat. It is designed to be seen only in two dimensions. What I love more is the idea of a three-dimensional tapestry—a thick brocade with qualities that look like tapestry if viewed superficially, but with layers of interwoven threads that add strength and quality—visible only by careful study. Understanding what brocade is, we can scrutinize its intricacy and appreciate its overwhelming complexity. We can stand back to take in its full beauty and meaning, knowing there is always more than what meets the eye. This picture of life should come as no surprise, as it has been recorded in the Hebrew Bible. Human life is made in the image of The Divine—body, soul and spirit.

We Become What We Desire Most

Don Garlits is unique. While his identity and attributes were on display to his fans and his detractors, with a touch of irony he managed to turn his apparent weaknesses into strengths. The name "Swamp Rat" was not just a car. It characterized the legend of the man and his accomplishments. Don Garlits is an ordinary man who created an extraordinary life as he became, what I consider to be, a strong soul. Not perfect, but one, like a rich tapestry, that we can properly admire and emulate within certain limits. As

Garlits proves, where we begin in life or success at achieving our goals, is not ultimately important. The test is how we progress toward a goal worth pursuing.

What was it that Garlits achieved? How did he do it? Can it be sifted and proved? Can we emulate it?

I propose that by understanding what Garlits means when he refers to "links in a supernatural chain", by hearing his story and the story of others on the same journey, we can share and celebrate the good life of a "thoroughly decent man".

We imagine what we desire; we will what we imagine; and at last we create what we will. – George Bernard Shaw

The Irony of Real Success

The irony of Christian faith is that progress is never measured by the sacrifices that we make or what we have to give. Christian character is never determined by how important, religious, wealthy, clever or successful we are. On the contrary, these characteristics may make progress less likely and more difficult. Progress along the supernatural chain that Garlits speaks of, is always and exclusively about how much we are willing to receive. To realize our weakness by following Jesus, is to enable us to add link to link. Admission price to the Kingdom of God is, ironically, to admit that we cannot meet the cost ourselves. It is an upside-down kingdom where the highest honor is to serve others, where the meek inherit the earth, where the poor in spirit are those who will see God. Becoming a strong soul is a journey that begins and ends with admission of need. This is the encounter that set in motion the transformation of Don Garlits, and many millions of men and women who have realized that God's love is made available to them. It was this mystery that Garlits depicted on his dragster for the world to see and make sense of as best they could.

Beyond Thunderdome

In the upside-down kingdom, God's Speed usually means going slower to appreciate the scenery and to get more from the ride than we may have done otherwise. It means that relationships are more important than achievements, that peace is more important than progress and shared joy is the greatest form of pleasure. – *Hot Rod Theology*

God is Love

There are untold aspects to the symbolic cross and the catch phrase, "God is love". In their expansiveness they can leave us lost for words or resigned to unconscious complacency. What God's love accomplished in Christ's sacrifice is most richly expressed through stories—stories of millions who have believed and experienced these words to be true. The upside-down kingdom is entirely relational: between God and us, us and our neighbors, even us and ourselves. Its purpose is to get us up to speed, to slow down, and to live the best life possible. God's purpose for us is the transformation of our souls so that we may enjoy Him and He enjoy a relationship with us.

We become radically transformed by replacing the old ideas and images that we love with new ones. We are made to be like the God we don't know, by becoming like Jesus, who we do know. – Dallas Willard

We Need Heroes

People need heroes. Role models teach us how to be human. They show us how to behave so we can live satisfying and fulfilling lives with each other. As infants we have heroes with whom we build nurturing relationships, heroes whom we mimic. As we become fully-fledged, we act on our own initiatives and become our own agents, at least, so we think. Our first heroes are circumstantial, built into our lives by circumstances. As we gain independence we express freedom to choose by finding new heroes (for reasons that initially we often do not understand). Regardless of how we acquire them our heroes either benefit us or harm us. Ideally, heroes guide us toward a workable picture of life—not just how to relate to each other, but to the world of ideas, beliefs, habits and opportunities. As we gain knowledge and skills, we gain agency and become creative in our own right.

Did you know that birds learn their song from the flock? Birds formed away from the flock cannot sing. Similarly, we learn from other people. This analogy applies to capabilities such as speech and specialist survival skills. In addition, during our formation we learn about art, beauty and the experience and meaning of love, again, likely without yet understanding them. If we are blessed with good parents and families who loved us before we were born, we intuitively return love. Without it being explained we return love verbally, by touch, expression, tone of voice and emotion. As we grow, our heroes include siblings, cousins, school friends, neighbors and communities. Books and media guide us into further possibilities. Then we become learners in our own right. We seek out our own sources of information, we form our own priorities and visions of possibility.

Initially what we learn is mimicry: monkey see, monkey do. For instance, we duplicate sounds that become words, with their accompanying nuances of expression and emotion. Only after we have learned how to move and feel, long after we learn how to think, do words fill in the gaps of meaning. Even during teenage years much of what we learn is not conscious. If, however, as children we have been dealt a poor set of cards or if we have chosen our heroes badly, then we will most likely mimic attitudes and behaviours that are harmful and not life-enhancing.

Beyond Thunderdome

You may well ask why anyone would be interested in mimicking a Don-Garlits-like hero from another era? In this day of instant access to almost anything, anyone, anywhere, why care about heroes from the past? Whether we acknowledge our need for heroes or not, I believe they are more important now than ever. Overwhelmed by the volume of information available we must constantly choose what we think is beneficial as against what is not. If we were fortunate to have been nurtured at our mother's breast we are indelibly familiar with being simultaneously fed and loved, which will hopefully continue throughout childhood. This, again, is not an intellectual experience so much as an emotional one that, for most people, becomes the measure of all other relationships. Ours is an era when certainties of loving relationships (that teach us the need for personal responsibility and accountability) are being replaced with the politics of identity. These are times when who I am is about belonging to an advantaged or a disadvantaged group (that should either be brought down or lifted up to achieve justice and social equity).

If the present change of emphasis toward social justice is truly life-giving then there will be some social evidence to prove its advantages. Despite the rhetoric of progress, evidence is that the quality of life and social cohesion in particular, are going in the opposite direction. Alienation from friends and family leads to homelessness and purposelessness, these lead to drug and alcohol abuse, which feed despair and suicide. These are indicators not found in cultures that exist in ignorance or poverty. They exist in cultures that are wealthy beyond the imagination of previous generations. It seems that the wealthier and better-informed we become, the more nihilistic and despairing we are. Personal responsibility is slowly being replaced with personal rights that express themselves in abortion, assisted suicide and the assertion of my rights against yours. Tragically, with our loss of responsibility we are losing a sense of gratitude, humility, optimism and

Don Garlits. The Enigmatic Hero

dignity, leaving us with hopelessness and pessimism. Heroes to the rescue.

Heroes are now called different things. Certainly, some are still sports stars (but they are contemporary, not from the past). They may be called influencers, thought leaders, innovators, progressives (or transgressives). Some are coaches, mentors or role models. Usually, they will have a high public profile and be fashionably "cool," especially in entertainment or media, like the Kardashians. They may be business heroes like Jeff Bezos of Amazon, leading the online shopping revolution; or activist political leaders such as Greta Thunberg, influencing millions of young people against climate change and "complacent patriarchy". Almost universally, these new heroes will have a presence on social media where their followers are numbered in the millions. Are the heroes of this age life-enhancing? Will their ideas work to reshape the world for the good of generations to come? Will they be remembered for the good that they did? Even if they do influence millions, will their ideas provide benefits that outlast their popularity? Will they even be a blip on the time-line of history?

Beyond Thunderdome

Looking for something
We can rely on
There's got to be something better out there

Love and compassion
Their day is coming
All else are castles built in the air

And I wonder when we are ever gonna change it
Living under the fear 'til nothing else remains

All the children say

Beyond Thunderdome

We don't need another hero
We don't need to know the way home
All we want is life beyond the Thunderdome
"All we want is life beyond the Thunderdome"[3]

Is there something out there better than love and compassion? I think the evidence is that there is not. If so, then it is true that we do not need another (new) hero. Perhaps we do need to return to past heroes whom we may have rejected as having nothing to offer.

Mixing the Sacred with the Profane

Mixing sacred and profane jars our senses. It suggests that incompatible things such as oil and water can be joined. (Ironically, they can be mixed but only as Don Garlits did, using an emulsifier to create a colloid of the normally incompatible substances.) Drag racing celebrates such contradictions. It harnesses raw power to achieve a safe mix of speed and risk. Garlits adds further dimensions of contradiction as he personally goes bravely, where angels fear to tread, both literally and metaphorically.

Don Garlits is an enigmatic man—*mysterious and impossible to completely understand*. Widely known as a tough guy, hard scrabble, hard-working pioneer; a fierce, un-relenting competitor; a bad loser with an explosive temper; a multiple-championship-winning racer; also, a designer and innovator. Not many know how his life is further embellished by his contradictions as: a passionate friend, an unrelenting competitor, a thinker and a dreamer, a fighter, patriot, and a political activist. Sometimes he is a man of prayer and of deep Christian faith. He is also a believer in

---

[3] Graham Hamilton Lyle, Terry Britten, (Warner Chappell Music, Inc.), BMG Rights Management.

extra-terrestrial aliens, a gun enthusiast, and an extraordinary husband, father, grandfather and great-grandfather. Sometimes he is shockingly-irreligious and profane. His incredible focus, courage and persistence have been proved by a willingness to suffer the extremes of pain and despair for what he believes to be true.

Garlits' status as a leader, plus the complexity of his character, have enabled him to become Big Daddy. Many see him as a leading actor in the drama of human history and hero to successive generations of motorheads across the globe. As the tough-guy aviator Chuck Yeager represents the "right stuff" image of the jet age, so Don Garlits is the right stuff of the mechanical age of cars. The age of machines is rapidly being overtaken by the digital era, where machines merge with computers—mind boggling to us who belong to a time past. But heroes like Don Garlits live on.

We Get the Heroes We Deserve

It is one thing that Garlits has been celebrated as an inaugural member of his own country's Motorsports Hall of Fame of America (whose mission is to "further the American core values of leadership, creativity, originality, teamwork and spirit of competition embodied in motorsports"). It is another thing altogether, to be similarly recognized in Great Britain, the nation that gave us the industrial revolution. (This honor was first granted when Garlits was invited to visit the UK in 1964 to demonstrate drag racing with countrymen Tommy Ivo and Dante Duce—a visit considered instrumental in bringing drag racing to Britain.)

Our dependence on heroes dispels the notion that individually we have all the resources required for a satisfying life. To realize our potential each of us must reach beyond ourselves for inspiration and power whether it is to ancestors, the dark forces of fear, a religious creed, science, or the political power of the state. It may be in the might of an army or in wealth. Whatever the source, each of us reaches out to a greater power to escape the limits of our ignorance and fear. Often this power will be a mere mortal whom we venerate, like Don Garlits. Ideally it will be beyond that—the perfect man to whom Don Garlits reached. The art for us is to distinguish between heroes who are human like us, and those who are transcendent. Because it is true that we become like the object of our worship.

Idolatry

My Don Garlits story is a cautionary tale, a warning to myself to be wary of idolatry from which we all suffer to some degree. Idolatry is where we fixate on the part, not the whole. Where we put all our eggs in one basket with our hopes focussed disproportionately on one picture of reality, choosing an immediate bowl of meal rather than a sumptuous feast if we wait. This is a crisis of faith because our vision of possibilities is not big enough, especially where God's promises to us are involved. We do this when we idolize Don Garlits or Ayrton Senna, without seeing them for what they really are; the idealization of our desires. Despite incredible abilities and achievements, they remain imperfect beings, unworthy of our worship. However, when we properly understand their strengths and weaknesses, the experience of ordinary hero "worship" can help lead us to the one who alone is worthy of our adoration.

The Myth of Self-sufficiency

Mysteriously, we each choose to take a path in life that we don't fully understand, which by the way, is the definition of faith. As consistent patterns emerge over a lifetime, we recognize the formative forces of desire and destiny. These forces (our emotions, imaginations, senses and intellects) are a combination of primal instincts and consciousness. They enable us to perceive the world around us and choose our path. Consciously or unconsciously we adopt patterns—archetypes—as our own. In the worst case, we create gods in our own image who are mere mortals like us. When our attachment to the stories of heroes is well explained, as I will attempt to do throughout this book, we begin to see ourselves as storytellers writing our own narratives (with a beginning, a middle and an end) into which we cast ourselves in the lead role. As our story begins we are consciously or unconsciously working our way toward an imagined goal, inspired by an idealized vision, usually embodied in a person.

Stories of heroes are re-told throughout history in great literature, myths and religions of ages past. Even today, in addition to sporting heroes we still have Superman, Batman and the Joker as heroes—archetypes of good and evil, not just for children. Ancient Greeks had pantheons of badly-behaved gods, complimented by true heroes such as Alexander the Great, who dominated enemies to become figures of adulation. While some of these heroes are historic, some are figments of imagination representing what we hope to be true. Hero worship is a well-known phenomenon necessary as a source of vitality and meaning for human life. Both our real or imagined heroes signify the way we think about ourselves and our place in the cosmos. As we hope and dream, such insights can be used to our advantage and our stories becomes interwoven with theirs.

While we behave as if we are ultimate masters of our own destinies in this enlightened age, we are not. Many of us exist in the fog of delusion, accepting the unquestioned beliefs and conventional wisdom of our era as the real thing, to the exclusion of other narratives or points of view. However, the common knowledge of the era, (the *zeitgeist*) in which we are born, changes with time.

Beyond Thunderdome

For better or worse, sages of the day interpret it for us.[4] Enduring against the odds and proven by time, we have heroes like Moses, Isaiah, Solomon and Jesus. More recently Shakespeare, Tolstoy, CS Lewis, Tolkien and JK Rowling who tell stories and interpret the meta-narrative. Insights we gain by their tales are merely words until processed through our imaginations and tested in the reality of our own lives, as CS Lewis suggests they must be. With some help, ultimately it is for us to discover our own story. That is the purpose of this book.

For more than six generations, the world over, Don Garlits has inspired motorsport enthusiasts to follow him into an automotive career, perhaps as a mechanic, a car designer, a builder or a race car driver. How do I know this to be true? I am one of them. I was introduced to Garlits and the California hot-rod craze as a 12-year-old, when, with my vacation pocket money I purchased a *Hot Rod* magazine. But I am not alone in my hero worship. Since then, I have spoken to others across the globe who, influenced by Garlits' many feats, seek to emulate him. Men like multiple African American Top Fuel world champion, Antron Brown. His followers recognize him as a pioneer who began with nothing other than raw talent and opportunity; a self-starter with the chance to innovate and set records over a long career. Garlits' appeal to me and so many others is that we can imagine ourselves doing at least part of what he did. His is such a powerful source of motivation, all the more clearly seen with the benefit of hindsight. We relate to the legend because he was an underdog who became "world's greatest...". He has helped me and many others to find our place in the enlightened industrialized world of my era.

---

[4] Such as the neo-atheists of today, led by Richard Dawkins, who claim that our cosmos is the blind, purposeless result of nature and time. Against such despair we have the prophets, the seers and sages of history, some of whom have proven to be false.

Don Garlits. The Enigmatic Hero

The mills of time grind slow, but they grind especially fine. – Helen Garlits

Unlikely Theologian

My purpose in writing is not just to produce another sports star biography. Rather, it is to better understand myself and help others like me to discover why people like Garlits have so much power to influence. In so doing, I want to explore whether my hero-worship robs me of my potential or does the opposite. Is it life-giving or life-denying? Is it creative or destructive? Does the hero give us life beyond a dystopian Thunderdome or are we seduced by one who has also been seduced by a lie—the blind leading the blind into an abyss? I believe that it is in the pursuit of the mundane and natural that we begin to see a transcendent, higher purpose.

When I began to write this book about seven years ago, I visited Garlits at his museum in Ocala, Florida to interview him. To my surprise, as I will later explain, it was an enlightening experience confirming the truism that we should never meet our heroes. Meanwhile, I wrote another book: *How Good is the Golden Rule? Learning the Language of Love.*[5]

It has taken until 2020, to realize that this present book is about the universal archetype of heroes, as seen through my experience, with Garlits as my exemplar. I am an ordinary man of my era: husband, father and grandfather, mechanic, engineer, teacher, consultant to the automotive industry; a bloke who loves life and cars, and loves God. Initially, it was Garlits' Swamp Rat dragster image that drew me to him. Later, it was the conjunction of cars and God that reactivated my interest. As I now have the luxury of reflecting

---

[5] Freedom Publishing Books. Recently revised and retitled as *The Golden Rule. A Panacea for every Pandemic.*

on my life, that convergence and contradiction has remained with me, which begs the question of relevance that I hope this book will answer.

I have had a very satisfying life that I am seeking to understand and explain both in the practical and religious sense. I share my experience with you because I would like you to have an alternative to the common narrative, that life is a meaningless puzzle resulting in death and then...nothing. I hope to convince you that life itself is a source of high adventure and satisfaction. Despite the difficulties that we each encounter, success is to discover that we are made for a Divine purpose. We are not intended to be clones or robots, but to find a place in a purposeful cosmos, as sons and daughters of The Most High God. We are invited into his family to become fully-fledged partners in the business of fulfilling God's own creative purposes.

Why We Need Heroes

Hero worship begs deeper questions relating to human agency. And, although this book does not pretend to be high philosophy I do make claims about human motivation that are more than just my own. In the pure sense, "human agency" is defined as *the freedom or ability to act according to your own will.*[6] While it is possible to have free will, we are influenced by the times in which we live, our country of birth, our parents, friends, education, religion and many other sources. So, can we be confident that we are not just puppets responding to someone else pulling our strings? There has been on-going discussion about agency ever since the Enlightenment paved the way for our modern, industrialized, technological world. John Locke was an English philosopher and physician, widely regarded as one of the most influential of Enlightenment

---

[6] Wikipedia.

thinkers, and commonly known as "the Father of Liberalism," who maintained that freedom is based on self-interest, to which I agree. This is the beginning of a process implied by the teaching of Jesus and Paul. Philosophers Immanuel Kant, Friedrich Nietzsche and Sigmund Freud, among other teachers and thinkers, have further shaped how most people in western democracies consciously or unconsciously think and act today.

My point is, because of the complexity of modern society and the way that conventional wisdom infiltrates the common mind, we do not fully understand our motivations. While these many influences are real enough, I believe that none of them ultimately determines what I must believe for myself. This, to me, is the basis of real freedom. Even if you put a gun to my head I can still choose what I want to believe to be true, and therefore my own beliefs and behaviors that shape what I think, say and do. This explains why, in essence, I have chosen like Don Garlits, to paint a cross on my life, with the words, *God is Love*. I attribute my success and survival to my choice of the hero that Don Garlits also chose.

Chapter 2 Tampa, Florida

> "Surely the fate of human beings is like that of the animals; the same fate awaits them both: As one dies, so dies the other. All have the same breath; humans have no advantage over animals. Everything is meaningless."
> – Eccles 3:19

The Ford V8

The birth in 1932, of both the Ford V8 car (known as a deuce) in Detroit, Michigan, and Don Garlits in Tampa, Florida, determined that this would be a significant year in automotive history.

Just a little deuce coupe with a flat head mill
But she'll walk a Thunderbird like (she's) standin' still
She's ported and relieved and she's stroked and bored.
She'll do a hundred and forty with the top end floored.
She's my little deuce coupe
You don't know what I got
(My little deuce coupe)
(You don't know what I got)
– "Little Deuce Coupe"[7]

---

[7] 1963.

Don Garlits. The Enigmatic Hero

If You can Make it in California, You can Make it Anywhere

When Brian Wilson, the creative genius of the Beach Boys wrote the song "Little Deuce Coupe", he displayed an artist's insight into the impending global impact of the nascent, hot-rod culture and Southern Californian influences more generally. In his 1982 book *Megatrends*, John Naisbitt predicted that California would become one of the bellwether states for major trends in the future of the United States. The Golden State is the birth-place of an amazing array of social trends that have shaped the modern world. This phenomenon is not limited just to movies and popular culture. Consider such current trends as lifestyle, fashion, entertainment, celebrity, sexual behaviour, bio-technology, information technology and dot-com. For automotive design there are North American, Japanese, European, Korean, and German design studios in California. Much of the Western world compliments Californians by mimicking them, the results being massive change to economies, politics, affluence, lifestyles, and perhaps even decadence. Many of these influences are to do with the dismantling of traditional hierarchies, the rise of individualism, access to information and the democratisation of what were previously, inaccessible bastions of privilege located elsewhere. Curiously, among the major social trends that have changed lifestyles, is a style of modern, Christian religion that also had its inauguration in California. In 1906, a one-eyed, African-American preacher, William J Seymour, ignited a do-it-yourself movement in Azusa Street, LA. This became the Pentecostal/charismatic renewal that has globally changed the face of Christian faith to become more expressive and participatory, more democratic and spiritually-motivated.

Of more universal appeal is the result of Fred Terman's work in his role as dean of Stanford University's Engineering Department. During the1930s, Terman was tutor and mentor to William Hewlett and David Packard, who created Hewlett Packard, one of the first stakes in the ground at Silicon Valley. This phenomenon has generated far greater wealth and benefit to humanity than the first Californian gold rush could have ever hoped. Hewlett and Packard risked all to achieve a gold-rush dream, making products initially coveted by Walt Disney, then Hollywood, then global businesses and now all mankind.[8]

Tampa, Florida

In 1950, the Californian influence had spread east to Florida, where 18-year-old Don Garlits was imbibing the heady mix of color, fumes and speed in the darkened streets of Tampa. His eyes feasted on Grady Pickel's, bright red, 1938 Ford convertible hot rod. This message of automotive anarchy was conveyed by Robert Petersen. (Peterson was to become the LA-based, mega-entrepreneur publisher of *Hot Rod*, the world's, largest circulation, automotive magazine that led the movement and spread the message to the world).

She's got a competition clutch with the four on the floor
And she purrs like a kitten till the lake pipes roar
And if that ain't enough to make you flip your lid
There's one more thing, I got the pink slip, daddy

And comin' off the line when the light turns green
Well she blows 'em outta the water like you never seen
I get pushed out of shape and it's hard to steer
When I get rubber in all four gears
She's my little deuce coupe. You don't know what I got

Hot-Rod Prophets

Hot rodding is a phenomenon of the age when mechanization became accessible to the common man. In pursuit of excitement

---

[8] "Life in the Smart Lane", *Qantas Magazine*, November 2013.

and visual impact he could achieve a dream formed in Hollywood, but realized in his own back yard. Propelled by visions of "Kookie" Ed Burns driving a hot rod (in episodes of the 1950s TV show, *77 Sunset Strip*) or by hot rod outlaws (in *Highway Patrol*, starring Broderick Crawford), hot rodding evolved to become an obsession for the generation who shaped the modern world. While many hotrodders went on to take regular jobs, some in the automotive industry retained their first love. Others started all-consuming careers in aerospace or business, leaving hot rods far behind. Brilliant engineers like Ed Winfield or Clay Smith and equally-brilliant marketers such as George Hurst or Ed Iskenderian, became the innovators and the names behind companies spawned in the 50s and 60s—companies still flourishing today. A few, like Mickey Thompson and Robert Petersen, created huge enterprises and fortunes from hot rodding while enabling a generation to have-a-go at creating their own high-performance machinery from old car parts. Millions of young men grew up reading the world's, most-read car magazine, *Hot Rod*. A small number raced professionally, while a few, some scratching to exist from one race to the next, ended their lives tragically in terrible drag-strip accidents. A tiny number, like Garlits, became enduring champions and outstanding examples of human drive, inventiveness and pure survival.

The genius of democracy is that it gives people freedom to choose not only their political ideals and representatives, but also other passions and perhaps even less-noble pursuits. It is the truly free nations that have spawned free expression to pursue passions that have motivated incredible creativity, productivity, passion and enterprise. This free expression oils the wheels of free enterprise and prosperity and perpetuates freedom in its most pure form. (This partly explains why, until very recently, democracy, capitalism and hot rods were not found in the Eastern Block or China.)

Tampa, Florida

Drag racing may not be listed among the most professional, prestigious, career goals, but increasingly, some so-called "high callings" have been debased by unimaginable scandals. In fact, the extent to which some fall is proportional to the unreasonably-high expectations that we put on them. Politicians, bankers, priests and ministers of religion, even sports champions, are among those who have brought themselves and their profession into disgrace by turning out to be human, and just as subject to frailty as we know ourselves to be. We may well be restrained in our judgement of those who have fallen, because we recognize in ourselves the tendency to judge those whose behavior reminds us of our own, often well-disguised shortcomings. But it is disappointing when our illusions of greatness become disillusions. What does take us by surprise, though, is when the opposite happens. When someone whom we thought was not up to much, perhaps a person in a lowly janitor's job, turns out to be a saint or a hero. Or, when someone who has personally failed us becomes one that we look up to as an example of true greatness. An example of this on a grand scale is the emergence of Australia as a successful, modern nation and an attractive place to live, when only 200 years ago the only way most people would go there was in chains at the King's pleasure. Certainly, the discovery of gold in the 1850s helped this transformation, but there were other forces at work that transformed criminals into pioneers of democracy and freedom.

Deep Roots in Dry Ground

Don Garlits grew up knowing hard times. In 1927, his parents, Edward and Helen Garlits, as wealthy newly-weds, and in the light of Edward's health problems, moved south from New Jersey to Tampa, Florida to try their hand at farming. Unfortunately, their new venture was not a success as bank failure during the depression emptied their savings. Then followed a demand from the Department of Agriculture to destroy their orange groves due to fruit-fly infestation, with no recompense. This double jeopardy sent the family into retreat from their large mansion to a tool shed with a dirt floor on a small, "truck" farming property outside Tampa. Following a period of great upheaval and unhappiness, Helen divorced Edward when he was arrested for violence against her and his harsh discipline of ten-year-old Donald. Edward Garlits was an interesting personality. He was an energetic, creative engineer who participated in the development of the electric fan and electric iron for the Westinghouse Company. But his real interests were more esoteric: long-haired, tee-totalling free-thinker, atheist, nudist, and advocate of alternative medicine. He ran a health food store and restaurant. At age 38 he left his first wife and three children to elope with Helen Lorenz, a 16-year-old who worked in his store. As non-conformists often do, Edward attracted the ire of authority and was run out of the state by a judge who believed that Edward's nutritional advice constituted practising medicine without a licence. Edward later opened an engineering and welding shop in Tampa. He died in 1966 after a long illness, the result of a drunk driver ploughing into his car. Don and his younger brother Ed learned their appreciation for machinery as they watched their father maintain his farm vehicles. He allowed the boys to attempt fruitless repairs on a discarded T Model Ford truck or to repair friends' bicycles for pocket money. Don maintained contact with his taciturn dad from whom, Don recognises, he learned the "tough discipline of workmanship".

Don had deep affection for his hard-working mother Helen. She was pulled out of the eighth grade to care for her younger siblings when her mother died. Garlits said of her, "She was a working mom before there were working moms, picking strawberries for one penny a quart to supplement the family income". Following her divorce from Edward, Helen married Alex Weir and moved to Lowry Park in Tampa, where they bought a small dairy farm running about 50 cows. "Mom raised calves and washed bottles for the milk delivery route. Ed and I were paid $10 a week to milk the cows." Don claimed he was haunted by cow-milking nightmares. Helen later became known as the "Orchid Lady" for having founded the Tampa Bay Orchid Society, and was listed in the National Orchid Register for her accomplishments in the intensely-demanding art of creating hybrid orchids. The hard life was salutary to Don and Ed. Joined at the hip, they shared farm duties using the disciplines and skills learned from their parents. An early-learner who could read and write before he started school, Don was a sombre, restless spirit and, with his brother, richly enjoyed and benefited from the farm experiences. Garlits says of his teenage years that he was no "philosopher struggling with angst from the devastation of war". Rather, he was a young man responding to the excitement of emerging adulthood. He left school, got a job, joined the National Guard, became mobile, discovered girls and pitted himself against the world of opportunity with an all-American, can-do attitude and a chip on his shoulder.

Hot Rod Dreams

Don and the Ford V8 engine shared a birth year and an emerging destiny. As a 17-year-old, with help from stepfather Alex, Don bought his first Ford, a 1940 V8 sedan. His inspiration was his high-school, metalwork teacher and closet hotrodder, Howard Fowler, who used hot rod magazines from California as his textbooks. This "school lesson" was a revelation. To his enchanted students Mr Fowler demonstrated modifying cars to increase their performance and resemble the enviable, Californian style. Suddenly Don's passions were fully engaged: independence; freedom of travelling with increased power and speed; imagining where, with whom, how far, and how fast he could go. Upon graduation from high school, with no clear career goals, Garlits, at his mother's behest, took a respectable, bookkeeping job with the Tampa-based, Maas Brothers Department Store. But when Alex noticed the onset of depression resulting from Don's new vocation, he wisely suggested that a job making better use of Don's mechanical inclination would be a remedy. Alex had a brother who successfully operated a small, body-repair shop. Thinking that automotive repair skills may be useful to fulfil his hot-rod dreams, Don readily agreed to this temporary job at lesser wages. There was another unanticipated cost. His then-fiancé, Virginia Gunther, dumped him when she saw he had few prospects, as, not only did he take a smaller wage, he was also working as a "grease monkey". (No doubt, Virginia reflected upon this decision when they met again at their high-school anniversary 50 years later.) This temporary job soon evolved into the bottom-rung task of preparing cars for painting with Ferman Chevrolet, accelerating not his technical career so much as his hot-rod aspirations. For, it was here that he met his slightly-older, work-mate Grady Pickel, street racer and hotrodder par excellence, who became Garlits' new alter-ego and hot-rod mentor.

In his 1990 autobiography *Big Daddy*, Don recalls that, while his acquaintance with Grady Pickel sparked his outlaw, hot-rodder period, it did nothing for his spiritual development. But such a nuanced view is wisdom in hindsight. Grady Pickel was not only Don's introduction into street racing but also into the intoxicating world of first-hand, home-grown, high-performance cars. This was in contrast to some far-off, European vision of aristocrats engaging in gallant contests with pure-bred machinery, or even the gritty heroes of Indianapolis, who were driving made-in-California, Offenhauser-powered, speedway roadsters. There and then Don began to dream of modifying his own car with available resources. This do-it-yourself mentality was to become a Don Garlits' hallmark; the shade-tree drag racer from Florida with a hot-rod vision of creating beautiful, fast cars out of "junk".

Tampa, Florida

Racing "Rich Kids" on the Streets of Tampa and St Petersburg

The new, hot-rod buddies Grady Pickel and Don Garlits, went street racing at night in Tampa and across the causeway to meet the "rich kids" of nearby St Petersburg, heading to Triplett's Drive-in to seek out Charlie "King" Hogan, who was the guy to beat. Across the continent in LA, the hot rod vision had simultaneously materialised when the guys and cars came out at night to cruise the drive-in diners and race each other on the streets. The maximum kudos was not so much to beat another hot rod. It was to out-run new iron from Detroit, or better still, an expensive, high-performance import from Europe. The idea of taking a home-built machine up against European thoroughbreds was already well-established in LA by many hot-rod pioneers including Ernie McAfee, Max Balchowsky and Duffy Livingston who raced hot rods against Ferraris and Jaguars on California road racing courses. Ak Millar went one better, when he ran his fabulous "Iron Horse" hot rod against international competition in the Mexican Pan American road race, and then in the famous Italian 1000-mile road race, the Mille Miglia. (Indeed, it should be noted that 1962 Formula 1 World Champion Phil Hill, and all-American, good-guy, Formula 1 Indy racer and race car constructor Dan Gurney, were both Californians who had ascended to the heady world of European motor racing via hot rods.)

Young Garlits' dreams were more parochial. His first ambition was to become the guy to beat in local competition. Later he would challenge the established Californian stars as a hotrodder who designed, built, maintained, drove, campaigned and promoted himself to international recognition and acclaim. It would be some years before he travelled overseas, not to serve homage to the Europeans, but to show them the way to unanticipated performance with his home-built, hot rod dragster. The first awakening of street racing is what inspired much of Don's development for the next half-century, as post-war freedom took hold, and opportunities to build and race cars moved from being the domain of the privileged few, to the many. For the next three years hot rodding was more precious than life itself. Garlits discovered that King Hogan had established a drag strip on a little-used airfield at nearby Zephyrhills. He was soon spending every waking moment living the life of a hot-rod bum, and every cent he earned looking for junkyard parts to feed the all-consuming need for speed. The possibility of beating King Hogan on his home turf was beginning to materialize.

This clandestine hot-rod life was precarious. On one occasion Don came home from a drag strip with his racing number still displayed on the car. His anguished mother reminded him that he was "still not too old to be whipped", at which his compassionate stepfather intervened; "Don't touch the boy. If he wants to race, let him race". Alex Weir's compassion for Don is deeply significant. In kindness, he sought to encourage and guide his stepson when the opposite could have easily been the case. And race he did. Fearing ridicule from his mates, Don traded his big Ford V8 four-door family sedan for a much sportier 1940 Ford convertible fitted with a 1941 Mercury engine. This enabled him to race the 26 dangerous miles both to and from, and then the competitors at King Hogan's drag strip at Zephyrhills, or slightly better-organised events at nearby Lake Wales. Eventually, fitted with a Cadillac V8 engine, Don's car ran 17.5-second elapsed time for the quarter-mile, burning up transmissions, clutches and tyres as dispensable commodities in the quest for supremacy. "I just loved it", explained Garlits. "I liked the idea of two cars lined up, side by side, not bumping into one another. It was one person against one person, one machine against one machine. There was a winner and a loser. It was real simple."

It was Don's meeting of Pat Bieger, in 1952, that was responsible for his next and most transforming awakening. Pat, about to graduate from Hillsborough High School as an honour student, was from a respectable, Christian, Tampa family. Suddenly, Don had an entirely new interest. Only 20 years old, Don showed up at Pat's home driving his hot rod Ford convertible with a Cadillac engine, only to find that her father "didn't like my looks one bit". Don's infatuation with Pat caused him to weigh the wisdom of a hot-rod, street-racer career against his newly-realized, romantic intentions. In order to pursue his new love and gain the approval of his prospective father-in-law, he immediately sold his Ford convertible in favour of an unmodified, 1950 Ford, two-door sedan. "I had to finance that Ford for $500", Don said. "When I drove to work in that plain-Jane Ford, the guys wanted to know how much I got for my hot rod. I confessed that I had to pay them." Garlits' new ride duly impressed Pat's father. "The day I met [Pat] was the best day of my life. I took one look. She was the girl of my dreams. We went dancing, bowling, to the beach, and finally got married in February, 1953." Tragically, the wedding coincided with Alexander Weir's untimely death.

With Pat working as a secretary at the Tampa Chamber of Commerce and Don working nights at the American Can Company, they found a house to buy. During finance negotiations the realtor presented them with an outrageous down-payment and interest rate. In response to Garlits' surprised protest, the salesman sneered, "Listen my friend, a guy like you will never get a house any other way". An indignant Don Garlits exploded with rage yelling, "DON'T BET ON IT BUDDY". He stormed out, dragging Pat in tow, promising her that she would have a house if he had to build it himself. And so he did. Buying a vacant lot in Tampa, Don designed and built a two-bedroom, concrete-block home with his own hands. It demonstrated an emerging Garlits' characteristic of frugality and dogged determination in the face of any suggestion that there was something he was not capable of doing. The disproportionate size of garage to new house suggested that hot rods were still on Don's mind. He began taking notice of hot rod magazines belonging to his work mate, Billy Herndon. Garlits, the new-look, reformed, street racer lasted only a couple of months until a Sunday drive with Pat to Bok Tower took them by a drag strip. After innocently enquiring if Pat would like to see the cars Don took advantage of the opportunity to make a few runs in their two-door, Ford sedan, garnering a class win and a plastic trophy. "Pat really liked it", he insists. "It was a family deal, not all black leather jackets." But the top eliminator of the day was his old nemesis, King Hogan, whose 1927 T model roadster was now fitted with a V12 Lincoln engine.

Born to Race

I live with fear, but sometimes she lets me race. – 1970s bumper sticker

With rekindled dreams of beating King Hogan, Don's compulsion to be fastest guy in Florida was quickly renewed. This led to a series of chassis and engine changes emanating from the oversized garage and backyard. Successive versions of the family car morphed into hot rods and then a dragster. Much to the annoyance of his neighbours whose street had become "hot rod central", the house became the shade-tree, engineering workshop from which emerged the new cars of his "Strokers" hot-rod club-mates. Now working at Craig Wheeler's body shop, Don learned valuable metal-working and welding skills from his journeyman/mentor. Craig was an old family friend who took Don under his wing, allowing each new skill to be put to good use at home. Don was now earning enough to fund his next car. Rather than continuing to compromise the family transport, he bought a 1927 model T roadster that was to become a dedicated race car. The model T, bought for $50, was soon fitted with his flathead Ford V8 engine that had been hopped up with Offenhauser finned aluminium heads, triple Stromberg 97 carbs, and a full race camshaft. This upgrade was a disappointment. Don still ran a relatively high 13-second elapsed time (referred to by drag racers as ET), while the King was now running low 13-second ETs. No amount of questioning would separate King Hogan from his speed secrets. He dismissed enquiries about his car's performance from the rabble of acolytes, including Garlits, who sought his advice. Unknown to Hogan, this offence backfired, motivating Don's burning desire to dethrone the King.

From Hotrodder to Drag Racer

Garlits noticed that Hogan's car always left the starting line better than his. He figured if he could leave the line the same, he would have a better chance of success. Using basic high-school physics, Don lengthened the chassis of his T Roadster to achieve the simple expedient of adding relatively more weight to the rear axle. In the process he removed the rear springs and welded the axle directly to the frame. All at once Don hit on the formula for drag-racing supremacy in Florida by beating Hogan with a 12.5-second ET. After three years of trying to dethrone the King, Hogan was defeated. Don's hunger for supremacy was satisfied, at least for the moment. Success bred further success. Don abandoned any pretence of his hot rod being road-legal, and turned the T Roadster into an all-out dragster. He removed what remained of the body, shifted the engine further back in the chassis and fitted the driver's seat under a crude, square-sectioned roll bar. The driver would now sit behind the rear axle to aid traction, just like in the Californian magazines. Perhaps it was not as pretty as west-coast examples, but the elements were there.

Hitting the Big Time

Don was now running successfully all over the state in this new, dragster configuration and was ready for the 1955 National

Hot Rod Association (NHRA) "Drag Safari", to be held in Lake City, near Jacksonville, Florida. This inaugural event was one of several regional meets promoted by the NHRA, reflecting the style of founder, Wally Parks, to clean up the image of drag racing with safety rules and good organization. Not being one of the NHRA regulars, Don had to run the gauntlet of what seemed to him, to be nit-picking technical inspections that sought to find fault with his junkyard dragster. He finally passed inspection late on Saturday afternoon just in time to make one successful qualifying run for the eliminations on Sunday. Up against his friends George Breen and Joe Travis and his old rival King Hogan, who had replaced his Lincoln V12 with a Chrysler V8, Garlits beat them all. In the final against Joe Travis, whose car failed, Don gained his first NHRA Top Eliminator win with a top speed of 108.17 mph in 12.1 seconds.

Much to Don's chagrin, *Hot Rod* magazine (then closely-aligned to the NHRA, due to Wally Parks being the editor), contrary to normal practise, did not publish photos of the winning dragster and driver of the Drag Safari event. His machine did not fit the desired image of a professional race car, to say the least. This insult would become grist for Don's hot-rodder mill, as the idea of beating the "rich guys" with a homemade, junkyard machine, gained further appeal. Don was to carry this underdog label throughout most of his career. He preferred to make do with low-cost parts rather than compete in the same, high-dollar terms as his rivals. The Strokers Hot Rod Club celebrated Don's victory by awarding him a dainty tea set. They thought that having achieved his goal, Don would now retire as there was no prospect of his ever being able to beat the Californians with their high-dollar, professionally-built cars. Little did they know. Rather, Don's hot-rod dreams of a career as a dragster builder and tuner were just taking root. Don's quest had just begun.

Tampa, Florida

Pat's Intuition

With innumerable race wins attributed to the flathead V8, and the proliferation of speed equipment available for it, Don believed that the newer, overhead-valve, six/eight-cylinder engines from Detroit, would never threaten flathead supremacy. This notion was tested when, to improve the coupe's towing ability on the narrow, two-lane, back roads of the Florida peninsula, he swapped the engine in his 1939 Ford coupe tow car—a flathead, for a 331-cubic inch, Hemi V8, scavenged from a wrecked Chrysler for $400.

A very serious Don Garlits, pictured in 1957 at age 25, already with more than 300 wins to his credit. In all likelihood, there were many more to come during the next 57 years (GARLITS COLLECTION).

When his dragster transmission broke at an event at Mac Dill Air Force Base, just for fun, Don substituted the dragster with the Chrysler-powered tow car, only to find the coupe ran 14.0 seconds ET at 114 mph, against the flathead-powered dragster's 12.5 seconds at 108 mph. During the trip home Don mentioned to Pat that whoever fitted a Hemi to a dragster was going to be the guy to beat. To this Pat replied, "Well, you'd better put one in your dragster straight away." Needing no other approval, Don performed the switch immediately. The dragster, now powered by an unmodified, Chrysler engine, immediately ran 10.5 seconds at 128 mph, beginning a new era of Hemi engines in dragsters for Don Garlits. Pat's intuition to back her man's judgement and encourage him to overcome the latest obstacle or to do exactly what he had just dreamed up, would come to the fore many times during his career, perhaps none so inspired as on this occasion. Whether or not Pat was taking Don's bait is open to conjecture, but the pattern of Don deferring to Pat's judgement and approval was, by now, a well and truly established formula for success. This was a winning formula not just for a poor-boy's drag-racing career, but also for his marital relationship, and eventually for life in the fullest sense.

Enter, the Hemi

Unbeknown to Garlits, there was growing evidence regarding the potential of the Chrysler Hemi engine from many sources including the NASCAR speed trials at Daytona Beach, Florida and on the Bonneville Salt Flats far away in Utah. Also on the international scene, the all-American sportsman Briggs Cunningham made it onto the cover of *Time* magazine for having run his eponymous, Hemi-powered sports cars to class wins at Le Mans, France. Ironically, Cunningham achieved an outright win in the 1953 Sebring 12-Hours in Florida, with cars built nearby in West Palm Beach. There was also an article in the May 1952 edition of *Hot Rod* magazine by Chrysler engineer, James Zeder, saying that the Hemi was the way of the future. It is unlikely that Zeder anticipated drag racing as the future of the Hemi, nor did Garlits immediately see "the writing on the wall". The revelation came as a surprise, as if the holy grail of drag racing were waiting to be discovered by the right person at the right time in the right circumstances. But Garlits certainly had a role in creating the Hemi's future as a racing engine.

The Hemi-powered, Chevrolet-framed car, labelled "Swamp Rat" by Setto Postoian in 1956. Note the high-mounted engine and body, the full-sized car steering wheel, the lack of any real driver protection, and the roughly, hand-fabricated, exhaust header pipes (GARLITS COLLECTION).

From the primordial swamp of the flathead V8 T bucket hot rod, sagging under the newly-imposed weight of the heavy cast iron Hemi engine, to what was to become the conventional, dragster design, Don invested in a Chevrolet frame from the junkyard for $50. Unlike the streamlined beauties that emerged from the race car workshops in LA, this revolutionary car still appeared primitive with its crudely-fashioned header pipes and handmade body perched up high like a praying mantis. But the ingredients were there: the long wheelbase, the driver seated behind the rear wheels under a roll bar, and the familiar, wide, Chrysler Firepower rocker covers that spanned the angle between the inlet and exhaust valves. These wide rocker covers required by the hemispherical combustion chambers were the first of many secrets to unlocking the power from production-derived V8 engines that were to propel dragsters for the next 60 years, with no end in sight. This was the start of a stellar career for the Chrysler Hemi engine.

Soul Evolution

Just as the tiny mustard seed becomes a huge tree, Don Garlits crafted an extraordinary life from an ordinary beginning. Reflecting the age and circumstances into which he was born, he cobbled up machinery, tested and innovated relentlessly. His accomplishments were born from what he envisaged, with what was available, made with his own hands. Garlits thrived on challenges that others said were beyond him. His energetic and creative intellect and dogged resolve powered him through setbacks and disasters. These gave him cause to think deeply about what he was doing. With encouragement from Pat, the one he most loved, the transformation of Don Garlits' soul was gathering speed. The evolutions of drag racing and of Don Garlits' soul are in many ways, parallel. "We were just a couple of kids", Garlits reflects. He and Pat lacked any concept of what lay before them as a couple or as drag racing pioneers. Neither could have anticipated the challenges that life would bring nor how they might respond to them. The emergence of faith as a source of inspiration and a bond between them likely had its origin in their individual early life experiences. Nevertheless, it was their synergy as a couple that categorically shaped them. Pat's determination was to share her husband's life and protect her family. Don's determination was to succeed and provide for Pat. Their evolution as a couple was a combination of these characteristics, this drive and these moments in time. Even today, six years since Pat's passing, Garlits' passion has overcome his grief. Getting on with life, he has married Lisa Crigar, (a "good Christian girl", the type that Pat selflessly recommended he should marry). Garlits is a survivor, who stared his own humanity in the face. On the basis of the collective challenges of the quarter mile, he has become an enduring marathon winner—a strong soul who has taken on the lessons life offered. His personal evolution involved the transition from a rabid, win-at-all-costs drag racer, to the man whose life was highly celebrated 60 years later. This is how a soul evolves, as we shall see in Don Garlits' life; from foolish risk-taking and youthful-exuberance, (to which the Ecclesiastes reference in this chapter alludes), to going where no man has been before, to ultimately becoming an elder statesman whose soul is being transformed.

Revolution of East Vs West

Each one of the United States of America exemplifies its geography, history, leadership and social trends. California had been home to the aircraft manufacturing industry during WWII. When the war ended and was no longer intruding into daily life, some of the remaining aircraft technology coming from trend-setting Californian minds, was re-directed into the design and manufacture of race cars. It is significant that Championship speedway cars were designed and built in southern California rather than in the eastern states where the ultimate contest was run each year, at the Indianapolis Speedway, in Indiana. Harry Miller, Fred Goosen and Frank Offenhauser were West-coast, engineering and motor-racing entrepreneurs who designed and built racing engines to be used by Indianapolis Champ cars and also by the smaller Midget speedway cars back in LA. The cars themselves were also built in LA by fabricators including Frank Kurtis, Eddie Kuzma and AJ Watson. In the pre- and post-war periods this creativity and competitiveness was put to the test several times a week in the LA area. Timber speedway velodromes for Midget racing abounded close to downtown LA, Hollywood and Pasadena. With population explosion, the land occupied by these venues became choice residential property and the timber death traps were displaced. The speedways went but the engineers and innovators remained, and race car design and manufacture continued. While speedway cars of various kinds continued to emerge from LA, hotrodders began to seek out the skills of car designers and fabricators. Among the most prolific of these was Mickey Thompson, a restless night reporter for the *LA Times* who seemingly never slept, enabling him to accomplish incredible feats of hot-rod innovation. Among other feats, Thompson was attributed pioneer of the slingshot dragster, and the mighty four-engine Pontiac V8 Challenger I and II land-speed record cars that achieved 406 mph in 1960.

Mickey Thompson's dragster, built by craftsman Bob Sorrell, illustrates the difference in concept and execution between California and Florida. The Chrysler-powered slingshot was Thompson's second Chrysler-powered car. He used his first Chrysler dragster to set a land-speed record of 294 mph at Bonneville, instead of completing a trip to the NHRA National drag race championships in Great Bend, Kansas. This car, featuring a steel-tube frame, later to be covered with a streamlined aluminium body, was powered by a fuel-injected Hemi. It had magnesium rear wheels and the pioneering, slingshot driver location behind the rear axle centreline.

By comparison to Thompson's masterpieces, Garlits' dragster was a crude device with a wrecking-yard Chevrolet chassis. The car that became Swamp Rat 1 had all the dragster elements but lacked sophistication. Fitted with a Hemi engine and rear-seated driver, the crude header pipes and the homemade body, the differences to professionally-built, Californian cars were conspicuous to say the least. But pretty does not always win where persistence does. Painstaking development gives better results over time. While racers like Mickey Thompson had already moved on to their next project, Garlits was still sharpening his saw, making incremental improvements for speed, safety and reliability. This combination of dogged hunger for success coupled with his courage and fertile mind was a winning combination.

Chapter 3 The Rat Gets the Cheese

"Cast your bread on the surface of the waters, for you will find it after many days."
– Eccles 11:1

Gathering Pace

Following Garlits' Lake City NHRA Drag Safari win, local pace picked up. But Garlits was left feeling a bit overlooked in the national drag racing scene. To correct this oversight, he wrote to the California-based, drag racing newspaper, Drag News, to complain about the lack of coverage of Florida-based events. At least he thought he deserved some wider recognition for his win.

As Don campaigned locally, developing both car- and race-craft, his interest in the West Coast was fed by a regular diet of news about Mickey Thompson, the Bean Bandits, the Chrisman brothers, Ollie Morrison, Cook and Bedwell, the Cortopassi brothers and their Glass Slipper dragster. Don also followed the exploits of his new hero, Calvin Rice, whose increasing dominance was attributable to a Chrysler Hemi running on nitromethane-fuel.

News from Great Bend Kansas

Don was not yet ready for national competition. But he was keenly-interested in the inaugural, NHRA National Championship drag races running in September/October, 1955, in Great Bend, Kansas. Chosen for its location in the center of the continent, it was far from ideal from a spectator-access and facilities point of view. Nonetheless, it attracted more than 300 competitors from all points of the compass, indicating the growing appeal of the sport that matched the best the nation had to offer. The field included Calvin Rice, from Santa Ana, California, who entered his beautiful, Chrysler-powered, JE Riley Special, slingshot dragster. This car was among the first to be professionally built in the Californian, race-car tradition, by craftsman Melvin Dodd, (featuring a tubular chassis with a streamlined, aluminium body enveloping the whole car, including the driver). But after qualifying commenced, the highly-anticipated event was rained out and eventually resumed in Perryville, Arizona, some weeks later. Confusingly, Rice's car, powered by a supercharged Chrysler Hemi, started the event in Kansas, only to win the event in Arizona, repowered with a flathead Ford V8. Proof of the importance of the chassis design, was that, although flathead V8-powered, Rice's dragster ran 143.95 mph in 10.30 seconds.

Early in 1956, after running local events and observing results from afar, Garlits sold his car to school friend, Art Malone for $500. His sights were set on a new dragster and a place in the big league.

Although the merits of a purpose-built dragster were now obvious to Don, practical reality and his lack of experience in chassis building led him to ask for help. Dave Phillips, fellow Strokers club member, who had commenced but not completed the construction of a slingshot, recommended a modified, Chevrolet frame rather than a custom-built chassis. Hoping to overcome that disadvantage with more power, Don modified another 1954 Chrysler Hemi engine with a hand-made, inlet manifold, to accommodate six, Stromberg 97 carburettors, inhaling air and gasoline.

Although the new car did not have all the speed secrets of the latest Californian machines, Don and brother Ed (who had returned home from military service to help Don) were pleased with their handiwork. The dragster featured a yellow-painted,

The Rat Gets the Cheese

The Calvin Rice Chrysler dragster, styled along speedway car lines (PHOTOGRAPH BY STEVE REYES).

aluminium body, with crudely-shaped exhaust pipes that pointed to the ground ahead of the rear wheels. Initial runs at Fort Myers, Florida, confirmed that the car was at least a local contender ready to race all over the state. With this new business venture Don was one step closer to a career in drag racing. Don's drag-racing success and increased profile among local racers enabled him to open Don's Garage, a body-repair and hot-rod workshop in Tampa. This was a further step toward a drag racing career which he precariously balanced with paid customer work and participation in local race meetings. Creating a business was an ambitious undertaking for a young, married man. But Pat was financially supportive, with a good job at the Tampa Chamber of Commerce. Besides, customers were knocking at Don's door, prepared to pay for his latest hot-rod-speed secrets.

More Bang for Your Buck

Seeking the next speed advantage, Don was ready to try the magic elixir of high performance called nitromethane. Nitro, known as Fuel, was commonly used as a dry-cleaning solvent. Nitromethane is a liquid containing oxygen molecules. Despite its low energy value, it can produce huge, power gains. An engine powered by nitromethane is no longer limited by the amount of oxygen in the air it breathes, or how many revs per minute it can achieve. Power is now determined by how much fuel can be burned to increase the size of the bang. To demonstrate Teutonic superiority, nitro had been used by the pre-war, Auto Union Grand Prix cars which were sponsored by the Nazi regime. Don Garlits correctly observed that these radical cars resembled hot-rod dragsters in more ways than the use of nitromethane. Designed by Ferdinand Porsche, and fitted with rear-mounted V16 engines, Rootes' superchargers, zoomie headers, dual rear wheels, and limited-slip differentials for traction, they were unbeatable. Legend has it that LA speed-equipment manufacturer, Vic Edelbrock Snr, was given a gallon of nitro that he dynamometer-tested in a V8-60 powered speedway Midget, racing-car engine. It generated a huge power increase. Adding credibility to the story, Edelbrock employed Indy winner, Roger Ward, to race his nitro-fuelled Kurtis Kraft midget against the dominant, purpose-built, Offenhauser-engine midgets. Ward beat the Offys twice in a row, both at Gilmore Stadium in LA, and again at San Bernardino the following night, before others also realised the advantage he had gained from this funny-smelling fuel called nitro. Nitro was introduced to drag racing and Bonneville Salt Lake speed trials by Joaquin Arnett, the brilliant, pioneering, Latino racer. Arnett had co-formed the ironically named "Bean Bandits Club", of ethnically-diverse racers.

The Rat Gets the Cheese

The team, using nitromethane and many other innovations, plus outstanding workmanship, overcame the disadvantage of having to use junkyard parts against their wealthier rivals.

AATA World Series, Cordova, Illinois

By getting the new business on an even keel and perfecting the art of running modest amounts of nitro during the summers of 1956-57, Don was ready to test himself and the car against all comers. He entered the inaugural American Automobile Timing Association, "World Series" event, in Cordova, Illinois. The competition included the dominant Californians, Emery Cook and Cliff Bedwell. This duo was looking for competition far afield due to the recently-imposed ban on nitro at NHRA-sanctioned drag strips. Predictability, nitro use had increased car speeds and Emery Cook's 166.97-mph run at LIONS Dragstrip in California, early in 1957, caused some strip promoters to have second thoughts about safety. This led them to lobby Wally Parks, of the National Hot Rod Association, against the continued use of "rocket fuel". The ban by the conservative founder of the NHRA was contrary to the very ethos of drag racing. It was an invitation to other drag-race promoters and associations to fill the void by allowing the now-illicit "Fuel" at the well-attended, AATA World Series event.

This was an event he didn't win but it convinced Garlits he could make a living out of drag racing. The hottest car in the country in 1957, was Cook and Bedwell's dragster. It ran 168.85 mph in California, fitted with a 354- cubic-inch Hemi and the revolutionary, Bruce's Slicks racing tires, featuring seven inches of wide, soft rubber. Cook and Bedwell's advantage was that Emery Cook was Joaquin Arnett's brother-in-law.

Don Garlits. The Enigmatic Hero

Encouragement from a Competitor

Also included in the field were Gary "Red" Greth and Lyle Fisher, of Tucson, Arizona. With their friend Don Maynard, they built the ground-breaking Speed Sport rear-engine, Hemi-powered roadster, a 160-mph, top-eliminator threat. Also vying for top honor, was Serop "Setto" Postoian, a wiry, Armenian racer from Detroit with a big reputation. Setto ran 9.36 ET at 158.17 mph from a nitro-fuelled, 392 Hemi that was to stand as the low time of the meeting. But Cook and Bedwell had previously run 168.85 mph in 8.89 seconds in California, with the right balance of power and traction.

Fuelled with anticipation, and having driven halfway across the country to get to the event, Don was completely off the pace with a 12.43 ET at 133.33 mph, slower than his NHRA Drag Safari time from two years earlier. Demoralised, embarrassed, depressed and baffled, Garlits was ready to give up, when he noticed Emery Cook was available for a chat. Don admitted that he knew only how to run 25% nitro. Cook graciously explained to Garlits the detail of how to modify his carburettors to increase the percentage of nitro from 25% to 95%, which he and Cliff Bedwell had been doing for some time. Perhaps, reflecting on the history of the use of nitro to overcome a disadvantage, Cook may have been keen to encourage its successful use. Whatever Cook's motivation, Garlits, to his credit, accepted the freely-offered advice and went to work with revived hope. Making crude, overnight modifications to the carburettors, the results were still depressing. The car left the line with a surge of new power but faltered halfway down the strip with a loss of fuel pressure. Now desperate, Don took further advice from Emery Cook and fitted a hand-operated fuel pump to obtain 10-psi fuel pressure before he launched off the line. Pumping furiously during the run to maintain pressure, he instantly increased his speed to almost 150 mph.

The Rat Gets the Cheese

Grateful for their advice, but making no concessions when it came time to race, Don lined up against Cook in the eliminations, only to foul the first run by anxiously red-lighting and bringing on a re-run. Cook ran a higher rear axle gear than normal to try to win the $1000 top speed prize for the meet. But chastened by his haste, Don carefully waited for the green, and won with a 9.92-second pass against Cook's 10.12 seconds, much to Cliff Bedwell's chagrin. This spelled an end to their partnership. Emery Cook's mistake was not the assistance he gave to Garlits. His mistake was, at a decisive moment in matching himself against all comers, he discounted Don as a serious competitor. Cook's underestimation of the desperate tenacity of his rival was a mistake that many others would continue to make. His kindness, however, made a lasting impression on Don, who later returned the favour. With renewed confidence, having beaten his heroes, Don next lined up against Setto Postoian, applying all his concentration and willpower to the race. Both cars left the line together. But the race was not restricted to the first few feet, and his more-experienced competitor inexorably drew away with the greater power of his bigger engine. Although Garlits lost to Setto, (who eventually won the event against Red Greth), Garlits' win against Cook and Bedwell was enough to convince him that he could run with the champions of the sport. "They were my heroes. I had their picture nailed up on the wall of my shop. When I outran them, I knew this was what I wanted to do."

The Next Step

Upon his return to Tampa, Don further improved his chances with a bigger, current model, 392-cubic-inch Chrysler engine relocated lower in the frame. The brothers fitted the new engine with the latest, hot set-up; a new, Weiand manifold underneath eight, Stromberg 97 carburettors, and an Iskenderian, 5-Cycle camshaft producing enough power to eliminate the gearbox in favor of a

Don Garlits. The Enigmatic Hero

straight drive, with a 3.27:1 final drive ratio. Still struggling with fuel supply problems, Don realised that his speed would improve dramatically if, for the whole run, he could just keep the fuel pressure up to the increasingly-thirsty carburettors. His unique solution was to pressurise the fuel tank with compressed air. Combined with bigger fuel lines this seemed simple enough, but it needed to be proven at the drag strip. The next race confirmed progress. Meeting at Kissimmee, Florida, Garlits performed a new, personal best time of 9.95 seconds at 156.52 mph.

News from the West Coast was that Red Greth had run 169.11 mph in his Speed Sport roadster, breaking the Cook and Bedwell record. This new record confusingly suggested that maybe the short-wheelbase, rear-engine, roadster configuration had even more potential than a long, wheelbase dragster.

Power to Spare

During November 1957, Don entered the car in an event on the high-traction, concrete surface at Brooksville, Florida. He was astounded by his first run with the improved fuel supply when, instead of the power dropping off as speed increased, the tires kept smoking right through to the finish line. Difficulty bringing the car to a halt confirmed that the run was much faster than usual. Don sat in stunned silence listening to the *tink, tink, tink* of hot metal contracting, and took in the emotional effect of the run. He was greeted by his excited crew with the news that he had run a record-shattering 8.79 seconds. But, as if to create dramatic suspense, no speed was recorded. His speed was beyond the speed calculation tables. (The calculation recorded the time taken to cover a 132-foot trap, to obtain the average speed over that distance at the end of the quarter mile. It is now measured by the time taken to cover the last 66 feet.) Employing every ounce of his native cunning, Don asked the event organisers to report the elapsed time to the

The Rat Gets the Cheese

West Coast periodical, *Drag News*, with a request to calculate the speed from the 132-foot, speed trap time.

Iskenderian Calling

Tellingly, the reply came not from the newspaper, but from the ever-vigilant, camshaft manufacturer and hot-rod-marketing genius, Ed Iskenderian. With his signature greeting, "Hi pal!", "Isky" was calling to offer congratulations for Don's record-setting ET and speed. And by the way, was there any way he could help? Reeling from the fact that Iskenderian, the great LA-based speed merchant, had even bothered to call him, Don asked what the speed was. To which, Isky replied, "176.40 mph. The fastest speed ever run over a quarter mile...", again offering any assistance that might be required. As his composure returned, Don gratefully agreed that for the upcoming International Timing Association event in Chester, South Carolina, some tires, spark plugs and T-shirts with the record speed printed on them, might be useful. To this Iskenderian readily consented. As if the drag racing fraternity were anticipating this result, news of the speed broke like wildfire in daily, newspaper, sporting pages. Drag racing publications carried front page articles and advertisements from Iskenderian camshafts, Weiand manifolds and Bruce's Slicks, claiming their products' role in the record-setting run. Suddenly, Garlits had a reputation to protect as competitors and detractors on the West Coast were calling the speed at best, a fluke, if not a fake, produced by a sub-standard car on a suspect track. Despite the growing disbelief from competitors, Don's self-belief was renewed enough to ignore the taunts, at least for the time being.[9]

Promoters claimed the big event in Chester to be the richest ever for Fuel dragsters. The meet bought out Setto Postoian, Bobby Sullivan's new "Pandemonium" dragster, and the Arfons brother's Green Monsters, both fitted with huge aircraft engines, one driven with a propeller. This car crashed in an horrific, cart-wheeling accident at about 150 mph to provide a salutary warning that drag racing was indeed a very dangerous business. Don's concern for his own safety was reinforced during a test run when a brake-line failure at high speed caused him, in a panicked response, to push in the clutch. With no brakes and no engine retardation, the dragster hurtled onward. He was saved only by the long strip which allowed the car to run for almost another mile before coming to rest in a bog. Meanwhile, Pat, who had gone to pick up Ed Iskenderian's package of goodies from the post office, was involved in a minor car accident. Shaken but not injured, she returned to the track only to find that Don had also crashed, and much more seriously than she. This combined trauma likely caused the miscarriage of their first child, shortly after their return home.

Slick Business

Adding insult to injury, as he washed the mud off the dragster at a local farm, Don heard the distant loudspeaker announcement that Setto's 169 mph was the speed to beat. But good fortune was again on hand. The event was attended by another character that would become instrumental to Don's success. Marvin Rifchin, was

---

[9] Ed Iskenderian's influence remained an integral part of the drag-racing culture for the next 60 years. Isky seemed to enjoy the joke of his exaggerated, advertising claims of uniqueness for his "5-cycle Hyperbolic" camshafts. The only hyperbole was that his "fifth-cycle" was overlap that every other camshaft manufacturer also used.

The Rat Gets the Cheese

an Easterner who founded the M&H Tire Company to provide tires for his own speedway race cars. Finding resistance to his new drag slicks, against Bruce's Slicks, which Don and all of the other top racers were using, Rifchin was impressed to find Don already using M&H Cruiser, oval track tires as a cost-saving measure. Rifchin gave Don a set of seven-inch M&H drag slicks, made in the same mould as the Cruiser oval track tires, with the promise that a properly-designed drag tire would be just the advantage that was needed. The new tires made the difference, and gave Garlits just enough to beat Setto with 170.71 mph in 8.95 ET, winning both Top Eliminator and top-time prize money. Don hoped this result was close enough to his Brooksfield record to silence the critics. But to his dismay, it was quite the opposite. Californians refused to believe that a hick from the swamps of Florida could beat them at their own game. Don had to wait his time to teach them a drag-racing lesson closer to their home.

Good Losers Don't Win

It was the final event of 1957—the Florida Central Timing Association annual championships, in Kissimmee. Don was competing for Top Eliminator against a small field of dragsters including Floyd Albritten, of Miami, who was running an Oldsmobile V8 dragster on gasoline. To overcome the disadvantage of gas against fuel, Don, full of confidence, agreed to a 60-foot handicap in favor of Albritten, only to break an axle halfway down the strip, causing him to lose the race to the less-powerful car. Don angrily loaded the car onto the trailer, living up to his reputation as a bad loser. When Albritten and his crew walked up, apparently to rub salt into the wound, to Don's surprise, Floyd held out a fistful of cash with the comment, "Here Don, you deserve this as much as I do". Don paused just long enough to feel guilty for his anger at losing to the sportsman at his side. He justified his attitude with the truism, that *good losers don't win*. But while Don recognised that his intense desire to win was his strongest asset, this incident made an impression on the emerging champion and he remained embarrassed at his lack of sportsmanship. Dragster evolution, in response to increased power, was demanding better traction, so Garlits further lengthened the chassis, fitted a lighter front axle and lowered the body to achieve a more aerodynamic, aggressive stance. The car was now sitting on a narrowed, Oldsmobile, rear axle complimented by up-front, hand-laced, wire wheels. It looked less like a praying mantis and more like an "anteater searching for lunch". This image of what was to become Swamp Rat 1, began to appear in magazines and advertisements carrying the news to a world of speed-crazy enthusiasts.

The New Year of 1958 commenced with painstaking development. Revising the car took longer than expected before it was ready to run again at Kissimmee. It produced an unremarkable 163.53 mph, 9.87 second ET. But the race confirmed that, as the science of speed advanced, competitive times were more consistently achievable.

A further boost to both Don's ego and the lure of racing for a living arrived by post; a letter from the Red River Timing association of Wichita Falls, Texas, offering $450 to run against some of the top stars of drag racing at their Southern Invitational Regional Championship in May, 1958. Don and Ed turned up to find the field filled with now-famous drivers and cars including Texan, Bobby Langley, the Cook and Bedwell car with new owners, Lyle Fisher, now driving the Speed Sport roadster, NHRA champion Melvin Heath, with a tube-framed, supercharged, Hemi dragster and Jack Moss, with his twin-engine, Chevrolet dragster. Don posted a 160.71 mph, 9.28-second run in practice, to better the Texan record. Garlits was now the man to beat. With rising confidence he used this early advantage to demoralise the field by setting improved times and speeds with each run. Now that all his nitro-powered rivals were eliminated, the final obstacle was

The Rat Gets the Cheese

to run against the Top Gas car of Jack Moss. Moss wisely conceded the run due to declining light. He knew he could not beat Don's times. This brought both Top Fuel and Top Eliminator prize money to the $450 inducement to appear at an event in which Garlits would have run for nothing.

Flushed with success, Don further consolidated his performance from Kissimee by recording three, back-to-back runs under nine seconds, running 8.97, 8.99, 8.99. This earned him hoped-for and well-deserved top billing in magazines, but also, more scoffing from west coast racers. Now, able to repeat performances reliably, Don ran again at Chester to win the second International Timing Association meet. He easily beat Bill Douglas, Setto Postoian's substitute, when Setto's engine blew up. Upset at being beaten, Setto stirred the publicity pot by claiming that Garlits could not possibly run 176 mph. To settle the matter once and for all, whether or not Don's times were real enough to beat the Californians, it was essential that he race against west coast cars. The increased business at the shop that followed the new-found notoriety was welcome, but the distraction of customer work, building engines and modifying cars made preparation of the dragster more difficult. Only by working around the clock was the problem solved, not that the Garlits brothers were ever afraid of hard work.

Like gunslingers meeting in town at high noon, the opportunity for a long-anticipated showdown came in a letter from the promoter of the Freeway Dragstrip located near Houston, Texas. The track, situated midway between California and Florida, was announcing a special meet to allow the speed titans a clash to resolve the dispute between East and West. Don and Ed stopped doing customer work long enough to prepare the car according to the now-proven formula, except for fitting a new camshaft and valve springs from Iskenderian. The Garlits brothers arrived in Texas to find an imposing field: Romeo Palamides from Oakland, California, with his beautiful, expensive-looking, fuel-injected Chrysler rail driven by Pete Ogden; Jack Ewell, driving the magnificent, Kamboor and Jado Special, fitted with a bored-out 500-cubic-inch Chrysler; and Red Case, in the Cagle and Callahan, rear-engine, fuel-injected, Chrysler-powered roadster, similar to the Speed Sport machine; plus local Texan cars including Bobby Langley. All were on a mission to beat Garlits. To the amusement and jeers of the crowd, when the battered-looking, Swamp Rat engine was fired up with plumes of castor oil smoke, it exaggerated the contrast between the beautifully-painted and waxed, professionally-built cars and Garlits' home-built car. The taunts only worsened when the car's agonisingly-poor performance reflected what the smoke had suggested. The crowd, needing no encouragement, started yelling, "Where's your 176 mph runs Garlits?". Their scepticism was rewarded with more slow runs and no competition to Langley's 161.29 mph at 9.2 seconds. When Red Case ran an easy 154 mph for his first run, Don, in desperation, elected to change the new camshaft back to the time-proven one it had replaced.

Clear, Texan sky and high, race-day temperatures, with the resultant poor traction on the track, brought out fans in huge numbers to witness the resolution of the long-anticipated, East-West battle. Garlits lost each toss of a coin to determine the running sequence. This meant that he had to face all three of the Californian cars plus Bobby Langley, to have a shot at top eliminator. Working his way through the field, the final confrontation was indeed, between Garlits and Pete Ogden; he in the glistening, high-dollar, Palamides' car with its beautifully-curved, fuel-injection trumpets and Don with the brace of old-fashioned carburettors. It brought back memories of Don's old hot rod versus the "rich kids" from St Petersberg. Against all odds, Garlits won! Clocking 165.24 mph at 9.13 seconds for Top Fuel Eliminator, leaving the Californians arguing among themselves about why they lost and who should have actually beaten Garlits.

The Art of Self-Promotion

According to Robert C Post, the social phenomenon of drag racing can only be understood by factoring in the effect of self-promotion and advertising. Drag racing is like a post-war continuation of the American tradition of barnstorming and Barnum and Bailey circus acts, rolled into an event that teenaged, hotrodders can readily aspire to and engage in. The sheer density of the population spread over the American landscape guaranteed that, as baby boomers became teenagers, thousands of pimply faces would appear in local workshops to get a glimpse of a hot rod, or hear an un-muffled, racing engine bark to life. Fascinated by the power, speed, noise, smoke, smell, acceleration and the glamor of drag racing, they youthfully dreamed of their own, hot-rod adventures. Young men could become hot-rod club members, pool their meagre funds and expertise to build race cars in their backyards, and achieve hair-raising speeds either on the streets or at local airfields serving as drag strips. Playing into this self-help, democratic melodrama were the event promoters and speed-equipment manufacturers. In the best tradition of the entertainment and promotion at which Americans excel, they pumped the hype of competition between cars and life-risking speed demons. In order to get spectator bums on seats, drag-strip promoters exploited competition between racers both on and off the track by creating a barrage of extravagant words and colorful, advertising posters known as "screamers".[10]

The master of the art of advertising-exaggeration was Ed Iskenderian. To sell his camshafts, not only did he pour fuel onto the fire between competitors, but he also taught a generation of

---

[10] Robert C Post, *High Performance: The culture and technology of drag racing*, *(1950-2000)*, 157.

motor heads the science of high performance through Isky advertisements in *Hot Rod* magazine. Adding intensity, the racers themselves played into the hype. They engaged in personal slanging matches with competitors using *Drag News* and other drag fraternity publications to offer offence and defence. All of this stirred the already-virulent pot of spectators, who thought nothing of making their passions known at the race track with cheers, boos, beer and soft drink cans hurled at the villain or the hero, depending upon whose side you were on. As Garlits dominated the Top Eliminator results, track promoters around the country offered him guaranteed starting money for match races at non-championship events. He exploited this by carefully selecting promoters and venues, and seeking local sponsorship. Reflecting on the economics of being a professional racer in the early days, Garlits claims that his motivation was pure competitiveness and survival. To illustrate the point he recalls his first run in California where he was offered a race for "pink slips". The prize was the pink-title ownership of a car that lost the contest. Garlits now regrets misunderstanding the offer, as he would have won hands down in that first instance.

Following Setto Postoian's well-publicised scepticism at Don's 176-mph achievement, the next opportunity to run against his arch rival was at the second running of the AATA World Series in Cordova, Illinois. Setto used the home-town advantage to good effect by recording 167.43 mph in 8.99 seconds, to which Don replied with the top speed of the meet at 170.13 mph. Setto eventually won the event when Garlits' clutch failed for the second time during the event. Top speed prize money alone was slim pickings for such a long tow but at least Setto was again silenced for a little while. Garlits next took the long swing into Chicago; Great Bend, Kansas; Caddo Mills, Texas; and back to Brooksville, Florida where he recorded 173.07 mph. Then he left again to run on a concrete drag strip in Montgomery, New York, fitted with new M&H 8.00 x 15 slicks. This resulted in an 8.36 second ET at 160.71 mph, providing convincing evidence of the superiority of the new, wider tires to achieve lower, elapsed times. These performances were backed up by a speed of 174.75 mph on the asphalt surface of Kissimmee, Florida. Then a further confirmation was at Brooksville, with NHRA officials present, to verify a new speed record of 180.00 mph at 8.90 seconds. Back-country drag strips where Garlits ran match races for money, were usually of very poor surface quality. When he ran at championship drag strips with a decent surface, his car handled like a dream. When Ed Iskenderian again mentioned to Garlits that the West Coast racers still did not believe this latest speed and ET, the time had come to meet them on their own drag strips.

West Coast Debut at Famoso, Bakersfield

Capitalising on the NHRA fuel ban, the Smokers Hot Rod Club of Bakersfield, north of LA, organised the inaugural United States Gas and Fuel Championship (later known as the Bakersfield March Meet), at Famoso Dragstrip, to be run in March, 1959. Don negotiated agreeable terms with the Smokers, additional appearance money from Kingdon Drag Strip, near Lodi, California, and a further meeting in Chandler, Arizona, with starting money totalling $5000. This was a huge amount, being held in safe keeping by Ed Iskenderian, as there had been previous instances of money not being paid. The "March Meet" is legendary in drag racing, known as the "Woodstock of drag racing", when virtually the whole town turned out for the event. This fostered a legion of motorheads including drag racers Tom "The Mongoose" McEwen, Cruz and Tony Pedregon, and Rick and Roger Mears (the brothers who went from being off-road racing champions to Indy Car racing, with Rick winning Indy four times).

Don, Pat and Ed made the trek to California for the first time, meeting their nemesis Setto Postoian en route from Detroit, along with a 17-year-old, aspiring drag racer named Connie Kalitta.

Don Garlits. The Enigmatic Hero

After meeting at Don Stillman's home in Arizona, they travelled in convoy to Inglewood, California. In preparation for the big event they enjoyed Ed Iskenderian's hospitality with a memorable Armenian feast. Ominously, the West Coast cars arrived at Famoso with their Chrysler Hemis equipped with GMC 6-71 superchargers mounted on top of Weiand manifolds, sitting underneath Hilborn fuel injectors and wearing M&H slicks. This was the configuration that had recently allowed Art Chrisman to run 181.91 mph in 8.54 seconds at the Riverside Dragstrip. GMC superchargers mounted in front of the engine, (originally fitted as blowers to General Motors two-stroke diesel engines), had been used for some time. The relocation to top-mounted and driven with toothed-rubber Gilmer belts, allowed changes in boost pressure as the supercharger speed varied with a change of pulley diameters. This was a significant performance breakthrough, despite the disadvantage that the supercharger obscured the driver's view of the track. Furthermore, Garlits set the Californian trend with M&H slicks and that completed the new, hot set-up.

With so much money at stake, the scene at the track was set by beer-can-throwing fans. The announcer Bernie Mather, wound up the fans with taunts, "Bring that piece of crap out here and see what it'll do, Don Garbage". To make matters worse, Garlits' car would not run well on the first qualifying day. Gary Cagle ran 180 mph, Art Chrisman did an 8.75-second ET, and the announcer incited the crowd with, "How did you like that one, Tampa Dan?". Eventually, Garlits ran 172 mph at 9.00 seconds, just enough to allow bets to be taken against his running any more than 170 mph or less than 9 seconds. The end of practice signalled the end of a miserable day and the beginning-of-the-end of the un-supercharged era for the Garlits' team. They could not improve on the run of 9.0 seconds at 172 mph, which was no longer competitive with the top cars under these conditions. The evening before Don Garlits' most important race of his career to-date, found him

The Rat Gets the Cheese

tearing down the engine at Ernie Hashim's Speed Shop, only to find a broken piston and a ruined engine block. Ed Iskenderian got on the phone, exhausting his contacts trying to find a stock, 392 Hemi, short block. They were left with no choice but to make do, fitting it with unsuitable pistons, con-rods and crankshaft. Race day dawned with an even bigger crowd to see the demise of Tampa Dan. As fate would have it, no sooner had the car been fired for the first of their elimination runs when calamity struck. A standard con-rod broke and oil was pouring onto the ground from the ruptured oil pan. Bernie Mather delighted the crowd with insults. To add insult to injury, the Eastern challengers were totally demoralised when Setto was beaten during an elimination round and Art Chrisman won the event with slow 9.36 at 140.50 mph. The final insult came when Don was accused of creating an excuse for losing by deliberately weakening the connecting rod to make it fail. Eight years later, in his 1967 autobiography, Don waxed philosophical; "The trip had been tremendously beneficial, mainly because it had forced me to make the switch to supercharged engines, whereas I might have fallen hopelessly behind men like Chrisman and Cyr if I had continued to race exclusively in the East... I learned that drag-racing competition was becoming so fierce that even the delay of several months in implementing the latest design advances could be a disaster."

That historic, month-long tour changed the lives of Don and Pat Garlits in another way. "When we got back, I don't think we'd spent $500 of that money because Isky fed us and we stayed at people's houses most nights. If you paid $10 for a room, hell, you were in a luxury motel! Gasoline cost about 18 cents a gallon. We had about $4000 cash, and my wife and I had always wanted a brand-new Cadillac. We'd wanted one from the day we got married. That was a real status symbol, and now we could get one." They eventually purchased real estate rather than the Cadillac which turned out to be an immeasurably-better investment decision. The supercharger era came and Don and Setto had to get on board to prepare for the Kingdon meet. With further help from Isky, Ed and Don built another new engine, a 454-cubic-inch monster with all the best gear: Forged-True pistons, C-T automotive crankshaft, Isky cam, boxed connecting rods and a 6-71 supercharger, but still with carburettors on a Weiand manifold rather than fuel injection. Don was unconvinced that the fuel supply problems with fuel injection had been solved. After the drama of Bakersfield, the Kingdon event was an anti-climax. The big guns did not show up. Garlits won against the Glass Slipper in the eliminations, to run against Setto in the Top Fuel final. It was an unsatisfying win that resolved nothing apart from further silencing Setto Postoian.

With a further two weeks to prepare for the Chandler, Arizona race, the crew returned to Iskenderian's shop to prepare for what promised to be another low-key event, apart from a match race against Jack Chrisman in the twin Chevy-engine, Howard's Cam Special. That was, until Don discovered that all the top Californians and Setto, who had changed his mind about running, had entered. Now there was a star-studded field with the single purpose of sending Garlits back where he belonged. Running 176 mph at 8.44 seconds in practice, the new combination of high horsepower and the M&H tires enabled Don to dispatch Jack Chrisman in the match race. Don then worked his way through the field, facing Chrisman again in the final for Top Fuel Eliminator. Garlits won the event against Chrisman, despite losing power due to a broken blower drive. The Californian trip had been a watershed both for Don and his competitors. They all realised that to remain competitive they had to keep up with the ever-changing, latest developments. Back in Tampa, Don prepared the car to run in Houston, Texas, by improving the blower drive and by fitting a new, high-capacity, Hilborn fuel pump, especially designed to run nitro. Testing the car at Brooksville confirmed the potential of the new set-up when Garlits recaptured the top speed record from Art Chrisman at 185.56 mph. In another of Pat's prescient interventions she presented Don with a new leather jacket, saying,

The Rat Gets the Cheese

"Don, this car is beginning to go so fast, that you just don't have enough protection. If you crashed, you'd have every bit of skin scraped off against the pavement. Those T-shirts you wear just aren't enough."

Doctor Cullen's "Spiritual Solution"

Disaster struck at Chester, South Carolina in 1959. Pat, pregnant again, stayed at home. Feeling confident with his new set-up, Don made a practice run of 177 mph and increased the percentage of nitro to see how fast he could go. Putting on his new leather jacket, Don ran the quarter mile. To cool the engine, he innocently switched off the ignition while still at high speed. Instantly an explosion immersed Don in flame as fuel in the manifold and supercharger exploded. This unprecedented phenomenon unexpectedly accompanied the fitting of the supercharger. Fanned by the speed of the car, the intensity of the fire grew. Don, shocked by the ferocity of the event, inadvertently kept the throttle partly open, feeding more fuel to the inferno. As he lost consciousness his foot relaxed from the throttle. The fuel was cut off and the fire extinguished. Don regained consciousness enough to stop the car, at which point excruciating pain kicked in. The supercharger that had given a tremendous power boost, was responsible for a new hazard. A high-speed explosion was enough to blow the supercharger off the engine, igniting an horrific inferno.

Saved, to some extent, by his new leather jacket, he could think only to ring Pat at home, lying to her of a little accident requiring a few days in hospital. But he would be alright if she would fly up to be with him. The truth was, "I nearly burned to death". "They were going to take my hands off. But I told them I would rather die." When Pat and Don's mother, Helen, arrived neither would sign the papers. Not wanting a death in his hospital, the doctor told them to find another place to die. So they did, in Florida.

Don Garlits. The Enigmatic Hero

Don recalls, "I rode from Chester to Tampa in a sleeping berth. I weighed just 80 pounds, all skin and bones". At St Joseph's Hospital, Tampa, a hand specialist, named Cullen, bent Don's fingers one by one, stretching the skin and making them bleed. "Good circulation!" he said. "Get this man to surgery." "I woke with both arms in troughs of saline solution, where they remained for 30 days until the new skin started closing in."

Doctor Cullen was, in fact, the best-trained surgeon that could have been available. He was a hard-bitten MASH surgeon fresh from the Korean War where he had attended to dozens of servicemen with tragic burns. (His war demons and shaking hands were only ever stilled long enough for surgery by the precaution of a fifth of rye whiskey.) Devastated by the fire and slow recovery from his injuries, Don concluded that his drag-racing days were over. He told Ed to sell his racing equipment and spare engines. But Ed didn't sell anything. Depressed and filled with regret for his situation, Don could only anticipate a future with useless hands and a face like an Egyptian mummy. When old schoolfriend Art Malone visited un-announced with his wife, Lorraine, he enquired as to Don's condition and future plans. Garlits' reply was a tale of woe. He was finished as a racer and the dragster was up for sale. Already experienced as a circle track racer, Art saw an opportunity, and suggested that he drive the car at least until Don recovered. Don reluctantly agreed to give the proposal some thought, considering that at least it may be possible for Art to fulfil existing contracts and the AHRA Nationals at Kansas in September. Don was release from hospital. Ed repaired the car, running it only on alcohol to limit the power, and the crew went to Kissimmee to trial the new driver. Art squeezed himself into the cockpit designed for a much smaller man, ran three times, all within the 165-mph, nine-second bracket, and won himself a job as a dragster driver with a one-month agreement to share prize money 50:50.

The Rat Gets the Cheese

With Ed running the shop and Pat's pregnancy progressing well, Don accompanied Art on a long drive to Sanford, Maine. By the day his health and enthusiasm for racing returned. In preparation to run against Setto Postoian and Red Greth in the Speed Sport roadster, Don taught Art the tricks of the drag racing trade, including the secret, that *most races are won off the starting line*. Beaten in the match race by the experienced Postoian, who ran a record-setting 182.92 mph, Art requested another run after the competition had finished. In an effort to improve top speed he wanted to trial a new technique of leaving the line without smoking the tires. With the day drawing to a close, and to a dwindling crowd, the loudspeaker announced a new speed record of 183.66 mph. This beat Postoian's three-hour-old mark and also broke Don's old, world record set in Houston. By accident, another leap of progress. Art discovered this speed-record-breaking technique because, in the cramped cockpit he could not get his foot fully off the clutch. Although this was still not the way to set low-elapsed time, it was a crowd pleaser, effective in getting top speed. By the time the AHRA Nationals came around, the car had been modified to accommodate Art's large frame, and he had run the car several times in preparation for open competition. Deliberately smoking the tires in time trials to gain the fastest ET of the meet at 8.23 seconds, was good for morale but bad for the engine. It was showing signs of stress. The final run was against Chris Karamesines, also known as "the Greek", who was driving his Chizler dragster. Karamesines was to become a perennial in the sport, commencing in the early 1950s, and still competing for Top Fuel in 2016, when he scored a round win at Gainesville, Florida, defeating number-one qualifier Richie Crampton.

The Making of a Rat

Setto Postoian was by now milking the advertising hype for all it was worth to gain match race bookings. He was incendiary

Don Garlits. The Enigmatic Hero

about a dubious speed of 195.65 mph attributed to Malone, in a match race series at Dunkirk, that Postoian had actually won. This prompted Postoian to return to his old form, taking a full page in *Drag News* to accuse Garlits and Malone: "No wonder they call you 'the Swamp Rat', you are only in the sport for what you can get out of it. You shoot your mouth off about safety, then take a green kid and put him in the biggest-blown fueler you can possibly make...", and demanding that Garlits explain how a record-setting speed can be set while losing a race. This was music to the ears of the Californians who now derided Garlits as "the Swamp Rat"—a much better insult than those previously-used affronts. Malone, who quickly developed a taste for the hype and publicity, immediately painted "The Green Kid" on his helmet to keep the pot boiling. The final event, just before Christmas, 1959, was a showdown and a nice finish to the difficulties of the year, with the added bonus of the birth of Don and Pat's first daughter, Gay Lyn. The ever-vigilant promoters adopted the "Swamp Rat" tag to goad Setto, who resisted the bait by not turning up. But other top contenders came from all over the USA with a map published in *Drag News* to show where the cars were coming from, including the home state "top dogs" from California. Running in eliminations against local hero Art Chrisman, of the Chrisman family drag racing dynasty that had never been beaten at the track, Art Malone won. The crowd went into uproar and pelted beer bottles and cans at Don and Ed Iskenderian who were helping with the car. Using every advantage, and then some, Malone was next scheduled to race the Cyr and Hopper dragster, when Ted Cyr came looking to see what set-up they were running. Spotting Don's 9.00 M&H Racemaster slicks, and not knowing that they were an experimental compound, Cyr asked Don's advice, as to which tires he should use. Knowing well that Cyr's existing 8.20 tires were better than the normally-available 9.00's, Don replied that the 9.00 tires were the best for the track. With this advice, Cyr changed back to the inferior 9.00 tires which determined Malone's easy win. Further cementing his reputation as a tough competitor, Don rationalised his position by saying, "If you are looking for good advice don't ask your opposition!"

The Rat Took the Cheese

The story of the Riverside event ran in the next issue of *Drag News* with the magnificent headline, "The 'Rat' took the cheese". The cheese, in this case, was a rare variety. Don had negotiated a percentage of the gate with the organisers, resulting in a tidy sum of $7000. The irony of this headline reflected the reality of the West versus East competition and the gritty persistence of the man for whom the insult was intended. By now, the "Swamp Rat" nickname had gained currency with race promoters, rivals and drag racing insiders, and with Don himself, when he adopted the slur as a compliment and painted the name on his car, thus creating the lineage of more than 30 Swamp Rat cars, with no end in sight.

Ed Iskenderian's role extended to more than just supplier of home-cooked meals, camshafts and T-shirts. In addition to providing cash to keep the show on the road, he also got his hands dirty helping with the dragster and fixing the fuel pump on Don's Cadillac tow car during the event, not to mention being pelted with beer cans. But of even more importance was his encouragement. Certainly, the extra business from drag-racing customers was welcome, but Ed was a racer's racer. A great collector of memorabilia (he refuses to discard anything), Ed was more interested in counting the people he influenced and supported in the sport, rather than counting the dollars through the cash register. Iskenderian had long-accumulated friends, including Garlits, who would, many years later, declare respect and affection for the man they called the "Camfather". Winning relationships is an even greater accomplishment than winning championships. Ed

Don Garlits. The Enigmatic Hero

Iskenderian was among those who helped Don Garlits at the beginning and was also among those, more than 50 years later, who recognised, that in reality, Garlits filled the shoes of Big Daddy—the greatest of all drag racers. In some cases, it took Garlits a long time to realise how important friends were to him. We all take each other for granted, especially those who are closest to us.

Chapter 4 Safety Fast

> *"Whoever digs a pit may fall into it, whoever breaks through a wall may be bitten by a snake. Whoever quarries stones may be injured by them; whoever splits logs may be endangered by them."*
> – Eccles 10:8-9

Drag racing seemed to push the boundaries of common sense without good reason in the post-war period. It engaged competitive instincts to an extreme, sometimes to a deadly conclusion, with youthful Californian hotrodder buddies racing on city streets. Despite his best intentions to sanitise hot rodding, Wally Parks, the paternalistic founder of the *National Hot Rod Association* (drag racing's major sanctioning body), appeared to have confused the issue of safety. By initiating the NHRA motto, "DEDICATED TO SAFETY", he attempted to improve the "bad boy" image that street racing had created for hotrodders as it is was already abundantly clear that they were dedicated to speed rather than to safety. Safety was only ever a consideration once the question of speed was answered. Notwithstanding the resulting mayhem, it was this hot-rod optimism that inspired technologically awakened young men and women. It was they who created wealth and explosive growth that came with the post-war boom of productivity and babies. But with unrestrained optimism also came restraining conservative forces, including those of William Randolph Hearst, via his newspaper, the *Los Angeles Examiner*. In a campaign to protect society from the perils of reckless abandon caused by hotrodders, Hearst labelled hot rodding as, *social rebellion and an unwarranted risk that inevitably causes harm, with no social benefit.*

Don Garlits. The Enigmatic Hero

Danger Calls

There are only three true sports; Auto Racing, Bullfighting and Mountain Climbing. All the rest are children's games at which men play.
– Ernest Hemmingway

According to the maxim attributed to Hemmingway, drag racing might be the ultimate expression of auto racing as a "true sport". Top Fuel drag racing is akin to strapping yourself to a rocket and, for a few seconds, exceeding the rate of acceleration that astronauts encounter on their trip into space. Science predicted, due to friction of rubber tires against road surface, that cars would never accelerate at more than 1g (the acceleration due to gravity), reaching a maximum of 170 mph in the standing quarter-mile. To achieve current speeds of over 320 mph and 3.7 second elapsed times over 1000 feet, (reduced from 1320 feet in 2008, after the death of Funny Car driver Scott Kalitta), Top Fuel dragsters accelerate momentarily at up to 8g, compared to a relatively low 3g for a space rocket. Regardless of the measures of performance, drag racing was created not by rocket scientists or engineers but by backyard, amateur mechanics who had no real concept of the limits imposed by the science they were challenging. Robert C Post states, "The greatest single difference between a craftsman and an engineer, is that the craftsman nearly always designs 'in the material', transferring his conception directly from a mental image through his hands, straight into the trial or the finished object".[11] By contrast, an engineer turns an idea into a drawing in order to first contemplate the science.

Drag racing's popularity endures partly because it represents the ultimate human harnessing of power that can be attempted without the resources of NASA. The fact that it can be done is

---

[11] Robert C Post. 194 *High Performance. The Culture and Technology of Drag Racing 1950-2000*. John Hopkins University Press.

reason enough for professional racers and weekend warriors alike, to put themselves in harm's way somewhere in the world every weekend. Drivers strapping themselves into wheeled missiles just for fun illustrates the dilemma of an individual's freedom to deliberately put him/herself at risk. It suggests that this is how humans behave when motivated by the passion for discovery, adventure and competition, to say nothing of money, machismo (read "sex"), or power.

The Necessity of Risk

I have come to see that all human progress involves risk. The supply of food, shelter, comfort; the quarrying of stones for the construction of dwellings; the harnessing of water; or the manufacture of machines as simple as a lever to move a rock—all involve risk. Often the risk is easy to control; perhaps risky simply because we have not done it before. I have heard it said that risk is created by "an uninformed step into the unknown", or, in some cases, "an informed and foolhardy step". Risk becomes apparent when we take that step and see first-hand what can go wrong. Inevitably, taking risks and learning from the experience to control them is a necessary human undertaking.

NASA knows a lot about risk management. When things go wrong many people suffer. Accordingly, enormous effort is made by NASA to manage risk. Even so, things still go wrong. To avoid what has become known as the potential cause of great harm, that NASA has dubbed, "The Complacency Syndrome", NASA has developed a responsive concept of "The Normalisation of Deviance". By being on the lookout for complacent attitudes at every level, this discipline tries to make the unknowns of NASA activities as safe as possible. The technique works by getting people to speak up about their concerns rather than rely on *group think*. Group think thrives, because if no one complains, there is a shared assumption that everything will be okay. This parallels the prevention of what I later describe as a "wheels up landing". When our mistakes become apparent, be they made out of ignorance, foolhardiness or complacency, we have an opportunity to learn to prevent them from happening again.

Learning from Failure

Psychologist, Carl Jung coined the term the collective unconscious, which points out that we, (either individuals), or a group as large as a society) can do something significant and be blinded by our own success, failing to see what we have excluded from our consciousness. Our blindness can be ignorance or arrogant presumption—the sense that we know everything we need to know. Such attitudes often bring us to peril because our success masks the new problem we have created. Success teaches us nothing other than the salutary recognition that we have confirmed what we thought to be correct. On the other hand, catastrophe alerts every fibre of our being to find out what went wrong and to avoid the situation happening again.

You only learn through mistakes. – Antron Brown interview[12]

"Safety fast" is the right motto for motor racing. The ideal of "safety first" simply does not jell with the reality of the racing experience where advances always involve increased speed or efficiency precariously balanced against the benefit. If we really believed in safety first we would make no progress, for fear of unknown risks. The need for risk is not restricted to sport. Stephen M R Covey's book, *The Speed of Trust*, begins with a quote from Jack Welsh, the CEO of the international conglomerate GE, who challenges risk-averse thinking. "If you are not fast, you are

---

[12] 2012 NHRA Top Fuel champion.

dead." Speed and its associated risk are the very life-blood of business. Speed allows the well-prepared to be "first and best to market". Rupert Murdoch is an even bigger risk-taker whose motto for senior managers is "high autonomy and high accountability". Inherent in the formula is the risk of failure, but the result is growth of a stellar, global, media and entertainment empire. Although motor racing has a good record for treating safety seriously, compared with mountain climbing and bullfighting, there have been many deaths among competitors and spectators alike. Among the worst was the death of driver Pierre Levegh, plus 80 spectators, at LeMans, France, in 1955. This tragedy resulted in motor racing being banned in some countries (including Switzerland)—a ban that remains in force today for most categories of the sport. Had the ban on motor racing been applied universally, humanity would not be beneficiaries of the safety controls that have ensued.

Despite the ever-present threat of harm, with simultaneous innovations in speed and safety, motor racing continues to thrive. Indeed, *progress requires risk*. Which begs the question, "How much risk is acceptable?". The language of business indicates that *business risk* is an inescapable reality instilled into company law. Business risk requires both investors and creditors to perform *due diligence* to acknowledge that they are entering into a risky activity, no matter how much they wish it were not so.

Risk-Free?

The attempt to create a risk-free environment has its own unintended consequences. According to my wife, (who trained as a specialist, early-childhood educator), a mother who keeps her baby off the floor and from eating garden dirt and snails, has a youngster who, come school-age, is more susceptible to common childhood illnesses. Children must be trained to take risks such as climbing trees, to know the proper fear of heights and to learn how not to fall. Some safety advocates and other risk-averse people take the moral high ground, insisting that safety should be the primary consideration for all human endeavor, including business and sports. For those who favor safety over progress, intentionally-risky behavior is unnecessary and therefore morally and socially unacceptable. A society that avoids learning from painful experiences creates the blindness of group-think, which is of grave concern to NASA. But this is not the most harmful aspect of being risk-averse. According to Carl Jung, quoted by M Scott Peck, "Neurosis is always a substitute for legitimate suffering".[13]

Australian, multi-millionaire, philanthropist, entrepreneur and adventurer Dick Smith is a great advocate for what he calls "responsible risk". At age 20, with a group of Rover Scouts, he climbed Ball's Pyramid, the world's tallest volcanic stack, (jutting out of the Pacific 700 kilometres north-east of Sydney). Smith now says that the experience of conquering his fear was instrumental in his later business success. Today he regrets that (for environmental reasons) this challenge is not available to young people. "They have to be able to take responsible risks. Otherwise, they might as well sit at home, drink alcohol and drugs and get obese. There has to be some sort of spirit of adventure in life."[14] Motor racing in general, and drag racing in particular, is an activity where risk is subordinate to the challenge of competition. Although no other justifications are required many are possible, including entertainment, human motivation, marketing spin and technical innovations that have found their way into road transport, and indeed into rocket science. But in the final analysis, as a society, we have a palpable need for speed that must be satisfied.

---

[13] *The Road Less Travelled*, 17.
[14] *The Weekend Australian*, (July 12-13, 2014).

Don Garlits *was in it to win it*. His risk was to make changes to his car that put him at a competitive disadvantage.

Faith and Risk

The paradox of courage is that a man must be a little careless of his life even in order to keep it. – GK Chesterton

Risk is required not just in sport or business, but in the adventures of life. Essential to all human existence and enterprise are the risks of faith. Faith, usually associated with religious belief, is not exclusively a religious concept. The classic, Biblical definition of faith from Hebrews 11 reads, "Faith is the substance of things hoped for, the evidence of things not yet seen". Faith is significant and purposeful; a "substance" that we cannot see, but which we "hope" is true, because we intend to act as if it were. Use of the term "substance" implies that our hope is the basis of significant, daily activity, not just a superfluous, abstract concept. Hebrews 11 goes on to say that "faith is required to please God". This, of course, is a religious concept, but an entirely logical one. It is God who cannot be seen or proven by scientific method. Therefore, for His pleasure to be realised in our lives, he must be the object of hope and the basis of behavior. This also speaks to the false dichotomy between faith and science. Science is about what can be replicated and proven by scientific method. Faith, however, which cannot be proven before it is exercised, is essential for us to achieve what can only be imagined/what does not currently exist, which, in some cases, takes a lifetime to accomplish. Faith, therefore, is required for all human progress, not just religious activity. One reason why faith and science are considered in opposition is that many deny the need for faith in God. The essential difference between faith and science is the timeline and criterion for proof. Science requires evidence or proof-of-repeatability in a laboratory, under controlled conditions. Similarly, faith requires confirming evidence, in my view, but proof in the mathematical sense is not possible in time and space. If it were, faith would require nothing of us, as God would be reduced to a creature like us instead of a supreme who dwells outside the material world to which we are limited. Ultimately, for people of faith, like me, there is no contradiction between faith and science because if God exists, then science belongs to Him. The risk of faith in God has already been taken. You just have to bet your life on it being true. Faith is the other side of the coin to risk. Ironically, the alternatives to religion require a substitute faith in science, reason, or some other thing, perhaps even in the hope that science will someday explain away any legitimacy for religious faith in a transcendent being.

Despite the implementation of increasingly-stringent risk controls, drag racing remains significantly out of step with a risk-averse point of view. Opponents of risk suggest that primitive man battling wild animals for survival has passed into history; the modern era should advance with caution; benefits to progress are not worth risk-taking. But there are new risks to encounter. (Fewer wild animals. More wild frontiers.) Not that safety awareness is exclusively a modern dilemma. The Teacher of Ecclesiastes warns: "If you dig a pit, you might fall into it...Whoever quarries stones may be injured by them...".[15] The Teacher also says, despite the inevitable hardships of life, "there is always a proper time and procedure for all activities".[16] In the pursuit of progress, a reasonable person must exercise a continuous, precarious and simultaneous balance of risk and caution.

Anything worth doing, requires faith. – Tony Schumacher[17]

---

[15] Eccles 10:8-9.
[16] Eccles 8:6.
[17] Seven-time NHRA Top Fuel Champion.

Safety Fast

Speed Costs. How Fast do you want to go?

Drag racing, and motor sports in general, improve the breed, but only at some cost. Competitive progress must be the goal, followed closely by a responsible approach to risk. Progress always requires a step into the unknown. Conversely, if we engage in activity where we know harm will definitely result, we are culpable and should expect to be accused of negligence. I contend that "safety fast" should be the motto of responsible progress, not "safety first". Task should predominate human achievement. Safety always follows progress, never leads.

Drag racing has generally shown a high degree of responsibility for safety. At times, it has gone too far to live up to its "safety fast" motto, such as during the 1957-1962 NHRA ban against nitromethane fuel. Garlits and others ran at events sanctioned by organisers who happily took advantage of the ban. Garlits' use of nitro was proven right by history when the ban was lifted. Top Fuel dragsters led the period of greatest innovation and drew the biggest crowds in the history of the sport. Safety was not abandoned as some feared. Rather, safety was inextricably linked with performance improvements. There should never be a forced choice between safety or progress alone. This presents a false dichotomy.

"The pursuit of speed and safety are in conflict. Any time you add speed, you better consider safety. ...For safety, there is no answer, there are only opinions." This is a remarkable insight from legendary dragster chassis builder, Don Long, in an interview in *Hot Rod* magazine.[18] Safety must be considered along with any performance improvement. But until the planned outcome, there is only guessing, at which time the bitter reality of experience must be accepted.

---

[18] February 2014.

Don Garlits. The Enigmatic Hero

The role of rule-makers is fundamentally important to human well-being. The NHRA, despite occasionally overstepping the mark, has done a good job of regulation, allowing the creative tension between speed and safety to continue. Societies need boundaries to determine what is acceptable and what is not, to provide freedom without unfair advantage. It is an essential feature of democracy that the proper enforcement of constraint is exercised on free enterprise. Had this been the case in 2009, the Global Financial Crisis may have been averted. In Australia, banks and financial institutions were subject to far greater restraint than in New York or London. This seems to be consistent in all human activity (except love), that restraint serves the common good. This is also what The Teacher means when he says that there is "a proper time and procedure for all things". Don Garlits, despite his many battles with the NHRA over rules and their often-paternalistic attitude, now says, "The NHRA is drag racing".

That the only purpose for which power can be rightfully exercised over any member of a civilized community, against his will, is to prevent harm to others. In the part that merely concerns himself, his independence is, of right, absolute. Over himself, over his own body and mind, the individual is sovereign. – John Stuart Mill

The mid-1950s were Garlits' pioneer, professional, drag-racing days. This era witnessed the transition of hot rods created from discarded Fords with hopped-up, flathead V8 engines in modified chassis, to the advent of high-performance, overhead-valve engines available from American car manufacturers. Don Garlits' first "rail" dragster was so-named for its two car chassis rails with the driver sitting behind a flathead Ford V8. To gain a weight advantage on the rear wheels, the driver's legs were straddled over the rear axle with only a minimal roll bar protecting the driver. There was no consideration for the driver's "family jewels" or feet, which were located on either side of the bellhousing that contained a flywheel and clutch assembly (with the potential to explode like a bomb at any time). When the Chrysler Hemi engine became available in wrecking yards, during 1954, Garlits fitted a 331-cubic-inch version into his rail, and established a benchmark for performance over the quarter mile with speeds immediately increasing from 108 mph pre-Hemi, to 128 mph in 10.5 seconds. So began the steady, hot-rodder, cut-and-try evolution of Chrysler V8 Hemi engines and dragster chassis, fettled by the instinctive hands of backyard mechanics. They were grease monkeys with little formal training in engineering, chemistry and vehicle dynamics, whose boundaries now extended beyond the limits of accepted science. Safety innovations during this period were many, for example, the use of parachutes for braking. The first recorded use of a parachute to slow a drag-racing hot rod was in a whimsical, Stroker McGurk cartoon by Tom Medley, that appeared in *Hot Rod* magazine. That trigger inspired drag racers to try it for real, and it worked! If parachutes had not been used, the continual increases in speed would not have been possible. There were few drag strips long enough to slow dragsters from speeds exceeding 100 mph by use of conventional drum brakes on the rear wheels. Dragsters in Australia during this period were controlled by the dominant Confederation of Australian Motor Sport, which required all race cars to be fitted with four-wheel brakes. This was impossible with dragsters, due to their extreme, rear wheel, weight bias and the consequent inability of front brakes to do anything useful. Against pointless regulation, Australian drag racers obediently fitted front brakes to pass inspection, then blocked them off to prevent the car destabilising.

Speeds and acceleration rates increased with the advances in power and traction, as racers tend to believe that you can never have too much power. The first weak link in the power train was the clutch, which in the early days was a heavy-duty truck item connecting the engine to the wheels. Excess power was dissipated by smoking the tires as the engine tried to overpower the friction between tires and road. The elimination of a transmission proved to be a major step forward, as clutch slip substituted for a transmission and tire smoke. When it was realized that both changing gears and smoking the tires were an unnecessary waste of power and time, speeds rose and elapsed times fell dramatically. The unintended consequence of this leap forward was catastrophic clutch failure when the truck-sourced clutch and flywheel explosions became common-place. Huge energy inputs into the clutch caused extreme overheating and eventual disintegration. The initial hot-rodder engineering solution was to improve heat capacity of the friction surfaces with heat-resistant, sintered metal clutch facings, and to enclose the rotating mass in a supposedly explosion-proof, heavy steel bellhousing, ominously called a scatter-shield. As power increased, with more nitromethane and increased supercharger pressure, so did the need to improve each weak link that prevented the new-found performance from being exploited. Safety innovations included increased chassis length for greater stability, greatly-improved tires, parachutes for brakes, stronger rear-axle components, and fully-floating axle shafts that prevented the wheels from falling off if an axle broke.

The engine remained the main source of increased performance, but every boost in power was matched with direct or indirect safety enhancements, some in reaction to disaster and some by design. Increasingly, ex-military servicemen entered the sport, bringing with them their engineering and design skills. Perhaps the most decisive innovation in drag racing history came in 1971, following a predictably-Garlits involved incident. The innovative, two-speed, planetary transmission exploded, cutting Garlits' car in two and severely damaging his right foot. Appalled by this carnage, from his hospital bed, Garlits dreamed up a solution to clutch and supercharger explosions. For years, drivers had suffered the barrage of shrapnel, and hot oil and nitromethane-fuelled infernos fanned by a 180-mph "breeze". His solution was to isolate the driver from the source of harm by relocating him in front of the engine.

An engine explosion inferno, in the driver's face.
(PHOTOGRAPH BY STEVE REYES)

This innovation, so obvious in hindsight, was not entirely original as there had been many rear-engine cars built previously, but not by competitors so committed to winning as Garlits. Even he wondered if the change was really an advance. It took his wife's convincing, and building another, front-engine car as insurance, before rear-engine rails became the universal solution. A myth emerged that rear-engine cars were impossible to control because at top speed they refused to travel straight. Garlits and his chassis fabricator Connie Swingle, realized that the problem was not the car, but the driver over-reacting with steering inputs. (Relocating the driver halfway down the length of the car meant he now needed less steering-correction inputs than when he was located behind the rear axle, using the length of the car to gauge steering corrections.) The solution was to reduce the steering gear ratio from 6:1 to 10:1, so the driver did not over-correct when only small adjustments were required. Garlits was later ridiculed for his adoption of an aluminized fire suit in conjunction with front-engine cars, but eventually, as lives continued to be lost, this type of fire protection became mandatory.

Proving the Pudding

The need to prove a concept is now well and truly established in many fields of endeavor, including motor racing, where the great innovators are not necessarily the great winners. History shows, winners need to be conservative when it comes to innovation for its own sake, as it is possible for the new thing to detract from the win. Above all, winners demand consistency of themselves and their equipment. They then look for incremental improvements to show real gains from new ideas, which is the secret to success for all great designers and engineers. Safety management might take the high ground to dictate terms of improvement and behavior. But it is always practitioners, like Garlits, who make real progress. Pioneers are people who take ideas and make them work, not just for the sake of innovation but for real improvement. In Formula 1 racing, which, in the period between 1950 and 1980, was killing several drivers each year, champion Jackie Stewart, applied his ample intelligence and steely resolve to improve safety, in contrast to many of his contemporaries for whom the risk of death was noble fatalism. Stewart's efforts have resulted in continuous change in car and circuit design to the extent that he could later claim, "There is no doubt that Formula 1 has the best risk management of any sport and any industry in the world". Some developments led to outstanding breakthroughs, such as the impact of rear-engine, Cooper racing cars on the design of Formula 1 and Indianapolis cars. Jim Hall's Chaparral Can-Am cars with their high-mounted wings, were bristling with innovation, as were Colin Chapman's Lotus cars, whose constant innovation resulted in several breakthroughs, despite several disasters, and a reputation for unnecessary compromise. A recent example of this is the development of the HANS device (head and neck restraint), developed by sports car racer, Jim Downing, and his crash-researcher, brother-in-law, Professor Bob Hubbard. The HANS device was invented following the death of a friend of Downing, whose car hit a sand bank head-on. (His basilar skull fracture was caused by his body being restrained, but not his head.) The device was initially greeted with scepticism. Less than 300 were sold in the first ten years of production, until the death of NASCAR speedway superstar, Dale Earnhardt, in 2001. News broke that Earnhardt's death was due to basilar skull fracture and would not have occurred if he had worn a HANS device. The following week 250 were ordered and they have since become mandatory in many codes of top-level motorsport.

The Unsquared Dance

Compared to his irresistible force of passion, Don Garlits' lack of technical knowledge and skill was no handicap. He naturally transitioned from hot-rodder to much admired and emulated champion drag racer. So it was with the legendary, jazz musician Dave Brubeck. Against his critics, he graduated from the conservatory unable to read music, but proceeded to create his signature, jazz classics, "Take Five" and "The Unsquare Dance".

There's a way of playing safe, there's a way of using tricks and there's the way I like to play, which is dangerously, where you're going to take a chance on making mistakes in order to create something you haven't created before. – Dave Brubeck

I conclude, that none of us should engage in or encourage pointless risk-taking where there is no benefit and almost certain harm. However, each of us should attempt the challenges life presents to us with whatever legitimate passion, motivation and wisdom we can gather and apply. Weigh up and control the variables enough to take risks. And aim for progress and rich, learning experiences.

Life is Risky. Give it Your Best Shot

Workplace health and safety has been of long-standing, professional interest to me, as I made my living from being a safety consultant and trainer for the past 15 years of my working life. The concept of doing what is *reasonably practicable* in relation to workplace safety, implies self-assessment of risk by the person responsible for the activity, while giving consideration to the welfare of others.

I propose that the riskiest activity any of us can embark upon, is life itself. In which case, responsible for ourselves, we are subject to our own assessment of risk. Unlikely to be hermits, we will encounter a series of very complex relationships, where what we do will impact others. If we are responsible for others and claim to love them, we will take this impact into account. We will be in discussion with them; we will acknowledge their view as to what is mutually good. This makes the assessment of risk not so simple. We are no longer the sole authority on how we should behave. Furthermore, we might acknowledge our ultimate accountability to God, the giver of life, in which case we are wise to consider what he thinks is best for everybody.

Regardless of whether your decision making is simple or complex, you will always have to take a risk that your decision is the right one. So, minimize the risk as much as possible and give it your best shot.

Chapter 5 Top Fuel

> *"What does a man get for all his toil and anxious striving with all which he labors under the sun?"*
> – Eccles 2:22

The Ford V8

From the first *thrump* of the 1932 Ford flathead V8 heard in public, the debate was over. The ideal engine for power and performance was this—the culmination of the commercial, engineering and industrial genius of Henry Ford, who, more than any other man, put the world on wheels. Ford enabled millions to own a car by constant improvement and price reduction resulting from production-line and quality-control techniques. He inspired successive generations to become engineers who designed, repaired or raced cars. The first V8 engine to be successfully mass-produced in large numbers was an immediate success, to the extent that the four-cylinder engine, 1932 model Ford was slow to sell and was eventually dropped from the Ford range. Despite the global depression, the already-overcrowded car market hungry for innovation immediately adopted the V8 for its superior power, visual and aural impact, and bragging rights.[19]

---

[19] The lack of change in the basic architecture of the V8 during 80 years is remarkable. The main evolution is related to moving the valves from the side of the cylinder bore and later the camshafts, to the overhead location. "Big Yankee V8" has become a byword and an icon by fulfilling automotive dreams for size, power and performance, sound, and low cost. The basic

Don Garlits. The Enigmatic Hero

Ford celebrated their V8 motif in 1967, by sponsoring the design of the Cosworth DFV V8 by Englishman Keith Duckworth, who was encouraged by the famous, racing-car design genius, Colin Chapman of Lotus Cars. The DFV incredibly utilized the dimensions of the small, cheap, but game-changing, short-stroke, Ford, four-cylinder, 116E Kent production engine. The Cosworth V8 has become the most successful racing engine of all time used in Formula 1, Indianapolis, LeMans, speedboat racing and many other applications. Evolution has resulted in higher engine speeds and outputs to the extent that the 2.4-liter, Ford Formula 1 V8 engine of 2012, is 33 percent smaller than the original 3.6-liter flathead but develops more than eight-times the power. In this case, the real difference between low and high horsepower for a given engine size is speed (the number of "bangs per minute"), reflecting that the true nature of all progress is to get things done faster. Evidence of this, is that the original flathead V8 developed its maximum power at 3500 rpm, compared to the 20,000 rpm of the 2012 Cosworth F1 V8 engine. While it is possible to double the size of the "bang" in the cylinder of a racing engine, compared to an ordinary engine, the difference in speed may be four-times as great.

There is another name that must always be included in hot rod history, that of Zora Arkus-Duntov, who created the evolutionary link between the flathead, Ford V8 and the Chrysler Hemi. Duntov, who later became recognized as the "father of the Chevrolet Corvette", is arguably America's best-pedigreed

---

design of pistons in opposite cylinders connected to a common crankshaft journal indexed at 90 degrees to the next crankshaft journal, remains the benchmark, not just in America, but across the automotive world. Testament to the superiority of the design is the inclusion of the Ford flathead V8 among the 10 Best Engines ever built and a letter from Clyde Barrow to Henry Ford, thanking him for the engine that powered his Ford V8 getaway car with his partner in crime, Bonnie Parker.

hotrodder. He was born in Belgium in 1909, of Jewish-Russian parents who moved to Berlin and then to the USA to escape the Nazi tyranny. Already accomplished as an engineer and car racer before they arrived in New York, Zora and his brother Yura, established an engineering company called Ardun, to manufacture components for Ford, including a hemispherical, cylinder head conversion for the flathead V8. The flathead, which by then was ubiquitous not only in cars, trucks, boats, army scout cars but in myriad other uses, lacked power and overheated chronically due to the long exhaust passage through the block. This was especially so in truck applications. No doubt Duntov drew upon his experience with racing engines to design and build about 200 sets of his conversion (just as overhead valve V8s from the major manufacturers were becoming common in the late 1940s). Hotrodders, being what they are, soon discovered the potential for the Ardun Hemi truck conversion to turn their obsolete flathead water-boilers into racing engines. In 1952, Don Clark and Clem Tebow used an Ardun conversion to power a run of 162 MPH at the Bonneville salt flats in a 1932 Ford roadster. Don Garlits, being an appreciator and curator of such history, has accumulated unused, Ardun conversion kits in his massive, private collection of hot-rod items and has rightly added Zora Arkus-Duntov to his Drag Racing Hall of Fame.

The Chrysler Hemi

Even more extraordinary than the flathead V8 evolution to the Cosworth DFV V8, is the evolution from the flathead V8 to the Ardun Hemi V8, to the Chrysler Hemi V8 design from the early 1950s that still powers dragsters. Hemi clones now develop 100-times more power than the original flathead, by increasing speed moderately, increasing the average combustion pressure as much as ten times and by the use of so-called power adders, including supercharging and nitromethane fuel. The Chrysler

Hemi V8, introduced to the market in 1953, reflects the very ethos of hot rodding and drag racing—that a backyard mechanic can take an ordinary, V8 passenger-car engine and turn it into something truly extraordinary, such as a Top Fuel dragster engine that will achieve amazing levels of high performance. Notice the pithy parable of what an ordinary person can do with their life? Transform it into something extraordinary. All it takes is the process of performance-modification in the hands of a diligent enthusiast, guided by the hands of a master mechanic.

Here is the source of the trouble. A Chrysler V8 Hemi that has blown its self out of the car, now sitting on the dragstrip (PHOTOGRAPH BY STEVE REYES).

The Little Deuce Coupe

The Deuce (as 1932 Ford cars are known, to signify the year of manufacture), are instantly recognizable for their elegant, radiator-grille design that has become an emblem of the most perfectly-designed car. The 1932 Ford cars were built in several factories in a range of variants for only one year, before the grille and body design was changed to the more "streamlined" shape of the 1933 range. But it is the Deuce grille that symbolizes the prototype of all hot rods. Of course, not all hot rods are Deuces. All Fords, plus many other makes of the era, including Chevrolets, Chryslers and some unlikely candidates such as Willys and English Fords, became hot rods on the streets of LA and on the drag strip. A Ford V8 Deuce coupe is clearly the ultimate Hot Rod, and arguably, the ultimate car. There are, of course, many other pretenders to the title, such as the T Model Ford, Ferrari 250 GTO, the E-Type Jaguar, Volkswagen Beetle, the original Morris and Austin Mini-Minor, and any number of modern super-cars such as the Bugatti Veyron. But, as a watershed of design and a benchmark of enduring influence and desirability, there is no peer to the Deuce, especially the coupe.

Don's Hot Rod, fitted with new old stock Ardun Hemi heads on a Ford side valve engine block (PHOTOGRAPH BY STEVE REYES).

To support that claim, we could call on the experience of a hot-rod expert, such as Pat Ganahl or celebrated hotrodders such as Chip Foose, the late Boyd Coddington, Jay Mays, or Don Garlits himself, but that would be like asking Dracula if he recommended blood as a tonic. Film Producer George Lucas chose a yellow, 1932 highboy coupe to represent youth culture in his hit movie "American Graffiti". Alternatively, we could turn to Adrian Newey, chief technical officer for the dominant, Red Bull Formula 1 car, widely-recognized as the greatest racing-car engineer of the modern era. Newey, as an old-car, motor-head racer himself, is said to love hot rods. But for passion and inspiration, it would be hard to go past Ian Callum, the British designer of Aston Martin and Jaguar cars, who is inspired by the purity and simplicity of the Ford Deuce hot rod that he has parked in his garage, and in particular, its signature radiator grille. Callum describes the '32 Ford grille as the hallmark of purity and sophistication of design that he tries to replicate in his contemporary work, and it shows. When some of Callum's fellow-designers "humor" him about his hot rod, he replies in the same way that many hotrodders do: *If the appeal of hot rods has to be explained, there is no point in the explanation.*

Hot Rod Evolution

Inevitably, the creation of powerful cars lures us into comparisons of performance, which of course means illegal street racing. In response to years of lives lost and bad publicity, Santa Ana garage and gas station owner CJ "Pappy" Hart, with his wife, Peggy, saw an alternative to his young customers blocking off deserted highways to race. With the assistance of the city fathers and the police, Hart established the Santa Ana Drag Strip at the Orange County Airport, in California, to become the first commercial drag strip. With the provision of basic facilities and rules, Hart and his wife held races every Sunday from 1950 to 1959, exercising a firm grip on competitors by the simple expedient of banning racers from the track if they were caught street racing. His efforts made hot rods safer and more respectable by getting racing off the street and in the process turned a dollar from the burgeoning sport. Their efforts were eventually recognised by the City of Santa Ana, proclaiming April 29th, in honour of his memory, as CJ "Pappy" Hart Day.

An equally-important social aspect of hot rodding from the era, was the drive-in diner or burger shop that became a destination to boast and to peruse cars after the races, or while cruising the streets at night. One such place, Mary's Malt Shop, in Main Street, Santa Ana, was a favourite location for boys to discuss hot rods and meet girls.

High Calling

It would be unlikely for an ambitious person to record a passion for hot rods and their drag racing skills on a curriculum vitae or a job application. Hot rodding, and indeed, drag racing, the sport it spawned, would not normally be thought to contain the elements of a high human calling. However, if we consider the elements in Don Garlits' case, he had an energetic, honest livelihood and career that entertained and inspired many with creative, highly-motivated problem-solving, breaking boundaries of science, engineering and human experience. Even hot-rod art is appreciated by more than just the automotive aficionados. In fact, the Specialty Equipment Manufacturing Association—SEMA, which runs a huge annual trade show, includes a section called Hot Rod Heritage Fine Art; and art galleries have included hot rods in exhibitions dedicated to the appreciation of fine automotive objects of art.

As 2007 marked 75 years since the Deuce was made, Ford Motor Company and others prepared a celebration for the occasion. Ford commissioned 100 Deuce hot-rod replicas to be made and sold. A panel of hot-rod experts selected the 75 most-significant, 32 Ford hot rods to be displayed at the 58th, annual Grand National Roadster Show held at the Los Angeles County

John Edgar's beautiful Ferrari, depicted here and driven by Carroll Shelby against MG TC, TD and TFs, created the need for professional racing that gave rise to the magnificent Can Am series.

Fairgrounds. Other events included "Deuce Week" at the LA-based Petersen Automotive Museum in February, at which the legendary hot-rod-loving band, ZZ Top played. The very exclusive, annual Pebble Beach Concours d'Elegance also honored the significance of the Deuce in automotive history.

European Influence in California

As World War II brought international conflict to the U.S., young servicemen experienced the international motor-racing culture of Britain in particular. They brought back European Jaguar, Aston Martin, Ferrari, Maserati, Alfa Romeo, Porsche, Mercedes Benz and MG sports cars to feed the post-war boom. Sports car racing in the U.S. was the prototype for professional drag racing, both of which had hot rod origins. But drag racing lacked the big dollars and European influence that sports car racing enjoyed.

Sports car racing was an amateur sport in which anyone with a suitable car could participate. Of course, it was soon dominated by the wealthy who could afford to hire the best drivers to get the best results. John von Newman, son of affluent German immigrants, thrived on European sports cars that he began selling and servicing at his new North Hollywood business (appropriately named Competition Motors). In August, 1947, von Newman's ambitions were further advanced by his becoming co-founder of the California Sports Car Club. Its first organized event held at Palos Verdes, was won by von Newman in his Jaguar SS100. Porsche and Ferrari cars were added to his growing franchise and racing team and he hired Englishman Ken Miles, for the 1956 season. Miles' well-established expertise with his modified, "Flying Shingle", MG racing car was irresistible to other, similar, wealthy entrants, including John Edgar.

We just wanted to have fun with our cars. – John von Newman

John Edgar was the exemplar for many. Well-funded professionalism was reflected in his huge, well-equipped, transporter; Ferrari race cars; and patronage of Carroll Shelby, Jack McAfee, Dan Gurney, Phil Hill and others, all of whom had hot-rodding roots, but were seduced by European exotica.

In January, 1958, John Edgar announced, against the strictly amateur ethos of the Sports Car Club of America, that he, Dan Gurney and Carroll Shelby were to become professional racers. Professional, sports car racing then took off in the halcyon period of the 1960-1970s. Dan Gurney won the initial, USAC Road Racing Championship in 1958, joined by luminaries including Lance Reventlow, Tony Parravano, Chuck Daigh and Phil Hill. Augie Pabst won it in 1959, Carroll Shelby in 1960, Ken Miles in 1961 and Roger Penske in 1962. Big events staged in California were the Times Grand Prix in 1958, and the Los Angeles Examiner sports car race in 1959 (to spawn what became the acclaimed, Can-Am

Series from 1966-1974). To this, many of the top, European, road-racing stars rushed in, sharing the rich rewards and glory of what is, perhaps, the most exciting, road-course series ever conceived.

The Hot Rod Invasion into Road Racing

As sports car racing transformed from being an affordable, strictly-for-fun thing to do with your car, to the Can-Am series; so hot rodding and drag racing evolved. Something you could do in your backyard and on the way to the burger shop became the high-dollar, high-status, professional sport of today. While some Formula 1 races were held in the USA from this period until today, despite the efforts of Phil Hill, Dan Gurney and several others, F1 never really found a home in this most automated of all nations. America created its own, unique, motor-racing formats for NASCAR Stock cars, paved-and-dirt-speedway cars of many varieties and configurations, and largely-ignored F1. Of all these, drag racing most fully reflects American style. European-style road racing remained in the background as a poor cousin to the main event. In fact it was hot rodding, in the form of V8 engines fitted to European-style racing cars, that invaded road racing and became Can-Am racing. For a while this threatened the superiority of Formula 1. Intriguingly, it was Bruce McLaren from New Zealand, with his combination of British motor-racing skills and hot-rodded, eight-liter, Chevrolet V8, who did the best job of defeating the insurgence of factory Porsche racers and Jim Hall's GM-funded and developed, Chaparral Can-Am cars. McLaren went on to dominate the championship until after his death.

Of all of the American motorsport disciplines, drag racing remains the most distinctly-American. Adopted in Canada, Mexico, Britain, Europe, Scandinavia, Australia, New Zealand and South Africa, drag racing remains unequalled by any other sporting spectacle for its projection of American character. Of all drag racing classes, Top Fuel is the ultimate American icon. The best examples of the commercial application of the hot-rod mentality are the Ford Cobra cars of the grand, self-promoter, race-car driver, innovator, car producer Carroll Shelby, recently featured in the movie, *Ford V Ferrari*. Born in Texas, and therefore removed from the hot-rod culture that he was to become part of, Shelby was a beneficiary of many hot-rod pioneers from both sides of the Atlantic. Initially, he raced a friend's MG TC and then a Cadillac V8-engined Allard, the product of the English, hotrodder Sidney Allard. This car introduced him to the British racing-car world and to Aston Martin, at whose factory he arrived unannounced to offer his services as a driver, eventually to win the 1959, 24 Hours of Le Mans together with Roy Salvadori. Shelby also drove a streamlined and supercharged Austin-Healey 100S for Donald Healey, setting 16 US and international speed records, in addition to two years in Formula 1. Carroll Shelby noted the accomplishments of other Californian hot-rod entrepreneurs who married American V8 engines into lightweight, racing-cars chassis (in particular, Lance Reventlow, who created the family of Scarab, sports and Formula 1 racing cars).

While Shelby was racing in Europe, he also noted the performance of an English GT car built by AC Cars, known as the Bristol. Three years later it would become the basis for the AC Cobra, that he, at one stage, assembled in Venice, California (in workshops belonging to Lance Reventlow, heir to the Woolworth family fortune). In 1948, at age 12, Reventlow had been introduced to the world of European motor racing when his mother, Barbara Hutton, married Prince Igor Troubetzkoy. Reventlow's new stepfather won the Targa Florio road race that year in one of Enzo Ferrari's first eponymous, sports racing cars, a Ferrari 166 Barchetta. As a teenager, Reventlow's money bought him the latest in exotic cars. This led to his involvement in motor racing and a foray into the heady world of Formula 1 and the British racing car industry. It was here, that he noticed the efforts of Brian Lister, who used a Chevrolet V8 in a tube-framed car he called a Lister "Knobbly".

Upon his return from Europe to LA, Reventlow drew on the experience of an army of hot rod and racing car geniuses, including Harry Miller, Clay Smith, Fred Offenhauser, Fred Carillo, Leo Goosen, Emil Diedt and Phil Remington. Among them were also Jim Travers and Frank Coon (learning the ropes of Chev V8 racing engines at Reventlow's expense before they became Traco Engineering). Well-established experts Dick Troutman and Tom Barnes designed and built the chassis with the aluminium body designed by Chuck Pelly. Ken Miles and Chuck Daigh assembled and tested the finished product on the track. The gorgeous, metallic, blue and white, Scarab sports-racers dominated U.S. road racing from their introduction in 1958, and were arguably the precursor to the fabulous Can-Am sports cars. In 1962, after having witnessed this revolution in sports-car racing, Carroll Shelby had AC Cars fit a 260-cubic-inch Ford V8 to provide a ready-made competitor to Chevrolet's Corvette. AC then air-freighted cars to LA without the engines, where Shelby fitted the engines and transmissions, (initially at Dean Moon's hot-rod shop in Santa Fe Springs, California), giving the Ford Cobra sports car impeccable, hot-rod credentials.

Top Fuel Rules

When it comes to the ultimate spectacle of hot-rod performance, Top Fuel dragsters are unsurpassed. They are the biggest, loudest, most powerful, fastest accelerating, most spectacular, most brash, most similar to professional wrestling, and most uniquely American of all motor sports vehicles. Along with a NASCAR race, the Indianapolis 500, and a Formula 1 round, a Top Fuel-dragster event is something that all true motor heads want to see at least once. One of the attracting factors in the televised contest, during a weekend NHRA Championship event, is when the top runners must first qualify. Over two days of intense competition, eliminations are worked through toward the Top Eliminator contest. Each element of the contest is there—nature, machinery, and competitors—written large in the names of the sponsors and the heroes of the sport. The other televised classes have their own appeal (Pro Stock, Pro Stock Motorcycles and Funny Cars), but there is no denying that Top Fuel rules the show. The theatre of each round of the 2020 NHRA Mello Yello Drag Racing Series 24 event season is created by the championship-points contest, held during the first 18-race section. The playoffs to determine the champion for the year include only the top ten drivers at the season's final six races. Each of the events held across the nation, is a celebration of professional drag racing, complete with huge, colorful, pantechnicon, tractor-trailer rigs, with temporary workshops attached. While TV coverage is the best way to see the competition and all the action, there is no other motor race event on earth to rival in-person attendance than a Top Fuel championship round.

There is as much spectacle in the pits as on the track. Cars are towed back after each round and engines are stripped and rebuilt in front of the adoring crowd. This "thrashing" to rebuild between rounds is an amazing experience to watch, especially as cars are re-assembled and engines started, to the great surprise of the unwary who might be standing just a few feet away from an 8000-horsepower monster when it roars to life. Aside from the cars, the drivers and the crew chiefs are all part of the entertainment. Larger-than-life characters abound, all trying to out-do each other during TV interviews and especially trying to out-do John Force, the celebrated grand master of rapid-fire hyperbole and self-promotion. Top Fuel drag racing is so part of the American cultural landscape, it is inconceivable that it could have evolved anywhere else. It reflects theater, geography, demography, culture, technology and traditions of this wealthiest and most-powerful of nations.

All the world is a stage, and all men and women are merely players. They all have their exits and entrances and one man in his time has many parts. – William Shakespeare[20]

To be a sporting competitor of any sort requires that one play according to the rules of the game. But to even conceive of such an undertaking, most essential is the opportune accident of one's place of birth. A Kenyan tribesman has no chance of becoming a Top Fuel drag racer, but a good chance of becoming a marathon runner. Life's circumstances create opportunity and motivation for the roles we play. Antron Brown, the sport's first African American champion, suffered no geographical handicap. He was born in Trenton, New Jersey and succeeded in motorcycle racing before turning to Top Fuel dragsters. Once competitors start on the path toward a sporting career, success depends on how well they play the role. Are they hungry and thirsty for success? Are they well-prepared? Does their passion even conceive of the audacious dream? Will they tolerate the hard grind of learning, the discipline of training, and the inevitable hardships and sacrifices required to reach their goal? A desire to succeed is the force that drives the development of qualities that are the making of a champion. Prize-winning qualities are almost unrecognisable until they are tested in the contest. According to Muhammad Ali, "Champions aren't made in gyms. Champions are made from something they have deep inside them—a desire, a dream, a vision. They have to have the skill and the will. But the will must be stronger than the skill."

This intangible desire to succeed that is so essential for success, resembles faith—"The substance of things hoped for, the evidence

---

[20] "As You Like It".

of things not yet seen". Could the same quality of hope, the same passion and commitment be required to succeed in the contest of life? This is not a game of sport. As William Shakespeare correctly observed, it is a game of life, and the players/actors are not play-acting. In real life we are the actors in a play of our own making. The Bible prefigures both Ali and Shakespeare when the Apostle Paul uses sport as a metaphor, not just for faith, but for life itself: "Do you not know that those who run in a race all run, but only one receives the prize? Run in such a way that you may win. Everyone who competes in the games exercises self-control in all things. They then do it to receive a perishable wreath, but we are imperishable. Therefore I run in such a way, as not without aim; I box in such a way, as not beating the air."[21]

An American Icon

Don Garlits and nitromethane-powered dragsters are synonymous. Similarly, dragsters are embedded in the soul of the United States of America. The U.S. extols big, loud, brash, powerful, exciting, hard-working, wealthy, determined, proud, insular, independent, frugal, moral and faithful people—just like Don Garlits, the ultimate Top Fuel Dragster champion. The role perfectly suited him in his time and place in history. The circumstances of America's international isolation during WW I and for the first part of WW II, is also a national characteristic reflected in motor sport. With some exceptions that prove the rule, the USA was reluctant to engage in top, international, motor-racing class Formula 1. They already had their own ultimate category, in the form of Indianapolis championship cars.

During my interview with him, Garlits relived the experience of driving a Top Fuel dragster in competition. He recalled the

---

[21] 1 Cor 9:24-26.

process of preparing the car in the pits, towing to the start line, the crew starting the engine, doing a burnout to warm the tires, backing up, getting positioned, the crew chief adjusting the fuel mixture, and being ready to "step on it" by anticipating the green light. Don mentioned that in the early days he won races by being better at the lights. In later years he had to be more cautious to avoid red lights, resulting in less wins. From the launch, everything goes "wriggly", with blurred vision and instinctive responses rather than conscious decisions; hoping the car goes straight and does not smoke the tires. Don related the early days of match racing when the crew was just he and Pat (with maybe some help from a local volunteer). These were the days when, to save the car, it was possible to run conservatively in qualifying. The days well before it was necessary to rebuild the engine and the clutch between rounds. "Maintenance" was checking the valve clearances, the spark plugs and maybe an adjustment to the fuel mixture. During match racing events it was possible to run just hard enough to beat your competitor and in some cases to "pedal" the accelerator and the clutch just enough to stop the tires smoking and steal the win.

In Pursuit of the Ultimate

Although the speeds and ETs of Top Fuel have plateaued due to rule changes in the interests of safety and the limits of physics, the pursuit of ultimate performance for wheel-driven vehicles competing side-by-side, remains the objective of drag racing. That they know only a little science has never stopped drag racers from this quest. Drag racing remains relatively unsophisticated by comparison to most other motor racing classes. This is not to say drag racing is unintelligent or easy, but it does not place high value on sophistication for its own sake. In fact, there are rules against that. The drag racers' performance criteria are always: "Does it work?" and "How fast will it go?" Never, "What is the latest scientific theory of what should happen?". Scientific limits remain, of course, as drag racing does not transcend physical realities. Nonetheless, drag racers challenge science with their persistence and inventiveness, in their search for the ultimate performance from cars with mundane design-origins and no pedigree. Until recently, when Top Fuel dragster speeds became too great for existing drag strip facilities, the hot-rodder quest to harness the most power to achieve the highest speed in the least time, remained the objective of the sport. Following the death of second-generation Funny Car racer, Scott Kalitta in 2008, the NHRA rules were changed to restrict speed and increase safety margins. Kalitta was qualifying for a Full Throttle Championship round when the engine backfired and caught fire at 300 mph, burning the parachute. As the engine kept running and delivering power through the seized clutch, the car ran out of shut-down area, impacted a heavy machine and fatally injured Kalitta. In response to this tragedy, the NHRA and the FIA mandated the reduction of Top Fuel drag strips to 1000 feet, and the development of a device that, in the event of a backfire, shuts down the engine and releases the parachute.

The Engine

The heart of a Top Fuel beast is of course, the engine. The prototype for a modern, dragster engine was a Chrysler Hemi, so called for its hemispherical, combustion-chamber design. Initially this concept was based on the French Peugeot, Grand Prix engine of 1911, as designed by Ernest Henry and later copied by many, including American Offenhauser racing engines. The hemispherical combustion-chamber design allows optimum breathing of oxygen and fuel at high revolutions, the key to ever-increasing engine output. Garlits and others discovered that the already-powerful Chrysler engine responded amazingly to modifications to increase horsepower. The basic engine architecture, first established 60 years ago (with the addition of oxygen-bearing nitromethane fuel, and later the addition of a supercharger to cram in even more oxygen and fuel, combined with powerful ignition systems), saw horsepower soar from the factory-standard 180-horsepower, to the previously-unimagined 10,000-plus horsepower of today. Top Fuel dragster design has seen a steady evolution from the 1950s, with speed increases and elapsed time reduction becoming incrementally smaller. Remarkably, the configuration of the Chrysler Hemi V8 still prevails with most of the basic dimensions and architecture unchanged. This design has been challenged from time to time, but it has proven to be the most suitable for its purpose. NHRA limits the engine displacement to 500 cubic inches, usually with a 4.1875-inch bore with a 4.5-inch stroke. The bore pitch has remained at 4.8 inches (from the later 426 Hemi), the V angle at 90 degrees, the camshaft location and crankshaft journal dimensions unchanged, similarly the 90% phasing of the crank pins duplicates the original passenger car design. However, the engines are now built specifically as racing engines. Adding greatly to strength, blocks and heads are CNC-milled out of solid blocks of forged-aluminium without water jackets. With no external heat dissipation for cooling, they rely on massive volumes of fuel during the few minutes that they run. The aluminium blocks are fitted with sleeves with combustion pressure, sealed by copper gaskets and stainless steel "O" rings, fitted to the top of cast iron cylinder sleeves. Compression ratio is about 6.5:1 because of the high boost pressure from superchargers that can be driven faster than the crankshaft. The forged-aluminium pistons are Teflon-coated, attached by tool steel wrist pins to forged-aluminium connecting rods, not so much for strength as for bearing and crankshaft reliability. The ductile aluminium material transmits less shock force through the big ends to the crankshaft itself, which is machined from a solid billet of high-strength steel. Dykes top rings are used with lower oil control rings to keep crankcase oil from entering the combustion chambers.

Two, 14-mm spark plugs per cylinder ignite the air/fuel mixture fired by two, 44-amp magnetos. Normal ignition timing is 58-65% BTDC. This extreme ignition advance is one of the unique aspects of slow-burning nitro. Legend has it, that in the early days of Top Fuel, an engine was mistimed with far more ignition advance than would ever have been normally used for a gasoline engine, or with nitro. Unexpectedly, the car produced vastly more power and speed. This caused some serious head scratching by the crew, who eventually realised that the incorrect magneto setting was the cause of greater power. The scientific explanation eventually followed, and what they had unwittingly unleashed became better understood. During a run, the ignition advance is brought back to about 25 degrees, after launch by a timing system. This allows the tires and the car to "settle in" for the remainder of the run. NHRA rules prevent the spark advance from responding to computer adjustments as this could be used to control traction. This would change the nature of the sport by requiring less skill from the driver and the crew. For durability and light weight, the 2.45-inch intake valves are usually made from titanium. The 1.925-inch exhaust valves are heat-resisting Nimonic 80A or a similar material. Valve seat inserts are ductile iron. The valve rockers and push rods are the original Chrysler configuration made from high-strength materials, particularly necessary on the exhaust side which must overcome very high cylinder pressures. At full power, the exhaust gases escaping from a dragster's upward facing zoomie headers, contribute about 1000-pounds of down-force blast. The engine of a Top Fuel dragster generates a ground-shaking 150 dBa of sound pressure at full throttle, equal to about 3.2 on the Richter scale. Despite wearing ear-plugs, spectators feel the sound in their bodies. Obviously, the noise is capable of causing permanent hearing damage if no hearing protection is used.

Don Garlits. The Enigmatic Hero

Supercharged!

The purpose-built supercharger is usually a Roots-type design based upon the very old two-stroke, GM Diesel engine blower. The supercharger is driven by a toothed Gilmer belt to transmit more than the 500 horsepower required to drive it at full pressure. Boost pressure is varied up to 5.0 bar (73.5 psi) by changing the drive belt ratios in response to track conditions. 200-psi Burst plates with a release pressure of 200-psi are fitted to the manifold to prevent the destruction of the blower in the event of a dreaded backfire. If one were to occur, Kevlar blankets cover the supercharger to contain explosion shrapnel. Fuel is pressurised to 500 psi by a mechanical fuel pump and injected through as many as 50 nozzles placed in the blower manifold and cylinder heads. Incredibly, the pump can flow 100 gallons per minute to supply the necessary power and enormous quantity of fuel. The mixture is controlled, in conjunction with the ignition and clutch, to pre-determined limits, varied in accordance with the atmospheric and track conditions. As engine speed increases, the clutch tightens and the air/fuel mixture is enriched, then leaned out to limit the available power.

This catastrophe is a bit more than a blower explosion, but it illustrates the potential for an engine to literally explode out of the car if the variables of performance are not managed correctly. The item to the right of the wing strut is part of the crankshaft, suggesting that its failure may have been the cause of this amazing vindication of rear engine dragster design.

The oil system has a wet sump containing 16 quarts of specially formulated SAE 70 oil that is changed following each round, when the engine is fully disassembled and examined. Damaged pistons, sleeves and bearings are replaced, along with cylinder heads and clutch components, and the engine is run for about one minute to warm up. When the valve clearances have been checked and the oil pan refilled, the car is fired up by a remote starter in the pits. A "lap" of the drag strip, including a burnout to warm the tires, amounts to a total of about three minutes. No computer-controlled functions are permitted. Data relating to exhaust temperatures, fuel pressure, fuel flow, crankshaft speed, rear axle speed, supercharger pressure and other factors are recorded to help tune the car's performance on the next run. The big power-management challenge is to avoid a loss of traction. Power transmission to the tires is controlled by a timed, hydro-pneumatic clutch system. A variable force on the clutch fingers controls the clamping load on up to eight friction discs and six steel floater plates. Pressure is increased to allow clutch slip for approximately three seconds into the run, when complete lock-up with the engine and drive train is achieved through a standard 3.20:1 rear axle ratio.

Performance

A Top Fuel Hemi makes more than 1000 bhp per cylinder, as a result of a Brake Mean Effective Pressure of almost 1500 psi, and a torque output of approximately 6000 ft-lbs. These amazing figures explain why the engines are so short-lived.

During the development of the sport, speed was the holy grail of drag racing achievement. As speeds plateaued with time (mainly due to safety considerations due to lack of run-off area), so elapsed time and first through the lights has become the sole objective. While speed ruled from the mid-1950s through to the mid-1980s, Don Garlits was usually the first to achieve the major milestones of 170, 180, 200, 240, 250 and 270 mph. Kenny Bernstein was the first NHRA racer to achieve 300 mph in 1992. Tony Schumacher was the first over 330 mph in 1999 and duplicated that milestone with the shortened 1000-foot distance in 2012. Numerous drivers have broken that record which now belongs to Brittany Force at 338.17 MPH. An article in Race Tech magazine, March, 2014, analysed the current performance of Top Fuel cars as they exceed 5.67G, to achieve 0-160 kph in 17.78 meters. According to Mike Lewis of Don Schumacher Racing, several drivers have recently exceeded 6G which occurs during the lock-up stages of clutch activation. Dragsters' chassis are made from 4130 chrome molybdenum tubing. They are now either built by Top Fuel teams or supplied by manufacturers with similar specifications; limited to a maximum wheelbase of 300 inches with no suspension (as chassis flexibility provides both controllability and traction). The rear wing produces around 8000 lbs force at the top speed of 330 mph.

Symbiotic Evolution

The symbiotic evolution of drag racing is fascinating. For instance, speed cannot increase consistently without corresponding safety improvements, but the need for safety and other improvements cannot be anticipated until the higher speed and its emerging problems are realized. Take engine block and cylinder head design for example; early Top Fuel engines used standard Chrysler components with coolant in the water jackets. Progressively, engines were run without water and engine blocks were filled with "concrete" to strengthen them. Eventually, when Keith Black Engineering, Milodon Engineering, Arias Engineering, and Ed Pink began making purpose-built heads and blocks, they started with sand-cored, aluminium castings. With the advent of affordable, CNC multi-axis milling machines, it was possible to make an entire engine from solid aluminium, without coolant passages. This development resulted in far greater strength that coincided with the massive increase in the amount of fuel that could be burned. This, in turn, was dependent upon twin spark plugs being fitted to the cylinder heads and greatly-increased electrical energy supplied to enable the spark plugs to ignite previously incombustible amounts of fuel. Many of these enhancements are to do with reliability of performance. In the early days, "one-off", record-breaking performances that occurred every so often were greeted with scepticism. In contrast, current Top Fuel performance demonstrates a high degree of uniformity across the whole championship field. The winner has usually worked out the traction-versus-power equation better than their competitors. Other than driver skill, such consistency is the result of many small improvements to variables such as design, materials, manufacture and tuning.

As usual, this interdependent, symbiotic evolution occurred over a long time. It was driven by cut-and-try hotrodders, rather than by scientists dealing in theory. However, with each new development an understanding of theory has become more essential.

Garlits the alchemist, measuring the nitro-methane alcohol mixture specific gravity (PHOTOGRAPH BY STEVE REYES).

Don Garlits. The Enigmatic Hero

Nitromethane Alchemy—Turning Fuel into Power

It has always amused me that the great physicist Isaac Newton, who made discoveries without which the modern world could not function, was a scientist, a theologian and an alchemist. Newton tried in vain, for many years, to unlock the secret that would enable him to turn lead into gold. Perhaps without such unrequited ambition he may never have made the discoveries that he did. For this reason alone, Isaac Newton's name could be added to the Hot Rod Hall of Fame. Traditionally, drag racers were not so good at science, at least not in the way that NASA rocket scientists are. While rocket scientists can take a scientific principle and apply it with precision to get the exact result they want, drag racers often acted in ignorance of scientific principles, but learned by trial and error to get results, sometimes at great cost to themselves. There is, however, one thing that they did have to understand, that Don Garlits began to learn at his first national contest in Kansas. It was there, that Emery Cook explained the basics of using nitromethane. At that precise moment, Garlits was a willing student to whom the teacher came. Garlits was desperate to learn the mystery of chemistry that enabled nitro to fulfil its promise of power.

The one scientific concept that Garlits and all subsequent Top Fuel drag racers have had to understand is called *stoichiometry*. If drag racers don't understand this principle, they cannot get their engine to run properly or get the power promised by the alchemy of nitromethane. In fact, improper use of nitro will, in the worst case, cause the engine to explode, perhaps endangering the life of the driver and spectators. Stoichiometric combustion has to do with the chemistry of turning fuel into power. It involves a balanced chemical reaction where the reactive elements are in the correct chemical proportions to release the products of the reaction. Of course, there are other mechanical and dynamic aspects of the use of nitro that must also be taken into account, but that is another subject. The use of nitro was a great mystery to most racers for a long time. Even now, the use of nitro requires a weather-eye on the barometer and atmospheric conditions. It is these, and a host of other factors, that determine how much power will be made, and whether a car will run slowly due to a lack of power, or "go up in smoke" and "overpower the track" because there is too much power for the available traction.

The old idea was to "tip the can" to increase the percentage of nitro, to boost power. But today, Top Fuel regulations limit the fuel mixture to a maximum of 90% nitromethane, with methanol usually making up the remainder. At 11.2 MJ/kg, nitro has a much lower energy density than either gasoline (at 44 MJ/kg) or methanol (22.7 MJ/kg). Provided the combination of elements is right, an engine burning nitromethane can produce vastly more power than the same engine burning gasoline, because the chemistry of nitromethane, which bears its own oxygen, allows for huge volumes of fuel to be used. In a stoichiometric reaction, the quantities of reactants and products form a ratio. To burn one kg of gasoline, 14.7 kg of air is required, compared to one kg of nitromethane, requiring only 1.7 kg of air. This means that an engine can burn 8.7-times more nitro than gasoline. Nitromethane also has a high latent heat of vaporization. It uses engine heat as it vaporizes, providing its own cooling, allowing Top Fuel engines to run without a cooling system. Power output can be increased by using very rich air/fuel mixtures. This also helps prevent pre-ignition, (something that remains a problem when using nitro). Pre-ignition can cause an engine to backfire and explode, blowing the supercharger off the engine. Due to the relatively slow-burn rate of nitro-rich fuel, mixtures are often not fully ignited. Some remaining fuel can be wasted in the exhaust pipe where it ignites on contact with atmospheric oxygen, and burns with a characteristic bright-yellow flame. As a result of all of these factors, a typical run may consume as much as 100 liters of fuel during warm up, burnout, staging, and the quarter-mile run. Management of the many variables is the basis of a Top Fuel crew chief's dilemma that determines success or failure. Nowadays, these complexities are made comprehensible by computer programs. Track-side laptops calculate and recommend blower overdrive, nitro percentage, compression ratio, ignition timing and other changes in response to the weather and track conditions. The weather calculations alone include temperature, humidity, wet bulb, barometer, altimeter, dew point, grains of water/cubic foot of air, track elevation, correction factors for altitude, vapor pressure, wind direction, and speed and track temperature. Most of these factors relate, to some degree, to the science of stoichiometry as it applies to drag racing.

Chapter 6 Don Garlits Meets "Big Daddy"

"I know the heavy burdens that God has laid on us. He has set the right time for everything. He has given us a desire to know the future, but never gives us the satisfaction of fully understanding what he does. So I realized that all we can do is be happy and do the best we can while we are still alive."

– Eccles 3:10-12[22]

Mickey Thompson was, without doubt, the greatest hot-rod entrepreneur of all. Amongst his amazing list of accomplishments was the slingshot dragster, mimicked by Garlits and every other Top Fuel car for the next almost 20 years. But running the next big innovation—the rear-engine dragster—was Don Garlits, at the Mickey Thompson-operated, Lions drag strip, in Long Beach, California. Vying for the Championship prize of $20,000, Garlits made the headlines that day, March 8,1970, but for all the wrong reasons.

Almost without moving from the starting lights, an explosion ripped the car in half—the transmission bursting through the steel safety shield and ballistic safety blanket. The force of the blast broke Don's left leg in five places and took the toes and most of the arch of his right foot with it. Flying shrapnel also severed the arm of Timothy Ditt, a young spectator in the stands. The sight of his bloodied foot brought Don a moment of perverse clarity.

---

[22] Good News translation

The end of his racing career flashed through his consciousness, morphing instantly to depression as he envisioned life as a cripple. Lifting Don from the wreckage was Tommy Lemons, with Mickey Thompson close behind. Thompson immediately arranged for Don to be treated at the Pacific Coast Hospital by a renowned surgeon, Dr Larson. Garlits and Tim Ditt arrived at the hospital at the same time. Dr Larson quickly assessed that what remained of Don's foot would heal, but to re-attach the boy's arm required immediate surgery. Garlits agreed without hesitation. (This act of kindness and the surgeon's skill resulted in a successful operation, enabling Tim, with a fully-restored arm, to become Don's pit assistant at the same event 12 months later.)

The Faith of a Child

In view of previous bad experiences with drug treatment, Don announced to Dr Larson that he would not be taking painkillers. Garlits was grappling with a multiplicity of problems: the prospect of the immediate end of his career; the financial and legal difficulties that he faced (as Tim Ditt was not insured); compounded by the sickening pain for which pain-killers were available, but promised their own demons. In a cold sweat, at about 4:00 am, the pain finally became unbearable. With no alternatives left but gritty resolve, he screamed out to God, "Father, help me!". Don recalls, that almost immediately he felt what he describes as, *the presence of God in the room*. He felt enveloped in a cocoon of warmth, as if "God was telling me that he loved me, and cared for me. And from that moment, for practical purposes, apart from when the doctor removed the staples, the pain left me". Reflecting on this experience, Don says, "Because I had cried out with the faith of a child calling out, 'Help me daddy' to his father, God came to me and changed my life forever."

For Pat, who flew from Tampa in a state of high anxiety, this event was a tragedy that unexpectedly became a triumph. Don's encounter with the Divine was a fresh start. He began to share Pat's long-held faith in God more deeply. What had just threatened to end Don's career was instead, the beginning of a new phase of unprecedented achievement in drag racing, plus a new dimension in his relationships with his wife and with God. For Don, life up to this point had been a series of adventures, challenges, exciting and devastating events and opportunities, to which he responded instinctively. This, however, was a growing discovery of an unanticipated dimension. All the while, his pragmatism was the key both to his sporting success and his spiritual development, which he would not fully appreciate until some years later.

Don was comforted by daily visits from Pat and other friends. Fellow drag racer, Tom "The Mongoose" McEwen, came and shared Don's favourite TV show, *Star Trek*, and conversed about Don's hero, Albert Einstein. (Tom gave Don a book about the genius and endowed Don with the nickname, "Albert".) From his hospital bed Don's despair slowly turned to optimism. He began to think about a less-risky future in racing by relocating himself out of harm's way. He knew that rear-engine cars had previously been tried and abandoned due to instability at high speed. But determination, with an increased emphasis on his self-preservation, drove him to continue with his career even at a disadvantage.

Garlits looks back on this series of events with a sense of surprise. While he would never have chosen to experience the events as they unfolded, he would, in retrospect, not have it any other way. The elements of crisis—to favour Tim Ditt, rather than himself and to call on God with child-like faith—fuelled his resolve to keep going with his dangerous career, albeit with a safer design. Furthermore, he was comforted by his wife and friends and inspired by the greatest genius of the twentieth century. These all served as elements of a script, in which Don became the writer, director and chief character; one of many significant occasions when Don said,

"God helped me". His decision to continue facing the challenges with renewed faith was critical. Far from his career being over, it had just begun.

In order to be prepared to hope in what does not deceive, we must first lose hope in everything that does deceive. – Georges Bernanos[23]

Finding Courage to Follow a Calling

"So I saw that there is nothing better for a person than to enjoy their work, because that is their lot..."[24]

The *fight or flight* response to the threat of conflict is intrinsic to being human. So, what motivates a person to engage in a sport that resembles war? Survivors of war describe the experience as *endless boredom interspersed with unimaginable chaos*. War heroes are those who, despite their fears, meet the challenge of fear (that Garlits sometimes describes as madness), and go back for more. The circumstances of life led Garlits to the place where he asked, "Do I have faith and courage to continue?". By choosing to go back into the fray, despite his fear, Garlits generated his sport into a business and more importantly, journeyed on to become a hero to millions of young men across the world. Garlits' calling, in this case, was not to be a drag racer per se, but to follow his passions, balanced with responsibilities to his family and those who relied on him.

In the early days of professional drag racing, the price of fame was to spend a large slice of life driving thousands of miles to get from one non-descript, dusty drag strip to another. It was usually the champ alone with his helper driving through the night, facing the prospect of a crash, a fire, or at least an engine-repair in a

---

[23] French author, (1888-1948).
[24] Eccles 3:22, King James Version.

Don Garlits Meets "Big Daddy"

motel parking lot...all for a cash prize or championship points and a trophy. This is not the champion portrayed in magazines; not the hero worshiped by devoted fans who idealize the excitement of competition and success. Fans see only the thrill of victories or the despair of spectacular crashes. Yet, it is these fans, these paying spectators, that keep the dream alive by turning up at events all over the country and beyond. It is these, predominantly young men, who idolise and emulate their drag-racer heroes. Don Garlits knew the highs of a big win accompanied by adulating fans and the lows of being pelted with cans and bottles because he beat the local underdog. Life on adrenalin, angst of competition, the grind of time-on-the-road, the roll of the dice-of-good-fortune, the need to put food on the table—were all part of the life of a drag-racing champion.

Becoming Conscious

Human history comprises stories of men and women who shaped their world, and influenced later generations for good or evil. Some visualize an ideal world and pursue it with enormous passion and cost. Others simply do what their character and circumstances dictate. As we know, not all who achieve greatness are born great. Some force their way into posterity one step at a time. Until their work is seen in hindsight, perhaps long after their time ended, there is no accurate sense of what they accomplished. Was their "greatness" born of genuine faith or dumb luck? Of course, faith and idealism do not guarantee the success that luck may bring. The driving force of a man may, in fact, be a folly of wishful thinking. Many of us are not conscious of where we obtain our guiding principles of life. Like inexperienced hotrodders we experiment with powerful concepts that we do not properly understand. We question reliable and traditional values with nothing to replace them other than yet another "new" idea. Don Garlits, however, was of an extraordinary species. Unlike jet-test pilot Chuck

Yeager, or Mt Everest-conquering Edmund Hillary, Garlits was an anti-hero. Hotrodders were a breed of outcasts with their dirty fingernails and anti-social behaviour, risking innocent lives drag racing on public streets. But step-by-instinctive-step, Don Garlits became conscious of a high-calling and a God who beckoned him. He was to inspire a generation and become the legendary, Big Daddy, Don Garlits.

While drag racing reflects many aspects of the brash American ego, it is at the same time generous, naïve, and perhaps, according to conventional wisdom, even foolish. These characteristics are all the more intriguing when they are observed in Don Garlits. He was certainly an intensely inquisitive and competitive, young man. But his success against competitors was in constant conflict with the need to provide for his children and tirelessly supportive wife. As a living specimen of contradictions, he is an ideal subject for the age-old study of human motivation. Among others Plato, Niccolo Machiavelli, Sigmund Freud and Carl Jung have asked, "What essentially makes us tick?".[25] Both the Teacher of Ecclesiastes and Jesus are distinctive as teachers who not only present, but scandalously resolve contradictions by revealing the universal human tendency toward vanity and self-deception.[26] For what was Garlits most remembered? What was his greatest innovation? Seven years after the Long Beach explosion, just after he had completed building Swamp Rat 24, Garlits nailed his colors to the mast by declaring the source of his motivation and inspiration. The painted cross and proclamation, "GOD IS LOVE" very eloquently expressed what men and women have discovered for thousands of

---

[25] Tensions within human motivation are explored in the likes of Machiavelli's, *The Prince*; and Sun Tzu's, *The Art of War*, where the contradictions are presented in the raw with a heavy bias toward an entirely rational resolution.

[26] This revelation has almost always earned the displeasure of the custodians of religion who turned out to be the greatest offenders. In the case of Jesus' revelation, He was crucified at the request of His own people.

Don Garlits Meets "Big Daddy"

years. In essence, it is what the Teacher of Ecclesiastes reluctantly conceded: *Motivation through God's love and wisdom are available to us as a remedy for ignorance, arrogance, pride and despair*. In effect, Garlits was saying, I have become conscious of what I believe is good about life and I am grateful for it.

Nailing his Colors to the Mast

A God-fearing, Top Fuel drag racer was not just unprecedented, it was contrary to the ethos of drag racing whose outlaw, street-racing roots were never far away. Not that the distinction of displaying his convictions of faith on the car would ever trouble a man like Garlits. He has attracted more than his share of detractors with an attitude of, "I don't care what they say about me". It has cost him millions, because he has turned down sponsorship offers that were contingent on his playing down the religious message. This he will not do.[27] When I asked him if declaring his faith was worth the cost, he changed the subject and said, "I'm now suffering more than I ever have in my entire life. This loss of Pat is taking me down. I just don't know what to do as I have tried everything I can think of, to include dating some very nice women, working on my projects and making appearances. I stay on my knees to God, but the hurt won't go away. Have you got any ideas? I'm desperate! This is nothing like physical pain. I can take that. This is mental. Sometimes, I think I'll lose my mind. Thanks for listening.[28]

---

[27] Nor will Garlits accept sponsorship from beer or tobacco companies, because of his concern for the image projected to children.

[28] I later followed him up to see how he was traveling. He said, "Thanks, right now I'm better; been on my knees every night!"

The cross and motif, to which the Navy objected.
(PHOTOGRAPH BY STEVE REYES).

When Garlits and Don Cook built Swamp Rat 24, the car was originally black, but it was repainted in blue and white because the US Navy was going to provide sponsorship. Don tells the story:

> They'd agreed to sponsor me to the tune of $50,000. However, I painted a cross on the cowl with 'God Is Love' written on the cross. And the Navy changed their mind about the sponsorship when the *LA Times* made fun of me for having the cross on the car. Over the two-year period, the blue and white car never had

Don Garlits Meets "Big Daddy"

a major sponsor, but won 24 out of 30 national event starts and total winnings were a whopping 600K! Seems like I didn't need the Navy money after all! I retired the car at the end of the 1979 season. Swamp Rat 24 had been in service for two years, had two back halves, one front half, but always the same body! It's in the Drag Racing Museum, totally original, the way we like em!

The practice of telling our stories is very important. It is both a way to clarify our own thoughts and an effective teaching method. People are interested in the meaning of a good story, but it is also a foil against dogmatic religion. By way of stories passed from one generation to another, the nation of Israel gave the world what they received "from the hand of God". These religious traditions and law were subsequently written down for posterity.[29] Our lives begin as a series of relationships initiated by our parents, then siblings, extended family, friends, neighbours and then the wider world. The purpose of religious faith is not to implement a perfect theory, but to create a story about relationships based on love. Religion, or *spirituality* as it is often labelled, attempts to explain the meaning, purpose and method of living a satisfying life. Therefore, if religious faith is not essentially practical, based in the tangible realities of our lives, it is useless. If it doesn't explain and facilitate satisfying relationships, first with our God, then ourselves and others, it is an illusion and a cruel deception. Don Garlits' most profound words were his simplest words. "Father, help me", he cried out from his hospital bed. GOD IS LOVE, even more profound, he inscribed on his car.

---

[29] It is deeply-ironic that over time the *literal word* recorded in scripture became more important to them than the *Living Word*, the message it was intended to convey.

God is love, recognises God's intentions for us and the means by which we are to approach Him. In gratitude for the life and sacrifice of His Son, Jesus, we are to love God in return—loving with all of our heart, mind, soul and strength. But before we can fulfil this first duty, we must be honest about ourselves, our weaknesses and our inability to meet even our own standards of goodness, let alone God's. This is a reasonable proposition (unless we consider *ourselves* to be gods). There is something/someone greater than us, to whom we are accountable. The question is, *Who is this ultimate authority*? An authority made in our own image leaves us vulnerable to unlimited self-delusion. Absolutes that we have uncritically accepted are very likely another person's delusion. If we acknowledge accountability to any authority, why would we settle for any, other than the Creator, God of love?

Fear God

If we are genuinely accountable to God and conscious of who He is there are many good reasons to fear Him. But as our relationship with him deepens, love expels fear. We who love life, or want to love it more, owe it to ourselves and those dependent on us, to make the most of life, live it to the full, and do the best we can to make our lives count for someone who cares.

The entire story of the Bible serves to express the same message as those words. From creation to the cross, the Bible is an account of God's offer to *help us*. And *God is love*, is the sentiment of his conditional proposal that we have no other gods but the One High God, and that we are to treat each other as we want to be treated. In my view, the basis of all human interaction with The Divine, is a plea for help. Secular culture introduces an increasing diversity of idolatrous options that obscure the possibility of God-consciousness. In addition to the traditional stumbling blocks of false religion and wishful thinking, the most pervasive of these

Don Garlits Meets "Big Daddy"

options is our own success and self-importance. Narcissism finds a welcome home in many hearts. How do we resist this onslaught? How do we fight this battle for our hearts and minds and for those whom we love and want to protect and influence? *Father, help me!*

He is no fool, who gives what he cannot keep, to gain what he cannot lose. – the diary of Jim Elliot[30]

---

[30] A Christian Missionary (1927-1956,) murdered by the Ecuadorian people to whom he went to minister.

Chapter 7 The Making of Don Garlits' Strong Soul

"There is nothing better for a man, than that he should eat and drink, and that he should make his soul enjoy good in his labour. This also I saw, that it was from the hand of God."
– Eccles 2:24[31]

Being Mean to Don Garlits

Don Garlits' 80th birthday celebration (The Rat Roast in Pomona, in February, 2012) was a rare insight into the mystery of the man. Don described the experience as, "hearing many true words spoken in jest". Several of his drag-racing friends and competitors took advantage of the opportunity to "be mean to Don Garlits". He was declared: driven, ambitious, opinionated, demanding, arrogant, tireless, hard-working, frugal, focussed, cunning, occasionally mean-spirited, restlessly-innovative, implacably-competitive and finally, outrageously-successful. What many fans and others did not know so well, was expressed at the Roast by fellow travellers who knew another side to their competitor. Tommy Ivo, the drag-racing TV and movie actor, recalled some of his many practical jokes against Garlits during their match-racing career; stuffing Garlits' zoomie headers with confetti, that showered him when he fired the engine; and

---
[31] King James Version.

pouring oil into the headers of his own car to lead Garlits into thinking Ivo's engine was about to explode. Perhaps Garlits had the last ironic laugh by saying, "I'm not a practical-joking kind of guy". Revealing another side of his character, Garlits also took the opportunity to square-off publicly with several people for things he did more than 40 years before. Garlits, known for his frugal preference of using old engine parts, had asked famed engine builder Ed Pink to supply an expensive, new, purpose-built aluminium engine for his dragster. When it did not perform up to his expectations, Garlits shipped it back to Pink without payment for freight. For this offence, he offered a simple apology: "I *am* sorry, Ed". Don's often-strained relationship with Top Fuel racer Shirley Muldowney reflected his disapproval of women racing. He expressed this none-too-subtlety by referring to the driver's seat as the "cockpit". But it was he who signed off her NHRA license. "I signed her license because she did a good job", Garlits admitted. "I never thought she'd amount to anything, but I was wrong. She's the best woman race-car driver, not just in drag racing but in any racing to date." Master of ceremonies Bob Frey, noted this generous approval as a milestone. "It took his 80th birthday for Don Garlits to admit he was wrong." Better late than never.

Garlits also apologised to Ed Iskenderian, the octogenarian camshaft grinder and hot-rod entrepreneur, whose patronage and $1000 sponsorship Garlits had spurned, in favour of another camshaft supplier who offered $10,000 for one year. But only the first instalment was ever paid. "I've learned that all the money in the world isn't worth a friendship", Garlits said. Then, looking right at Isky, he said, "I love this guy". Multiple-champion, Top Fuel and Funny Car driver, "The Snake", Don Prudhomme, spoke on behalf of many when he said, "He set the example for me in drag racing; he showed me how to be a champion. Don Garlits is the greatest drag-racer of all time". The emotion and nostalgia of the occasion was best summed up by the broadcaster and

The Making of Don Garlits' Strong Soul

announcer, Dave McClelland, known as "The Voice of NHRA", who showed his affection for Garlits with a simple kiss to his forehead. The remarkable thing was not that he needed to be reconciled with these people (he had already done this many years ago), it was that he wanted his confession to be on public record for all his peers and competitors to see. Don's demeanour raises many questions. What does it take for a man to openly admit his mistakes? Is this a sign of weakness or strength? Was Don more aware of the errors of others than his own short-comings? Was he also able to forgive those who offended him? Are bullies strong or are they weak? Was Don Garlits always a hard-nosed, win-at-all-costs racer who became a softie? Or did he have a tender heart buried deep below the fiercely-competitive, death-defying, contestant spirit that defines drag racing?

The Garlits' family (PHOTOGRAPH BY STEVE REYES).

Is Don Garlits a freak of nature? Tough competitors confessing their mistakes and professing their love for each other is not normal for drag-racing greats. It appears it is possible for macho, tough guys to harbor a warm heart and a strong soul. At the very least, Don Garlits is an extraordinary man whose motivations and accomplishments are worth exploring.

The Enigmatic Man

Over the years, many of Garlits' critics have questioned his status as Big Daddy of drag racing because, "he sees things differently to other people". This is both an accurate statement and a gross understatement. Garlits does not just see drag racing differently, he sees everything differently. From drag racing, to religion, metaphysics, extra-terrestrial life, the nature of the universe, politics, sexual relationships, racial relations, economics, energy utilisation and the list goes on. Garlits' enigmatic, contrarian position of not-going-with-the-flow, has not only worked to his advantage during his career; it is an essential characteristic of pioneers in any field who forge the way for others to follow. In any case, he is not the first imperfect saint, as any insight into Saint Peter will confirm.

I sent my illustration of Don Garlits: *The Balanced Man with a Strong Soul* to him for his comment. He replied, "I don't know, I think maybe we're going too far". In response, I explained how I wanted my book to be a tribute to him and Pat, and for their story of faith to inspire many. His reply is what I have come to expect:

> Warren, I'm just a plain, outspoken Christian that loves God and Jesus Christ. I'm not a Saint...I don't want this book to make me appear something that I'm not. This is hard to put into words and I'm doing the best I can. I'm not the Pope, or Billy Graham by any stretch of the imagination. I don't know what else to say," Don.

I replied,

The Making of Don Garlits' Strong Soul

"Thanks Don, that's what I hoped you would say. None of us are Saints of the big "s" variety. We are saints of the small "s" kind though, because of God's love and what He accomplished for us through Jesus...should we choose to accept it. Ecclesiastes is filled with paradox. So are the teachings of Jesus. I want to show that we all struggle with exactly this question, if we have had a real encounter with God.

By the way, Billy Graham and Pope Francis have both recently said that they are sinners, just like you and me.... I want to tell your story. Can I ask you to just keep reading what I send and tell me when I have gone too far."

"Warren. I will," Don.

Upon meeting with Don at his Museum of Drag Racing in Ocala, Florida, during May, 2014, he wasted no time in strongly reinforcing what he is and what he is not. When we arrived, Don was preparing to drive to a "cackle fest" nostalgia event in Michigan, where old dragsters are displayed and started-up to "cackle". As Eugene Kneebone and I got into Don's Dodge Challenger to run some messages, Don commenced with his favorite subjects, including the US government not backing its currency with gold, and aliens who came to obtain gold from earth to shield their atmosphere and guns.

DG   "YOUR [expletive deleted] [Australian] GOVERNMENT TOOK OUR GUNS AWAY FROM US." (Referring to the Australian government's compulsory gun buy-back, following the 1996 massacre of 35 people by a madman in Port Arthur, Tasmania).

WM   (Pause, while my brain goes into overdrive.)

WM   "That was an interesting time for me, Don. When my son (Brock) turned 15, I wanted to go hunting with him and his mates, so I bought two shot guns and a rifle to hunt rabbits. We had them for only a couple years, when we had to hand them back. But I am glad that I did, because there have been no mass killings since."

DG   "THEY'LL ONLY TAKE MY GUNS FROM MY COLD DEAD HANDS, AND THEN ONLY AFTER I GET A FEW SHELLS AWAY."

WM   (Stunned silence.)

End of conversation.

Don was at his dramatic best, testing me to see if I were just an idealizing sycophant or the genuine article, which I quickly made sure I was. I understand that celebrities have to play a role with adoring fans. I am sure they love this, or else they could not perform their role as hero. But adoration is tiresome and superficial. *If a tragic, aging fan from Australia wants to pour on the syrup, let's see what he is made of*—is what I reckon Don Garlits was saying to himself.

Don moved quickly to his next subject.

"THE GOVERNMENT WAS LOOKING IN THE WRONG PLACE FOR WEAPONS OF MASS DESTRUCTION. THEY SHOULD BE LOOKING BETWEEN OUR LEGS. EVERYBODY HAS ONE."

The new subject was about the need for population control to prevent the overuse of the world's resources. At this stage, he was, thankfully, no longer requiring a response from me, so I didn't attempt a defense. (I have learned from my own bitter experience, that my strongly-expressed views are usually the words that later, I have to eat. So, these days I try to make my words as sweet as possible—a problem that Don Garlits obviously does not entertain.)

Although I was prepared to some degree for the full force of Don Garlits (by what I had read and what he had said to me by email), I immediately abandoned my propensity to make Garlits fit the image I had created of him. Here was a new dimension for my parable of the strong soul. Over the years I have been simultaneously attracted to and repulsed by stories of success. I want to believe them but I hear the voice in my head saying, *"Don't swallow the hook, Warren. It's not that simple. Don't get sucked in to defining 'success' in pleasing words of poor-boy-makes-good."*

And forgive us our debts, as we also have forgiven our debtors. – Matt 6:12[32]

His Father's Son

It did not take Don Garlits a lifetime to be shown the error of his ways. As a 10-year-old he had his faults forcefully pointed out by his taciturn father. Don describes it as "a mean fit". It left an indelible imprint on the boy. Even at this young age Don shared some of his father's characteristics of being bad-tempered and demanding of the hired help and family members. Happily, he was not just his father's son. Don also shared aspects of his mother. Don portrays her as opposite to Edward in ways that a young man can identify, and seek to emulate.

Although well-equipped by his heritage and the freedom of farm life in the "land of the free", Don Garlits, like most of us, did not start life with a strong soul. Without speculating too much about the forces that shaped Don, it can be said that universally we

---

[32] The Lord's Prayer.

each respond to life's events and opportunities with the resources that are available to us.[33]

In addition to his quick temper, Don's obsessive drive, his instinctive engineering-prowess and his predilection for esoteric knowledge were, arguably, inherited from his father. Edward's interest in alternative lifestyles led him to radical conclusions about food, health and relationships, that had already taken a toll on his previous family before he married Don's mother, Helen. After Edward had bashed her and young Don in a fit of self-justified rage, she divorced him; giving Don confused memories about his father. Don's stepfather, Alex Weir, a Scotsman who had been a worker on Edward's farm, no doubt knew of his father's sharp tongue, and subsequently provided a contrasting model of warm encouragement and support.

Despite all of Don Garlits' idiosyncrasies, he has many revering fans beyond his now-aging competitors. They admire his pioneering professionalism within the sport during the nation-building post-war period. More recently, 16-time Funny Car Champion John Force, recorded his admiration and affection for Big Daddy both in *Hot Rod* and the *English Motor Sports* magazines. Eight-time, Top Fuel Champ Tony Schumacher and the three-time Top Fuel champion, Antron Brown, gave similar interviews at the 2014 NHRA Mellow Yellow Championship round in Atlanta, Georgia. What all these champions attest, is that Don Garlits paved the way for professional drag racers. He did this not just technically, competitively, commercially or by sheer persistence, but by establishing the legitimacy of faith in Christ that they, and many more top competitors explicitly now proclaim.

---

[33] There are aspects of our own individual behaviour that we do not fully understand. Nonetheless, we are without excuse for behaving in ways that we find intolerable in others. It is only reasonable to apply standards to others that we are prepared to apply to ourselves.

The Making of Don Garlits' Strong Soul

Tony Schumacher has an interesting take on Garlits' role in drag racing. Sitting in the Army-sponsored Top Fuel pit, he reflects on his long experience at the top of the sport.[34] Schumacher acknowledges that he is tired and that others will eventually take his place. Given this, he is unlikely to be impressed by false claims of any kind. "Garlits was the best. He changed the face of drag racing. You can't do what Garlits did without faith." Schumacher projects his own experience and position in drag racing when he says, "People without faith are not represented at the awards. You have to believe, to do things that are worth doing".

The 2012, 2015, and 2016 champ, Antron Brown, uses an analogy relevant to his situation when he says, "Big Daddy is the Michael Jordan of drag racing".

It's a fine thing to rise above pride, but you must have pride in order to do so. – Georges Bernanos[35]

Don Garlits' Championship Qualities

From the beginning of his hot-rod career, Don Garlits displayed the characteristics for which he is famous. His love of machinery, determination, competitiveness, strong ego and self-reliance made him a champion. But being a sports champion is "success" on a very narrow spectrum. It reflects very little about a person's quality-of-life beyond sporting accomplishments or the lives they touch. Don Garlits was distinctively known as a tough, uncompromising competitor and a bad loser. The problem looming for him, and for us all, is that when our work is done, what we have become and what we have accomplished is seen for what it is. Garlits has

---

[34] He influenced his businessman-father, Don Schumacher, to re-enter the sport. Don Schumacher Racing has become a dominating, mega drag-racing enterprise.

[35] (1888-1948).

always been celebrated for much more than his accomplishments on the drag strip. It was his qualities of determination, courage, compassion, conviction, persistence and enduring relationships, that earned him the title "Big Daddy—a thoroughly decent man". Even this accolade is insufficient, being only the praise of admirers. It is essential to have some further external measure by which to assess oneself.

Character determines how far you will go and whether you will still like yourself when you get there. – Don Garlits

How to Become a Champion

To succeed as a "champion", goals, self-confidence, expectation and mastery must rate in the superlatives. Competitors of any kind, who do not learn the lesson of setting goals beyond their mundane expectations, do not become champions. Small goals are never enough to overcome the roadblocks. Garlits candidly observes of himself, "I've just always been very competitive. When I was in school, I wanted to turn in the best paper. I wanted to have the fastest bike. My stepdad would give me a calf and give my brother a calf, and I wanted mine to be the best and the prettiest. I always wanted to excel at everything." Don's hero, Albert Einstein, knew that mastery of anything demands full devotion of strength and soul. For a soul to become strong, that same commitment to the task of personal growth is required.

Only one who devotes himself to a cause with his whole strength and soul can be a true master. For this reason mastery demands all of a person. – Albert Einstein

The idea of *strength through weakness* sounds like an intellectual riddle. *To love one's neighbour as one's self was a command fit only for effeminate weaklings*, was the dismissive attitude of Hitler's

Nazi regime to the Christian faith. Instinctively, we pursue our own advantage and make demands of others for our entitlements. Does a soul become strong by living instinctively? Or does a soul become strong by recognising its weaknesses and needs, and seeking help? Is meekness weakness, or is it strength? Before we answer these questions, perhaps we could attempt what one church suggested on its notice board, "Meekness ain't weakness, try being meek for a week". James, the brother of Jesus, ironically drives home the point when he says, *Rich people should take pride in [be meek about] their low position, because wealth will pass away and wilt like wild flowers and the rich man will fade away, even as he goes about his business* (i.e. wealth alone does not leave a legacy).[36]

Contrary to the popular saying, perception is not reality. Perception is our version of truth that needs to be tested for vanity in the harsh world of reality. – Hot Rod Theology

Real satisfaction depends on how much of our perception of reality has been tested. A friend of mine who is a pilot instructor has a teaching point that he calls, "Wheels Up Landings". By this he means, *pilots of aircraft with retractable undercarriage have either made a wheels-up landing or are going to*. This adamant statement suggests that pilots who have trained on light aircraft with fixed undercarriages, who are now flying aircraft with retractable under carriages, have already, or will eventually attempt to land without lowering their wheels, despite the presence of warning systems and even an instructor sitting alongside telling them what to do. The consequential fright that they give themselves when they finally become aware of their error, is what it takes to break the habit of not thinking about the landing gear. I think this is a truism. The problem we all have is that to become conscious of our ingrained imperfections, we need to "have the shit scared

---

[36] Paraphrased from Jas 2.

out of us". After that we can vigilantly make sure that we do not make the same mistake again. We have proved the benefits of compliance with safety procedures. In that case, our fear of failure becomes a strong source of motivation to break bad habits.

The more I see, the less I know for sure. – John Lennon

Don Garlits' Strong Soul

As we have seen, a soul is not just ego or even a sense of self, but the sum total of a person's passions. A strong soul is a paradox. It begins by being aware of the good it possesses. Simultaneously it knows its faults and desperately seeks good. At the heart of the process, is acknowledging the need to be transformed into the image of goodness—goodness personified in Jesus Christ, the source of life. Additionally, a strong soul relinquishes any sense of entitlement, superiority or privilege. It enjoys life and ensures that others enjoy their lives as well. Self-respect or *to love ourselves*, as Christ suggests, is fundamental to a strong soul. I have no doubt that Don Garlits has a sincere faith and is both a redeemed child of God and the possessor of a strong soul, tempered as it has been, in the furnace of drag racing. He has endured many challenges and temptations common to mankind, albeit, by his own admission, imperfectly. He is unashamed of his strong positions on a range of subjects that perhaps kept him from being successful during his 1994 run as a Congressional candidate for the Republican Party. As distinct from most of us, he cares little for political correctness or any sort of pretence. It should not surprise you to know that Don Garlits is a sinner in need of a saviour, and that he is not fully transformed. We are all in the same boat. (Don told me that his many shortcomings have been made clear to him over the years by his enemies and friends including his wife, and he needed no further reminding at 82 years of age!) Not that we should celebrate our shortcomings, but if we deny them, they become despicable secrets. I wish we all had the same strength of character to be as bold about our sins as is Don Garlits, who is not hypocritical in the sense of consciously wanting to appear to be something he is not. He is, however, inconsistent in applying God's love to himself, while doing the hard work of also applying it to others. Strength is not associated with shallowness. Strength is associated with depth of character, endurance when the going gets hard, discipline, and faithfulness to a goal or a person. Some of these qualities Garlits has displayed to a high degree. In particular he has persisted with honesty and endurance in his commitment to Jesus Christ. But in some areas, as we all do, he has relied more on instinct than has been good for him. My assessment, to the extent that it is valid, is that, in regard to endurance, Don Garlits' soul is of championship strength. Imperfect of course, but as strong and as sincere as many a good man may hope to become.

But the one who stands firm to the end will be saved. – Matt 23:14

What would be far worse than accepting that each of us is sinful, would be pretending that we are not. The utter devastation that is being wreaked within the Roman Catholic Church at present, is a result of sexual abuse of children, official corruption, money laundering and many other dark secrets that have been covered up for centuries. It is significant that Pope Francis, appearing at the Vatican when his papacy was announced, bowed his head in humility and shame for his church. "Pray for me", he said to the crowd. My confronting experience with Don Garlits caused me to rethink my own view of what I meant by a strong soul. This was a perilous moment. I had over-idealized him. Any book that is substantially autobiographical runs the risk of being self-indulgent justification, and mine was found wanting.

A strong soul is not perfect. If we think we are, we are deluded. One of the first steps to any sort of transformation is to admit that we are capable of self-deception and creating God in our own image. Transformation is a learning process. Inspired by a still, small voice, we must make new decisions each day based on our goal and what we learned yesterday. Transformation is about being the best we can be and getting the most of what life has to offer. The Teacher, Solomon and Jesus clarify that this requires us to unlearn much of what the world teaches. ("I am number one"; "I am so important, that the world owes me...") Like Don Garlits, we need to develop a state of mind that accepts the challenges, the disappointments of failure, and the triumphs of success. Such an achievement requires that we have someone to love, like Patricia; someone who gives their life, so that we might return the favor. If we do not have that someone, then we should make it our business to seek out supportive relationships based on the high calling that is usually reserved for marriage. If we are able to do this, we are able to learn our shortcomings and seek the help we all need to be transformed into the image of Christ.

Chapter 8 Godspeed

"I have seen something else under the sun; the race is not to the swift or the battle to the strong, nor does food come to the wise or wealth to the brilliant or favour to the learned; but time and chance happen to them all."
– Eccles 9:11-12

The Speed of Progress

That human history is speeding toward utopia is a hope clearly unfounded, as two world wars have more than proved. Western thinking was first dominated by the false hope that Christendom would make universal progress. The Enlightenment's equally-false optimism, to some degree, replaced these hopes. Whereas Christendom expected Christian governments to solve humankind's problems, the Enlightenment postulated science, rational thought and high culture could replace religious superstition, to achieve the same goal. The evidence of religious abuse of power—the Crusades, witch-hunts, and two world wars—have shown that we are no closer to a solution. The more recent failures of various dictatorships have provided similar testimony, counted in millions of lost lives. With the rise of education and science, religion has, to some degree, declined in the West. However, there are no signs of it dying out. Many Asian, African and South American countries are increasingly religious, well-educated and prosperous. Despite the successive failures of many ideologies, the democratic ideals of freedom, liberty and justice continue to progress. As prosperity grows in most countries, more people are better off (measuring in life span and health-related terms). Even so, the collective wisdom of the world was unable to predict or prevent the catastrophe of the Global Financial Crisis.[37] Much of what we now see as advancement has to do with: increasing speed, travel, communication, access to information, business dealings, construction, financial transactions, wealth creation, and medical intervention. While the benefit of progress is unarguable there seems to be a correlation and a cost in the increasing alienation of people from each other. Traditional relationships and meaningful connections are waning, emotional illness, alcohol abuse and drug-related problems are manifesting increasing despair.

Things always seem to get better and worse at the same time. – Mal Garvin[38]

Many voices of protest are saying that the cost of progress is too high. We face certain doom unless we address the speed-related crisis of energy use, carbon emissions and global warming, to say nothing of human misery.

Speed is tranquility.– Stirling Moss

Despite all we have learned and all the progress that humans have made, we do not have the formula for continued success and human satisfaction, at least as a popular idea to which the nations and the power brokers of the world might agree. I propose, that history proves progress and speed to be important where they

---

[37] It should be recognised that Christendom and Christianity are not the same thing. Christendom is a political theory about the use of so-called theocratic power and religious law. But it is not the teachings of Jesus Christ, or of Scripture. In fact, it could be said that Solomon and other Bible teachers predicted the opposite of what Christendom attempted and still attempts to do. Many eyes are on Pope Francis to see what progress he makes in dismantling the false hopes of Christendom.

[38] Australian Radio Broadcaster.

demonstrate a benefit to many, but they are not the panacea that we hoped for, nor will they ever be. I do not, however, discount human resourcefulness and our ability to solve problems of our own creation. This, after all, is the making of human history. We do seem to be able to solve most problems apart from the most elusive problem of evil toward one another. My use of the term "God's Speed" does not suggest that we should continue just doing what we already do faster or better. On the other hand, I propose there are other dimensions we should attend to first, before we blindly attempt more of the same that produces the same. God's Speed is an approach to dealing with reality in a new way—to recognize, as Solomon did, that our individual responsibility is to fear God and keep his commands.

God Spede

According to the Collins English Dictionary, *Godspeed* or *God spede* is an old English expression of one's good wishes for a person's success and safety, meaning: *May God prosper you.* To wish Godspeed is not about being the fastest or being the wisest, wealthiest or most powerful as was Solomon. Rather, as Solomon may have wished, *that we might make the most of our lives, knowing God's fatherly gaze as he watches over us and desires that we find satisfaction in Him and in all we do.* This was the missing element from Solomon's own life that led him to say, "All life is a meaningless vanity." I submit that our purpose is to discover what both Solomon and Don Garlits found–the remedy to despair; the panacea that enables us to live life with *God spede*.

Following the transmission explosion in Long Beach, California, that cut Garlits' car and right foot in two, Connie Swingle and TC Lemons began to repair the Wynn's Charger dragster. All this, despite Don's mother, Helen, extracting a promise from TC that he would not do so, and from Don, that he would never drive the car again. The awkward situation was resolved by TC, who agreed to buy the car from Garlits for Connie Swingle to drive at the AHRA Nationals in Bristol, Tennessee. Pat reluctantly allowed her still-recovering husband to attend the event with "the boys", provided that Don did not drive. But Swingle found, after a couple runs, that as he had not driven a dragster for some time, he was not fast enough to qualify for the field. Being at the event with the car and no driver, the temptation was too great. Disregarding the promises to his wife and mother, and afraid for his life, Garlits climbed into Swingle's firesuit and prepared to make a run. Instantly, as the engine fired, the anxiety and fear disappeared and he staged and ran the quarter mile to gain top speed and low ET of the event. Disappointingly, or perhaps providentially, Garlits was then eliminated when the engine spun a crankshaft bearing; (possibly the explanation for Swingle's earlier poor performance).

Back in Florida, having somehow squared off with Pat and Helen, Don once again adjusted his thinking (on the basis of a percentage of income) to drive the now TC Lemons-owned, Wynn's Charger slingshot for the remainder of the season. Electing to run at Indianapolis, Don red-lighted during eliminations, only to then witness Jim Nichol's car suffer a horrifying clutch failure that cut his car in two while running against Don Prudhomme for Top Eliminator. Such déjà vu was enough for Garlits, who saw the front half of Nichol's car come safely to rest while the back half tumbled down the strip with Nichols still in it. Although Nichols was miraculously uninjured, the experience again confirmed to Don that the only safe place for a driver was in front of the engine. Garlits still had not resolved the financial dilemma of continuing the sport that he dominated and from which he had made his livelihood. There was no uncertainty about Pat's opposition, but she had her own dilemmas—the struggle of having faith in her man coupled with awful anxiety every time he got into a dragster. In an attempt to resolve both his and Pat's fears and to accept the evidence staring him in the face, Don conceded that a new design would not be faster than the existing cars. He hoped at least to design something competitive while not being so utterly lethal as what front-engine dragsters had become.

This resolution was a measure of his character. Garlits was not overcome by fear, but he respected its message. His love for Pat and indeed his love for himself had been pushed to the limits, but this situation now demanded greater courage. Surrendering speed to safety, he faced possible humiliation of defeat and the contempt of his competitors and fans. His values were put to the test. Would he treasure his status as a drag racer more than his life? My definition of love proposes that *we want the best for another, at some possible cost to ourselves*. This definition also applies to how we love ourselves. Do we value ourselves enough that we are prepared to sacrifice something, especially our ego, to preserve our own lives?

Rear-engine Dragster Design Theory

The Indianapolis event was followed by a long drive to California with TC Lemons. They were headed to another match race against Don Prudhomme, at the Champion Speed Shop Drag Strip, in Fremont, near San Francisco. During the trip the detail of the new, rear-engine design became clear in Garlits' mind. After winning the first round against Prudhomme, the supercharger rotor exploded. Garlits was once again engulfed in 185-mph flames. Fortunately, thanks to his fireproof suit, he suffered only minor singes to his face. The supercharger explosion scattered shrapnel throughout the engine causing valves to bend and requiring a full strip-down and all-night-marathon rebuild to finish the job. The next day brought no good news. Garlits spun the tires and went up in smoke, allowing the Snake to easily win, and ending the contract to drive Lemons' car. The return trip to Florida provided an opportunity to discuss and finalise the design of the new, rear-engine car: it should be as simple and as light as possible without a transmission; using proven components, including the 426 Dodge Hemi and the Dodge eight-inch crown wheel and pinion. To bring this vision into reality, Don again engaged the best welder/fabricator in the business, Connie Swingle, who was champing at the bit for the new challenge. As always, there was a major obstacle to overcome. To date, all rear-engine cars that had exceeded 200 mph had crashed due to instability at high speed. This "challenge of the status quo" brought out all the naysayers with their predictions of failure, including friends, drivers, sponsors and fans. For further reflection, inspiration and design consideration, Garlits and Swingle took a case of beer and went clamming in the Gulf of Mexico to "clear their minds". Strategically this worked and soon Don was sitting in the driver's seat appreciating the unrestricted vision after years of staring at the back of a supercharger. A month of long days and short nights (with Pat supplying coffee), materialised the vision. The long, sleek, new Swamp Rat 14 car defied the potential to wreak havoc that front-motored cars had done for so long.

Years of dragster design and performance have proven them to be mysterious machines. Simple at first glance, there have been many design philosophies expounded over the years. Those designs that were successful, prevailed and became increasingly standardised, and the winnings counted, but only after the smoke cleared. Dragster design is always precariously evolving with considerations of symbiotic speed, safety and reliability. Speed does not come without new, unanticipated problems, as chassis-builder Don Long pointed out in Chapter 4. In this case, Garlits was going against his own calculated wisdom, only ever doing what made sense from a cost-and-performance point of view. Certainly, he had engaged his enthusiasm for the challenge, but his motivation was distinctly different from the well-worn evolutionary track he had created for himself and others to follow. This was a change in the interests of a new priority of self-preservation and it was as big a risk as he had ever taken. Once the driver location had been established, there were many theories regarding variables, including the length of the wheelbase. Previously, short cars with a wheelbase equal to the circumference of the tires, were said to be the answer. Discussions always included the total vehicle weight as against the chassis material strength, the transmission and clutch design, and so on. All of these variables were compounded by whether the car should be rigid or flexible. Even Garlits became confused at different times after having to "cut the rick rack" out of a new frame with a hacksaw to make a poor-performing car more flexible, in order to improve traction. Every design consideration in a dragster is predicated to speed, reliability and safety, as a result of applying extreme forces generated by the engine. As power increases, so traction becomes the problem. As traction is provided, more power is engaged in an ongoing game of cat-and-mouse, where drivers' lives are always at stake. At the first run of the new car at Tampa Dragway, conveniently located just down the road from the Seffner workshop, the supercharger belt broke and took out the throttle linkage that Swingle had just made. With another new linkage and a blower belt guard fabricated, Don's first pass in the car was disappointing to say the least. It did not handle at all well. Don described it at the time as, "an evil-handling bitch"—an expression of his frustration with what he had, all the while, suspected to be an insurmountable problem. Another foray to the longer St. Petersburg strip, with more braking and run-off area, produced the same result. The car alarmingly darted to the left or right at 200 mph, confirming the predictions of the naysayers, and defying the hopes that the team had invested in its work. To make matters worse, the car looked fantastic in press photos taken by Bob Smith of the *Tampa Tribune*, ramping up the expectations of Garlits' legion of fans and observers and making the crisis all the more acute.

This poor result was only slightly improved when, prior to the first public outing, a spoiler was fitted above the front axle. At this stage Don, TC and Swingle, were ready to give up. The only believer in the new concept was Pat, who continued to say, "Honey, if you believe in that car, don't listen to anybody. Just keep trying. You'll work it out."

Steering a Straight and Narrow Path

According to the hard-bitten racer Connie Swingle, there was a bit more to the story. TC Lemons was working on a new, front-engine slingshot, Swamp Rat 15, ostensibly as a promotional display for the Goodyear Tire Company. Having succumbed to frustration, Garlits and Swingle put the rear-engine car aside to help Lemons. The reprieve was a relief from having to solve seemingly insoluble problems with the new car. Swingle's version of events was that the new rear-engine car was actually pushed behind the shop (exposed to the elements), because they had given up hope that it was going to work—ever!

Pat, on one of her visits to the shop, noticed that the crew was not working on the rear-engine car, for which she required an explanation from the three naughty boys. After their mumbled attempts to confuse the inquisitor, Pat lost it. In single syllable words she reminded them once again, of the dangers of what they were doing with those lethal, old-design cars, and their failures in the challenge to perfect the new design. Whereupon they proceeded with the challenge, as Pat had convincingly suggested. With renewed motivation and more drag-strip testing, Don noticed that he was over-correcting the steering at high speed, when only small changes were required. When he mentioned this to Swingle, he said, "Why the hell didn't you say so, Gar?". Swingle immediately got to work on the Bridgeport milling machine to fabricate a new Pitman arm and longer steering arms on the spindles, to slow down the steering ratio from 6:1 (which was typical for slingshot dragsters) to 10:1. A return trip to the Orlando strip was a revelation. A new strip record of 6.8 seconds at 230 mph sent the previously-exasperated team of innovators into a head spin. After months of hard work and disappointment they realized they were onto a winner. Relishing the moment on the return drive to the workshop Swingle kept saying, "Gar, you gonna kill 'em". TC Lemons just kept smiling and saying, "Wait till the Californians see what the Okies built".

This episode confirmed that, while failure or an evil-handling car was a thing to be feared, these faded into insignificance compared to the prospect of Don disappointing his wife.

God's speed often says 'slow down'. – Dallas Willard

Swamp Rat 14 was the first continuously-successful, rear-engine dragster. It was to become the standard against which all other dragsters were constructed, but not until the handling problems were solved by Pat Garlits' resolve to make the cars safer.

First rear-engine car. An immediate winner despite no body and no wing. (PHOTOGRAPH BY STEVE REYES).

Two Better Than One

"Two are better than one,
  because they have a good return for their labor:
If either of them falls down,
  one can help the other up. But pity anyone who falls
  and has no one to help them up.
Also, if two lie down together, they will keep warm.
  But how can one keep warm alone?
Though one may be overpowered,
  two can defend themselves.
A cord of three strands is not quickly broken." – Eccles 4:9-12

It is highly unlikely that Don was thinking about Ecclesiastes at that moment, but he later reflects on the number of times providence smiled upon him. This phenomenon is often poorly understood. Divine providence is sometimes considered to be reserved for the favored few in religious vocations—priests and ministers of religion—but not drag racers. In reality, the principle of Ecclesiastes applies to very ordinary people doing very ordinary things. Solomon found that all his kingly powers and accomplishments amounted to nothing in terms of his satisfaction and enjoyment of life. Only when he admitted his dissatisfaction, his weakness, and his need for help, was he able to make progress in life. Having done this, he said he was able to enjoy his work, his family, his food and drink (making no mention of his grandeur or power). His satisfaction and pleasure were in the simple enjoyments of daily living. In my experience, for those couples with shared faith in God, Divine enabling through one's spouse is not an exceptional event. My wife and I have learned to live with the experience that, when one is down the other will be there to pick them up. This is beyond co-dependency or "dumping" our emotional needs on each other. Divine intervention is not miraculous, as we usually understand miracles to be. In most instances Divine intervention is essentially practical and relational—not some spiritualised ideal of holiness, but God's presence apparent in the very ordinary challenges of life—the outworking of the *Kingdom of God within us*.

Speed as a Measure of Progress

When Don Garlits was asked to define himself in a word, he replied, "driven". He could well have added, "I have always wanted to excel". Although he was capable enough, he was not equally motivated by school math lessons, or administrative tasks in the Florida National Guard and Maas Brothers Department Store. What captured Don's extraordinary motivation to succeed, were the things that captured his imagination (including unusual activities such as learning to play the piano). For the most part, these revolved around his relationship with Pat and his daughters, and the sport he loved. Garlits' need for speed was the predominate driving force in his life. More generically, human need may be described as "teleological", meaning to be *purposefully forward-looking*. As we have seen earlier in this chapter, social progress is a controversial topic because with every advance comes a restraining force, as if progress and restraint were two sides of the same coin. The concept of freedom and the ability to choose the substance of our own future hope, is fundamental to the concept of democracy. While some contemporary thinkers may have rejected the ideal of progress, it remains at the very heart of modern life in Western society. We strive for individual freedom (consistent with the democratic rule of law and religion), for improved health, welfare, comfort and wealth. We strive not just to improve our own situations but those of our family, our business and our society. Progress is dependent on aspects such as access to knowledge, technology and capital to invest. In turn, we gain freedom to choose our own education, politics, vocation, where to live and where to travel without restraint...all of which encourage progress. Christian faith implies that we are free to choose good or ill and free to perversely choose whatever we want. Conversely, we are free to be led by the revelation of Scripture and free to be inspired and enabled by the Divine Spirit. These freedoms are founded on Jesus, the Son of God. He sacrificed himself on the cross in our place, doing what we cannot do for ourselves—granting us freedom, if we embrace this salvation.

The Apostle Paul makes the emphatic statement: "It is for freedom that Christ has set us free". He continues to say, with very persuasive language, that faith in God is all about the freedom that Christ has gained for us. *If we strive to achieve a relationship with God through our own efforts to satisfy the law or a moral code, we alienate ourselves from Christ's free gift and fall away from grace. The only thing that counts is faith expressing itself through love.* Paul finishes this strong statement with perhaps the strongest words he could bring himself to use. "You were running a good race. Who cut in on you to keep you from obeying the truth?"[39]

God made me fast, and when I run, I feel his pleasure. – Eric Lidell[40]

Speed and Progress

Over the last 100 or so years, there has been profound technical, social, medical and political progress. The world we live in would be unrecognisable to anyone who was unaware of the merits of the internal combustion engine—arguably the single innovation most responsible for greater personal freedom. However, although there are more people with more freedom and more possessions than ever before, we are still threatened by environmental catastrophes, war, economic ruin and a bleak future unless we constantly reconfigure what we consider to be progress. Even if human inventiveness could solve all of our social, energy

---

[39] Gal 5.
[40] Chariots of Fire.

and environmentally-related problems, Solomon's wisdom would reign true; life is unfair, and unsatisfying. It is all repetitious vanity. Governments, kings and technocrats will never solve our problems for us. Individuals have more access to information than ever, but the problem is our lack of wisdom to know how to use the increasing mountain of information. Democratic freedom has become a fundamental human desire and a right for many. We want to choose for ourselves, to choose our hopes and aspirations for ourselves, our families and for our nations. We want freedom to do the work we find satisfying. We want freedom of ideas, freedom to believe, to strive and to love. We want to live a good and abundant life. God's speed is not just a way of getting things done faster for the sake of speed alone. Drag racing does have this goal as a measure of success, but there is much more to consider than speed, even in drag racing. God's speed implies making the most of the time and unprecedented opportunities available to us, for the greatest benefit (not just for ourselves, but for others, as ultimately our freedom and satisfaction is dependent upon the freedom of others). This is a parallel concept to the "abundant life" that is promised by Jesus, or the elusive "good life", that most of us seek by one means or another. God's speed is not just more of any one thing, because as Solomon discovered, more is not necessarily better.

The best things, in life are not things. – Art Buchwald[41]

The Living Word of God promises a higher quality, a better experience, more fulfilment, and a future hope. Thousands of years of human experience have taught us that the problems of life are not so much a lack of resources, as a lack of willingness, intelligence or goodwill to use our resources well, for ourselves

---

[41] Quoted by Donna Garlits.

and for the common good. Of course, the greatest resource available to us is love, applied with faith and hope. Of love, as distinct from other ideals or principles, it is impossible to have too much.

"But the fruit of the Spirit is love, joy, peace, patience, kindness, goodness, faithfulness, gentleness, self-control; against such things there is no law."[42] If it is true, that satisfying relationships are the holy grail of not just human experience, but of our spiritual relationships as well, why not cast off all restraint in the pursuit of this promise.

The Motor Spirit

Don Garlits' high-school yearbook entry compares him to a greyhound. Under his photograph Don records why this image might have been selected by his schoolmates to represent him. "A greyhound; then all I'd need to do was eat, sleep and chase rabbits." This characterisation became the reality of his life—eating, sleeping, and endlessly driving from one place to another in pursuit of the elusive rabbit-down-a-drag-strip. Greyhounds are bred to run fast but they are not much good at other doggy things. Perhaps it takes a certain type of animal characteristic to even contemplate a drag racer's life, let alone to begin it. In the early days, Don, Pat and brother Ed did everything they could to continue racing. They worked or drove through the night, suffered financial hardships, took risks towing dragsters thousands of miles on narrow roads, to say nothing simply of the danger of the sport—racing just to go fast.

Driven, I've still got it. At 82 years old, I still like to get things done.
– Don Garlits

---

[42] Gal 5:22-23.

Godspeed

Finding Meaning and Purpose

The constant theme in Ecclesiastes is also the central platform of this book: *when we find our sense of meaning and purpose in the midst of this confusing and vain world of many possibilities and pitfalls, we should go after it with all the energy and sense of purpose that we can muster.* Solomon had unlimited opportunity and power in his day, but he found that all his accomplishments and indeed his passions were futile, until he resigned himself to the line that I have quoted several times. "God has placed eternity in the hearts of men." Then, and only then, when Solomon acknowledged his accountability to God, was able to find the purpose for his life, because he was fulfilling the Divine calling for which his soul was created. While this new orientation solved most of Solomon's problems, he still needed some help with his many projects. When he accepted the help that was offered, he succeeded, but when he rejected assistance he failed miserably.

Balance between power and traction—we have seen this to be the aim of dragster performance. The crew chief's job is to optimise the variables to suit the atmosphere, the track and other conditions. When a dragster does not have enough power, it is said to be "bogged down" and when it has too much, it is "up in smoke". In the same way, the history of religion shows that some people become bogged down with religious theory and dogma and have no power to implement what they say is important. This remains true today, especially if we grew up in homes where theory was more important than its practise. Some fortunate people are unconcerned with the detail of religious idealism for its own sake, and just get on with the business of living a good life. Some may even respond to the Spirit without being deeply enmeshed in theoretical "spirituality". Then, there are an increasing number of people who remain hostile to any suggestion that an unseen, apparently irrational, spiritual force could influence humankind. But I have heard it said that there were no unbelievers in the trenches of the great wars. Excessive "religiosity" is a problem that Solomon does not have. He continually relies on his experience and wisdom to determine what he knows about God and his Kingdom. Not once in Ecclesiastes does he defer to his father David's many passionate declarations of faith. Solomon seems to say to himself; *I will use the experience of my life to determine what to invest my faith in, rather than to trust what someone else has told me.*

Although deep reflection about what we believe and how we behave remains very important, Ecclesiastes also says, "The more words, the less meaning"[43] and, "Of making books there is no end",[44] implying that in our search it is possible to overdo scholarship of all kinds. As an alternative, the Teacher recommends, "follow the ways of your heart and whatever your eyes see, but know that for all these things, God will bring you to judgement".[45] This is a stern warning about our potential for hubris and our ultimate accountability. A warning not to get "carried away" with self-importance and self-indulgence, especially of the religious kind. Solomon relies on his kingly inheritance and natural abilities as the foundation for his reluctant accountability to God. However, this is only half the picture. The missing element from his experience (as is often missing from our experience, especially that of dogmatic, religious people) is the presence and inspiration of God's Spirit.[46]

The Missing Essence

Wisdom takes Solomon only so far, and leaves him craving satisfaction. He does not have much time for the active, Divine

---

[43] Eccles 6:11.
[44] Ibid., 12:12.
[45] Ibid., 11:9.
[46] Spirit, or spirituality, is a measure of the effective power one has access to, to get things done.

agency his father knew—the agency of God that David mentions so gloriously in the Psalms, where he says, "...do not cast me from your presence, or take your Holy Spirit from me".[47] Solomon does mention God's Spirit (characterised by ruach or smoke), but usually in the context that it is elusive. He claims not to know the destiny of man's spirit, nor does he claim, other than in passing, to be Spirit-inspired as the prophets were. Taken as a whole, Ecclesiastes suggests that Solomon knows very little of the presence of God's Spirit in his life, nor does he have any insight into his soul becoming immortal. So, he is stuck with what can be seen through the eyes of his experience and intellect, not through "the eyes of faith". Solomon deprives himself of the certain hope that was available to him and is available to us. Those whose eyes of faith have yet to be opened, share Solomon's encounter with the reality of the world as it is. However, we are not necessarily limited to the same fate of spiritual despair. There is an alternative available to us. The gifts of God's grace, of which Solomon speaks theoretically, are the remedies available to us for the asking.

When the Old Testament records the giving of the Law, it also records man's consistent inability to keep the Law. The New Testament commences with the coming of God's Son, Jesus, whose objective is to fulfill the Law; to provide a means by which we may access grace, be empowered by the Holy Spirit and be reconciled to God. When Christ was crucified, the veil in the Jewish temple in Jerusalem was remarkably torn from the top to the bottom, indicating that the barrier between God and us had been removed.[48] "But whenever anyone turns to the Lord, the veil is taken away.

---

[47] Ps 51:11.

[48] According to Josephus, a First Century, non-Christian, Jewish historian, the veil was almost 60 feet (eight meters) high and four inches (100mm) thick. The book of Exodus tells us that the veil was made from blue, purple and scarlet material and fine-twisted linen. It was so strong that it could not be torn by two horses pulling it apart.

Now the Lord is the Spirit, and where the Spirit of the Lord is, there is freedom. And we all, who with unveiled faces contemplate the Lord's glory, are being transformed into his image with ever-increasing glory, which comes from the Lord, who is the Spirit."[49]

Christian teaching explains that the veil (representing that barrier between God and mankind), prevented direct access to God's Spirit. Jesus' death removed this barrier, allowing us direct access into God's presence, mediated only by our acceptance of Jesus as Lord.

The window behind Garlits' desk features this ironic combination of a stained-glass dragster displaying the cross, alongside an alien face. These images are a glimpse into the soul of Big Daddy, Don Garlits (MILLS FAMILY COLLECTION).

---

[49] 2 Cor 3:16-18.

Godspeed

Don Garlits describes his own religious experience: "I was no saint, of course, although I had started going to the Forrest Hills Baptist Church (when Reverend Crosby's cute daughter, Martha invited me); in fact, I even 'went forward' (as they called it) to accept Christ into my heart during a service—not because the other guys were doing it, but because I really believed."[50] None of this experience made much sense however, until he met Patricia Beiger. Undoubtedly, legitimate relationships are the stuff of the Divine. My own experience and that of many of my contemporaries, suggests that what we do as young men and women is almost entirely instinctive. We *eat, drink, sleep and chase rabbits* or whatever our passion is, until we are awakened by sexual impulses, when, hopefully we are ready for meaningful relationships. At this stage, most of us are not focusing on our religious duties. Passion and instinct drive us to respond in ways that are sure to test our sense of responsibility. If a mature approach is well-developed, we sell our metaphorical hot rod, and go straight to win the approval of our new-found love and those who love her, or him. Garlits more recently adds, "I would like at this time to state for the record, that I believe in the Supreme Creator/God and His manifestation on earth in the human form as Jesus Christ. Our Lord Jesus came to earth to teach the human race how to live in peace with each other and become a civilized, loving species". He goes on to say that he thinks some original Scriptures have been edited or left out as a result of tampering by the Roman Emperor, Constantine. Putting aside questions of scholarship, an even greater problem, he states, is how we as individuals understand and apply Scripture to ourselves. This we must do, because "faith comes by hearing and hearing from the word of God".[51]

---

[50] Don Garlits, *Close Calls*.
[51] Rom 10:17.

Don Garlits. The Enigmatic Hero

Both Solomon and Jesus teach that legitimate human passions are no less a Divine calling than the highest of human motivations. True, some of us have a special task to perform. Others aspire to common goals. God intends each of us to be fully-human within the constraints of His law. This intention is summarised by the requirement to "love God and our neighbour as ourselves". Our love of God is dependent on how we conduct our relationships with our parents, neighbours, spouses, girlfriend or boyfriend. With these minimal restrictions on our humanity we are free to go where our choices and circumstances take us. God's big-picture principles within relationships are to be enjoyed and be productive. We apply our motivations and passions within these limits as we listen for His voice. Consequently, we are invited and drawn into the very processes of God's re-creation that he has commenced. We participate with Him, not as robots, but as passionate, autonomous, adopted children—co-heirs with His Son, Jesus.

People like me, who love to race or watch others race, are called "motor-racing enthusiasts". Robert C Post, in his epic book *High Performance*, goes to great lengths to understand what motivates drag racers. Post concludes that it is never for money, technological challenge, or adulation of the fans alone, although all of these are important. It is primarily the pure exhilaration and naked enthusiasm for the competitive challenge that drives motor sport. These high-powered motivations are rightly restrained by other priorities and the life-threatening risks. Combine these, and in most cases, that is what prevents spectators from becoming competitors. Regardless of which "side of the fence" zealots are on, the single, big motivator is the elemental force of enthusiasm, which I maintain to be a Divine gift. The root of the word "enthusiasm" is *entheos*, or "possessed by God." But, in general, it is understood as, to *experience intense feeling of excitement or keen interest*. This word, like so many, has been secularised over time. Now, applied to that which inspires any creative, sporting or challenging human activity, it is more along the lines of simply *intense enjoyment*. When Don met Pat, he was immediately enthusiastic about her, more than he had been about anything before, including his hot rods. Enthusiasm is an essential life force. We each depend on it to add anticipation, excitement and color to life. While I am not proposing a return to religious fanaticism (for which the early Methodists were denigrated as "enthusiasts"), I am suggesting that passionate, energetic motivation to undertake a challenging task or vocation, is a high calling of our souls. Awakened by the Spirit, I have called this lively motivation, the "Motor Spirit". When we respond to this calling, experienced as enthusiasm, we begin an inspired journey. We might not conceive a path, destination, or purpose in any rational way, but we are compelled to begin with a step of faith into an uncertain future. It is the fortunate few who enthusiastically pursue a dream that transforms into a life's work. In the real world, it is not always possible to combine work with a passionate sense of purpose. But some who are highly motivated become the pioneers and innovators that shape the world in which we live. More common, of course, are most of us, who have regular jobs to provide for ourselves and our families, and who keep our passions alive with a "hobby" or a prevailing interest. We may still enjoy the work we do but our more intense passions may need to be sublimated by responsibility for what we love most. Happily for Don Garlits, his passions complimented each other and therefore did not cancel them out. When Pat encouraged Don, he was released to pursue with all his instinctive might *whatever his hands found for themselves to do.*

Is Spirit Divine or Malign?

According to Walter Wink's book, *Naming the Powers*, Spirit is *the essence*. Spirit is the interior; the intangible but "real stuff" of any actuality, including, families, homes, your city, your country and maybe even your dog, (at least according to Eccles 3:20). Spirit is intangible, in that it is elusive and unpredictable, like smoke or vapour, but "real" nonetheless. Because it is intangible and numinous, spirit transcends the limits of time and space and our most fervent attempts to harness it. Even when it is dormant, somehow our mysterious, intangible, individual spirit truly reflects who we really are. As spirit also represents the power to be and to do, we must always ask of any spiritual agency, "What is this spirit empowering me to do? To give life, or to take life away?" I am convinced from Scripture and my own experience that the Divine Spirit resonates with our spirit to empower, comfort, guide, teach, correct and encourage us as individuals, if we allow it. Conversely and ominously, if we permit it, our spirit can reflect such traits as arrogance, narcissism, contempt, despair, anger and destruction.

The wind blows where it wishes, and you hear its sound, but you do not know where it comes from or where it goes. So it is with everyone who is born of the Spirit. – Jn 3:8

As the Teacher makes clear, "God has set eternity in the human heart; yet no one can fathom what God has done from beginning to end".[52] This is either an eternal "spiritual" goal of faith that we might disregard, or a more intentional purpose for life that enlivens our soul. To have eternity in our heart is also an effective antidote to hubris—the delusion that suggests we can control everything ourselves. The Teacher explains that, when we choose to be accountable to God, we are spiritually awakened: our souls were made for relationship with God; our spirit responds to the Divine Spirit; we recognise the motivating, empowering and encouraging nature of God. And although we continue to be imperfect, the Spirit now enables us to become strong souls. We begin to live according to Divine purpose, to experience the high-performance life—the Good Life. But this is no free ride.

---

[52] Eccles 3:11.

Godspeed

Membership in this Divine family creates an obligation of accountability to God. Membership (as adopted sons and daughters of the Most High), also ensures that we have a truly awesome home in an eternal Kingdom.[53] Pardon my pun, but the "Motor Spirit" is not gasoline, petrol or nitromethane. It is the motivating source of impulse and power that enables us to become strong souls. When our spirits are enlivened by the Motor Spirit, our identities are no longer based on our own abilities, circumstances, or ego. Identity is now based on Divine grace, which we experience as an unexpected, free gift from God.

When teased at the Rat Roast about his well-known belief in extra-terrestrials, Don retorted, "I don't just believe in them, I've seen the sons of bitches". Don is eager to explain his "close encounters of the third kind" during dark nights on lonely highways and skyways. His belief about extra-terrestrials has many dimensions, including an interest in his favourite TV series *Star Trek*, Martians, space-time travel and similar esoteric topics well known to his friends and detractors. No doubt he acquired the taste for such things from his dad. Don had given me an explanation about how he believed aliens came to earth to mine gold, in order to create a sun-shield to protect their planet. When I asked Don if the giants called *Nephilim* who sought out human female partners because of their beauty (Gen 6), were extra-terrestrials from the Constellation Orion, he paused for a moment to see if I was winding him up (which I was not, as this reference in Genesis has always puzzled me). It is a field of ambitious speculation and study well beyond me or the scope of this book, but Don's views are available on the Internet for your discovery. (Incidentally, I agree with Don that it is somewhat arrogant for our race to believe that we are alone in the vast and seemingly incomprehensible universe.) Whether or not there is more out there than meets the eye, is open to further

---

[53] Paraphrased from Rom 8: 9-17.

discussion. Our immediate interest in Don Garlits' extra-terrestrial faith, though, is of a more traditional kind. On one hand, without any attempt to understand the extra-terrestrial realm, there are seemingly unlimited, unanswerable questions about the physical universe resulting from what we can see with our own eyes on a clear night. On the other hand, Don's belief in the extra-terrestrial transcendent God is not only orthodox, but his belief is testable in the real time of his own experience.

Of greater interest to me, are questions that children ask that cannot be answered by the greatest minds, such as the classic, "Who made God?". This is perfectly reasonable for humans to ask. We have done so from the beginning of time. We put these unanswerable questions on the back burner in the hope that they will be answered one day. Otherwise, if we become obsessed with them, it can hinder our progress in the things for which we can find answers, and that are really useful to everyday life. Just for the record, God was not made. He is Spirit who exists outside time and space in a realm that is, as Don Garlits suggests, beyond our comprehension, which is why we need faith to see him.

Spirit in the Sky

(I recommend you find this song on YouTube and crank up the volume.)

When I die and they lay me to rest
Gonna go to the place that's the best
When I lay me down to die
Goin' up to the spirit in the sky
Goin' up to the spirit in the sky
That's where I'm gonna go when I die
When I die and they lay me to rest
Gonna go to the place that's the best

Godspeed

Prepare yourself you know it's a must
Gotta have a friend in Jesus
So you know that when you die
He's gonna recommend you
To the spirit in the sky
Gonna recommend you
To the spirit in the sky
That's where you're gonna go when you die
When you die and they lay you to rest
You're gonna go to the place that's the best

Never been a sinner I never sinned
I got a friend in Jesus
So you know that when I die
He's gonna set me up with
The spirit in the sky
Oh set me up with the spirit in the sky
That's where I'm gonna go when I die
When I die and they lay me to rest
I'm gonna go to the place that's the best

When Jewish songwriter, Norman Greenbaum, wrote what was to become a rock classic in 1969, these Christian-sounding lyrics gave some concern: *"Never been a sinner I never sinned"*? He now says, "I just didn't know better at the time". I present this song as a further example of God "placing eternity in the hearts of men". Summarizing both the text in Ecclesiastes and this song, the word "spirit" has two primary meanings and applications. Our spirit is the essence of our character. The *spirit in the sky* is the elusive, Divine capital "S" Spirit of God. It is elusive because He remains the absolute sovereign, accountable only to Himself. Hence, The Motor Spirit.

Choose Life

If the choice is ours, why not do what the song suggests and choose to *go to the place that's the best*?

The Bible explains it this way:

"...through Christ Jesus, the law of the Spirit of life set you free from the law of sin and death."[54]

> Jesus answered, "Truly, truly, I say to you, unless one is born of water and the Spirit, he cannot enter the kingdom of God. That which is born of the flesh is flesh, and that which is born of the Spirit is spirit. Do not marvel that I said to you, 'You must be born again.' The wind blows where it wishes, and you hear its sound, but you do not know where it comes from or where it goes. So it is with everyone who is born of the Spirit".[55]

These texts explain how the often-misunderstood term, "born again", is the beginning of spiritual rebirth—a necessary step for all who seek God. Jesus secured the potential of this rebirth. And in exchange for a simple request from a repentant person, God is ready to give this free gift.

My experience as a grandfather has been a revelation of what grace means. "A free gift from God": as a definition, I could have given this answer maybe 50 years ago. But then, my *experience of grace* was more profound than its *definition*. Many religious people are held back by their attachment to the "letter of the law", which Paul says, kills us. "The letter" represents our confused love/hate relationship with strict obedience to Biblical law. We

---

[54] Rom 8:2.
[55] Jn 3:5-8.

know from experience and the teachings of Jesus, that this compliance does not save us. Nevertheless, many are fatally attracted to ticking all the legal boxes. We live self-righteously (intellectualizing and judging others, and pursuing our secret sins, especially when they are under the cloak of doing something good), rather than acknowledge our shortcomings, our ultimate accountability to God, and our need for his forgiveness and kindness that we call grace. The biblical notion of "salvation" or the need to be "saved" is foreign to modern ears. If you did not attend protestant evangelical Sunday school or were never bored enough to watch TV evangelists, you may find the term curious or objectionable, depending on your point of view. Although my wife has told me to find another term with the same meaning, there is not one. I could say, "redeemed", "gathered-in", "born again", but these only partially capture the meaning of "saved".

According to Christian doctrine, our need for salvation is the fundamental purpose of God becoming man. Jesus Christ, the Son of God, God incarnate came to save us from our sins. To be saved means to accept the proposition that requires we accept not only that there is a God, but that he, in order for us to be reconciled to him, became human, was born of a virgin, and lived a perfect life. We are required to believe that his life was so offensive to religious authorities that they accused him of an offence that he did not commit, and was crucified by the hands of his own creation. He was killed, buried, and brought back to life to live eternally. Does this seem plausible to you? Would you stake your life on it?

Chapter 9 Team Garlits

"Though one may be overpowered, two can defend themselves. A cord of three strands is not quickly broken."
– Eccles 4:12

Two are Better Than One

Many men have abandoned all responsibilities to feed their obsession with speed, but Don Garlits never did. Perhaps he knew it was not possible to achieve his goals alone. His strategy (if it was a strategy), and his later experience, demonstrate the practical reality of the quotation from Ecclesiastes: *that although one may be overpowered, two can withstand almost anything.* There is no doubt that Don Garlits is a man of many facets and contradictions. No one ever accused Garlits of being stupid (other than Shirley Muldowney, who did so for her own reasons). ...*Crazy like a fox*, maybe. His objectivity and relentless focus on the task in hand always showed. Is a man so completely given to speed in both passion and vocation, obsessed? Again, not so Don Garlits. Drag racing was obviously important to him, but it was not the primary objective in his life. This was best demonstrated when Don met Patricia. He immediately sold his hot rod and stopped racing to win her affection and to establish their relationship. From the beginning of their relationship, there were many occasions when Don deferred to Pat's judgement and intuition, not just regarding family matters, but in decisions that directly impacted his achievements and standing in the drag racing fraternity. From Pat's point of view, her complete trust in Don freed her to be his greatest support. Pat's trust was not just in Don's ability to eke out a living to support her family. For years she travelled to competitions with him all over the continent and abroad. She joined with him in his passionate embrace of a goal; to be the best, the fastest, the quickest drag racer in history. Shared single-mindedness is a great asset for great achievement.

There were only two of us at the beginning. There will only be two of us at the end. The rest is detail. – Elaine Mills[56]

It is this pragmatic approach that enabled Don to invest everything in his relationship with Pat. On the one hand, his steely focus, on the other hand, a long-term resolve. Don already knew what he wanted from his life. Above all else, he wanted a good relationship with his wife. Just how he knew this is speculation. Did he want to avoid conflict like he had experienced between his mother and father? Or was it the opposite? He wanted to emulate the relationship between his mother and his stepfather. Perhaps he had just figured out the nature of love for himself, guided by Sunday school lessons. Regardless, it was his commitment to Pat that enabled him to do what he did so well and for so long. There were certainly tensions in their relationship from time to time, (inevitable when two strong souls meet). As two become one, the rough, sharp points of contact wear smooth, like pebbles in a stream.

For all her support of Don, Pat was never a pushover. Not a compliant wife. By Don's own admission there were times when what he asked of Pat was unreasonable. She let him know the boundaries regarding finances, safety initiatives and other unwelcome intrusions into family life. On one occasion Pat took a strong position against Don teaching Donna to weld. According to Don,

---

[56] Wife of Warren Mills.

Pat said conclusively, "I have not raised my daughters to have grease underneath their fingernails". Considering Don's objection to women being around men's rough talk in drag racing, this should have come as no surprise.

She was tough, tougher than the rest of us. – TC Lemons

Anything that threatened the family was unacceptable to Pat. But within her clearly-defined limits, Pat accepted all the challenges of the relationship including single-handedly driving overloaded trucks with trailers attached, driving non-stop through the night to get from one drag strip to another, being the push-car driver at events where Don was both the mechanic and the dragster driver, and occasionally becoming a Super-Stock competitor herself (when the Dodge factory saw the benefit of two race-car drivers in the Garlits family).[57] Pat was the heart of the Garlits family. Don was the racer she supported. Pat was not Don's first girlfriend. He had previously been engaged to a girl who preferred clean fingernails. Pat, on the other hand, recognised Don's strong soul from their first meeting. If Don had married a lesser woman, it is unlikely he would have survived, let alone dominated in the way that he became Big Daddy.

Sandalwood Symbiosis

Sandalwood is an exotic species of wood found in Western Australia. Due to its spicy-sweet essential oils it is highly sought-after by the world's perfumeries, fetching up to $2000 per kilogram

---

[57] Donna Garlits states that women in Pat's mother's family grew up expecting to work hard. On Pennsylvania farms the wife would always have to work outside the farm, especially during the winter months when the frozen ground bore no income. Pat's parents owned a motel in Tampa, so Pat's mother always worked full time to support the family business, as did Pat.

($907 per pound). Sandalwood is also valuable because of its rarity. Growing wild in the wheat belt of west Australia it is strictly-controlled to prevent over harvesting. It is notoriously difficult to cultivate because it is symbiotically dependent on other plant life, without which, it will not germinate. Not to draw too long a bow about Don and Pat's symbiotic relationship, it is clear to me that this is how all good complimentary relationships should operate. It is shared goals, complimented by differences between partners that help marriages, or businesses to thrive. Don Garlits' speed secret was his relationship with Pat. She enabled him not only to endure, but to go faster, quicker, further, more safely and more successfully than any other racer in history. Furthermore, they did it together...for 62 years until her passing in 2014. In their experience, the faith, hope and love invested together and into each other, was returned many times over. Their relationship was rich with peace, joy and satisfaction. The level of confidence Pat invested in her man was rooted in her own sense of security. She was confident in her Christian faith that was established in childhood, nurtured in her devout family, and maintained in adulthood. It is easy to trivialise childish naivety, but as Pat's faith emerged it was increasingly-shared by Don. He saw the outworking of faith in her life and it directly impacted him. It was profound but simple. It guided everyday priorities and decisions, produced inspiration, and shaped values and behaviours to reflect the high ideals of following Jesus Christ.

Early in their marriage, Don won $450 at work in a game of pay-day poker. His workmates at the American Can Company would pool a part of their pay packet, and each week names were drawn from a hat for the winner to scoop the pool. Considering that $450 was more than 10 times what Don earned, this was a big sum for a young, married couple beginning their life together. It was this event that brought out the real character of Pat Garlits and gave insight into her priorities. At the time Don was a member of the Florida National Guard. He was likely, at a moment's notice, to be

Team Garlits

called into action in the Korean War. While they discussed making a down-payment for a house, Pat told him, "Honey, why don't you get that Mercury crank and pistons you've wanted. Enjoy yourself. You might not be able to later". Practical affection. The degree to which Pat returned Don's love made a lasting impression on him. "This is the kind of support I have always received from Patricia Louise throughout our entire marriage." As far as Don's part in this financial arrangement, at least initially, he did not allow hot rods or drag racing to be funded by either of their wages. Don's hobby was considered an extra-curricular activity funded by extra work and horse-trading outside working hours. Later, of course, drag racing became the sole source of family income, abetted by wise property investments.

While drafting this book I called in on Larry O'Toole, (who internationally publishes hot rod magazines and books), seeking some advice and assistance with my project. Upon arrival, Larry introduced me to LeRoi "Tex" Smith, one of the original writers of *Hot Rod* Magazine, who at 80 years of age, now lives in Castlemaine, Victoria, Australia. He continues to write about hot rods and drag racing.[58] As LeRoi graciously scanned the Introduction and the Table of Contents of my book, he pointed to this chapter heading, and said wryly, "Well, at least you've got one thing right". He was acknowledging what a small number of drag racing insiders already knew, that Pat Garlits was the unseen force behind Don Garlits' success.

Their marriage may have been a match made in heaven. But would either of them claim it was pre-ordained that drag racing would be Don's Divine calling and life's work with Pat as his offsider? For the most part, they were just doing what came naturally,

---

[58] Castlemaine, incidentally, is the self-proclaimed hot-rod capital of Australia, if not the world, for the concentration of hot rods and related business, per capita.

or unnaturally, as the case may be. Their passions and abilities were deeply-rooted in genetic, historic, geographic, environmental, emotional, psychological, relational and indeed, spiritual heritage. The most distinctive thing about Pat, apart from her good looks, her family background, her good education and her diligence as a student, was that she maintained her family's Christian faith. Not that Don would initially have taken much notice, but it was a shared element of who they were and who they were to become. Don says without guile, "It was love at first sight". They dated for eight months—dancing, bowling, the movies, water skiing, picnics at lakes and beaches. Drag racing was forgotten. "Hell, I never even mentioned it", he recalls.

The Paradox of Love

While love is often misunderstood because it is essentially paradoxical, an attempt at understanding it is very important. Humans have a strong need to love and be loved. But the need for love to be given before it can be received, is a subtlety that some never learn. Most of us begin by thinking that because love is such a basic instinct, true love just comes naturally—so say the poems and songs. But it is only *the need for love* that is a natural instinct.

If love is to work we must consciously make and apply a decision. For this to happen, the focus of our ego must switch from ourselves, to another (and that is no natural instinct). To love another, is *grace given* (and to receive love, is *grace received*). To give grace is a lesson that must be learned. This lesson is often deferred, because someone, such as our mother, has offered us love expecting nothing in return. But when we take the love of an equal who loves us, and do not return it, love dies before it is fulfilled. When we love another for our own reasons of ego, pride or status, rather than as a gift of grace (for them to receive with grace), our love becomes perverted and harms both of us, particularly the other. The tragedy is that this perversion of love is often unconscious in both parties.

During their brief courtship, they had great fun being together. Don attended the beaming Pat's graduation—obviously a proud young man. They were ready for what life had to offer. They saw in each other their aspirations for life, profound in simplicity.

Happy Wife, Happy Life

Any misgivings that Pat may have had about hot-rodder mates, were put aside when Don abandoned them for her. Pat soon saw that Don would do anything for her, including build a house with his own hands. When they happened to visit the drag races at Bok Tower after their wedding, Pat had no qualms in agreeing to "look at the cars", and "see how their car would perform", and she was delighted in the plastic trophy that Don gained for his efforts. His comment that "Pat loved the family picnic atmosphere", was no exaggeration. But what Pat really loved was Don. Donna Garlits expressed Pat's role winsomely, "She has been the buffer between Dad and everybody else. She was 'It's my way or the highway.' She'd tell Dad, 'We're doing this.' She looked after her family, her life".

Following their first big win at Bakersfield in 1959, Don thought it might be time to buy the Cadillac tow car they had promised themselves. "It just so happened that this corner lot near my garage was for sale for $10,000. I said, 'Honey, we could put the money down on that lot. With a few thousand dollars, we could have a building up. We could save that $125 a month that we're paying for rent, and we could have a concrete floor instead of dirt.' She said, 'We'll forget the Cadillac; let's get the lot'. Oh, that was a good move!", Don now reflects.

Pat Garlits' List of Credits

From the time Don Garlits and Pat Beiger met, she was the force who shaped her man with total support and her own amazing list of innovations. Pat's confidence that all would be well was based on her having seen Don's determination to provide for her at all costs. When the credits run at the completion of a movie you have some insight into the complexity and the cost of the production by virtue of the number of people and companies involved in the production scrolling before you. The credit list of Don Garlits' life would be extensive, but it would be dominated by one name—commencing with Patricia Beiger and continuing with Pat Garlits 60 years later. Donna compares her mother to King Solomon's idea of *the wife of noble character*. In summary, "Charm is deceptive and beauty is fleeting; but a woman who fears the Lord is to be praised. Give her the reward she has earned, and let her works bring praise at the city gate."[59] I imagine that when Pat Garlits' list of credits is rolled it will look something like the list I have created.

Closing Credits: in respect of Patricia Louise Garlits—wife, mother and matriarch

Encourager	Pat supported Don's return to racing soon after their marriage, perhaps because she understood that he was a passionate man, who would accomplish any task to which he set his mind. A terrifying fire in Chester, S.C., a horrifying clutch explosion at Lions in 1970, a blow-over in Englishtown in 1986, and the lean years, in the early

---

[59] Prov 31:10-31.

Team Garlits

	1980s—people thought they'd seen the last of him. She knew better.
Psychologist	Throughout Don's career, Pat understood him and his emotional need to keep pushing against the odds. She precariously balanced encouraging her man in his role as family breadwinner, and keeping him from harm.
Investor	Amazingly, it was Pat who proposed investing earnings and savings into hot rods, dragsters and property.
Financial backer	They would both arrive home from day jobs, to commence working on Don's early Ford "T" Bucket, hot rod dragster. Pat supplied coffee and, at times, slept in the car as Don worked. Numerous times Pat intervened so her tenacious husband would not jeopardise the family's financial security. She guided their real estate purchases and property developments and kept him on the narrow road to financial success.
Defender	Pat more than tolerated Don's Strokers Hot Rod Club mates by turning their home garage into a club workshop, where cars were built and tested at all times of the day and night, much to the neighbors' chagrin.
Advisor	Pat encouraged Don to fit a Chrysler Hemi engine to his dragster, when he explained the performance advantage it had given to his tow car.
Protector	Her timely-gift of a leather jacket to replace Don's flimsy T shirts (just before an unprecedented supercharger explosion and nitro-methane fire), saved his life.
Nurse	Following the fire at Chester, in June 1959, Pat refused the doctor's request to amputate Don's hands. She sourced a burns specialist to treat

	Don's burned hands and face, and nursed her recalcitrant patient back to health. She nursed his wounds and his ego when things went badly.
Hard worker	Pat produced meals, limitless coffee and did all-night shifts alongside Don in the home garage when building his first, drag-racing hot rod.
Racer	Pat drove a super stock 1962 Dodge at local drag racing events. More significantly, she had the racer's instinct, doing everything possible to win the contests she thought were most important.
Pit crew	Pat accompanied Don on countless road trips across the majority of the USA, England, Mexico, Canada, Australia, Scandinavia and Europe. She assisted as pit crew, took their two young daughters on the road, established boundaries to protect the family, and consulted with other racers' wives about the latest speed secrets. She travelled the nation's highways and byways with her man, riding shotgun. Fans came to know her from frequent photos in drag magazines.
Visionary	It was Pat who was there to hand Don the shaving cream and razor to shave his beard, after the historic win at the 1967 Nationals. She suggested that Don establish a museum of drag racing after visiting the British Motor Museum.
Home maker, mother	Pat single-mindedly cared for her family and prevented drag racing from threatening this most precious possession.
Wise counsellor	She insisted that Don persevere with the rear-engine dragster design when he had given up. Though she supplied endless amounts of coffee and encouragement, she finally put her foot down and insisted that Don retire from Top Fuel competition at age 71.

Team Garlits

Faithful wife   Pat overlooked Don's shortcomings; she tolerated his return to racing after saying he would quit. She tolerated Don working on cars, even on Christmas Eve, while all of the family waited for him. She remained dignified and gracious despite having good reason to be demanding and self-righteous. Pat was a graceful woman of faith who carried her Bible with her and influenced everyone she could.

Despite Pat's support for Don, her anxiety was never far from the surface. "Now that we have the museum established, Don's racing stronger, harder and faster than he ever has", said Pat, who has worried about him for her entire adult life. "That's the thing that scares me—with these speeds and experimentation, he's open to it now." Finally, Don relented. "I don't miss the Top Fuel cars any more. I came back in 2001, ran a best of 323.04 in 2003 at the Gatornationals, and hung up my helmet in September of the same year at the request of my sweet wife. She said the 300-plus runs were scaring her. I never drove again!" Don and Pat appeared not to have lost any of the passion they enjoyed when they first met. Don, for his part, was often torn between his love for racing and his love for Pat and the family. But of course, time and again, with Pat's encouragement, he continued to overcome defeat and achieve new levels.

She loved her man with all her heart, body and soul and never thought of anyone else but him. She was at Dad's side through every win, loss, crash, you name it, she was there. – Donna Garlits

There have been new recruits to Team Garlits in more recent years. In the early days, the girls travelled with their parents. Later they had their own families and careers—Gaye Lyn as a piano teacher and Donna as a math tutor. They have been involved with the museum and the family business from time to time. Donna is now the CEO of the museum and Gaye Lyn a board member. Donna's daughter Sarah, became a live-in nurse to Pat. Donna's son Rodney has become Don's understudy and travelling companion to cackle fest events and is now the father of Braden Garlits, perhaps a future drag racer. Sarah, who is now enrolled at the University of Asheville, North Carolina, says of Pat, "She was the glue that held the family together, the heart and soul of the operation who ran the company and the business. Pat is the reason the family are Christians. She loved God and always carried her Bible with her".

Pat's Passing

As Pat struggled with Parkinson's and dementia, Donna said her dad made time to be sure she was comfortable. He fed her and helped her around their home. "He never sleeps", said Garlits' eldest daughter, Gaye Lyn Capitano. "I am so proud of him. He's caring for our mother, an awesome task. I hope I have that kind of energy when I'm his age."

Pat passed away on the 2nd of February, 2014.

In Don's office, there is a box of hundreds of cards and letters of condolence from all over the world, from people who knew of Pat and respected her as *a wife of noble character* who lived a good life.

> Dear Friends,
>
> My dear wife of nearly 61 years left this world and went over to the other side at 5:53 pm, this afternoon. She has been suffering a lot these last few days and it was a Blessing to see God take her into His care. I will miss her very badly, but will be with her sooner than I realize, as time is very different here than over there. She passed at home with her two Daughters at her

side and me holding her hand and a little Yorkie dog on each side of her. She went without making a sound and this house is going to be very quiet for a while. I had "Glenn Miller" playing in the background, as that was her favorite "Big Band". I will let everyone know what the arrangements will be when I know myself. Thanks for all the Prayers and support through this terrible ordeal. Sincerely,

Don's Friends

There are many people associated with the Don Garlits legacy. Pat was the one constant, but there was a large group of friends and associates who were significant over a long period or made a lasting impression in a short time. Initially, it was Garlits and Garlits. Brother Ed joined Don to build and race cars and to run the garage and speed-shop business during Don's long absences while he was competing. Then there was Garlits and Malone, when school friend Art Malone drove the car while Don recovered from burns. Then Garlits and Taaffe, Garlits and Swingle, Garlits and Lemons, Lemons and Garlits, Garlits and Cook, etc. But very few could stand the pace, commitment and sheer endurance required to keep the show on the road.

No one does it alone. – Antron Brown

From the time Garlits commenced running more-than-local events, help was needed to build and maintain the car, drive to and from events, push-start the dragster, service the car between rounds and share the disappointment of defeat or the spoils of success. The following list of helpers includes only the main players, particularly in the early days when there was no money for wages, and most of the work done was for love. By his own admission, Don Garlits was always and still is a hard taskmaster—of himself, his hired help, and at times, those close to him. The standard he set for himself was the standard by which he judged most others, except for Pat. (Even then, he expected a lot, which she happily gave, most of the time.) Garlits' relentless demands on others often worked against him. Many joined him on his mission, only to grow tired of the pressure, leave after an incident, and return at a later time to share the excitement. Some stories suggest that, at times, Garlits' standard differs from what his Christian faith requires—the high standard to "treat others as you would have them treat you". Garlits appreciates those who stuck by him, as arguments were soon forgotten on both sides. Tommy TC Lemons gave his utmost to drag racing and worked with Garlits for most of his working life. Lemons' low-key delivery was a necessary foil to Garlits' unrelenting competitiveness. Famous for his dry wit, Lemons was a quintessential story-teller, particularly of jokes against himself or Garlits, of whom he said, "He can be a tough, son-of-a-bitch, but he's soft with me. Wasn't always that way, but he is my friend..." One of Garlits' demands of himself and others (including Pat) was to drive marathon distances without rest breaks (often after working for days on end, with only cat naps to prevent falling asleep on the job). On many such occasions, driving and sleeping were taken in shifts.

Don's relationships with his hotrodder assistants was always complicated by the fact that they often wanted to drive the dragsters. But none of them could drive as well as "the old man". Garlits was not just a driver, he was also the innovator, designer, engineer, fabricator, welder, mechanic, tow car driver, chief cook and bottle washer. There were others who could do all these tasks, but no one could do all of them so persistently-well as Don Garlits. When a few, such as Art Malone, Connie Swingle, and Emery Cook did drive successfully, some thought they had *become* Don Garlits and wanted to run the show. Garlits' first preference was to design, build and work on the car and if possible, let others drive, but when there were appearance money-contracts to fulfil and thousands of miles to drive between events, Don did it himself. Typically, in the early days, a Garlits team mechanic may have earned $125 per week, when typically mechanics were earning $50 per week. This was good money provided they didn't mind living on the road and working 24 hours per day, seven days per week. Not that they always worked so hard. But when the car was damaged and had to be repaired before the next event, hundreds if not thousands of miles away, they stepped it up.

Most significant among Garlits' helpers and friends are the following, presented in alphabetical order of the first names:

Art Malone

Art Malone was a younger, school friend who kept popping up in Garlits' life at critical moments. As a boy Art was a big, timid kid. Don defended him against bullies which cemented a life-long friendship that stood the test of time. They both rose to help the other in times of need. Following the Chester fire, Malone offered to take over the driving role. Garlits agreed, which prevented the need to breach existing contracts and sell the racing equipment to keep the wolf from the door. Malone, a building contractor, became a racer in his own right, buying dragsters to run and win in national competition including the 1963 US Fuel and Gas Championships at Bakersfield, California. Malone who was also a speedway fan, had a car built (powered by a Chrysler Hemi) to win a $10,000 prize put up by Bill France, to be the first car to lap Daytona at over 180 mph. To further prove his versatility, Malone also ran at the Indy 500 twice in Andy Granatelli's Novi, finishing 11th, in 1964. Malone then inspired Garlits' return to the NHRA US Nationals in 1984, after a long absence, going on to win the event, plus the 1984 NHRA Championship finals at Pomona, California. Malone later became a dragstrip owner and a patron of the sport when he convinced Garlits to update Swamp Rat 26 and to enter (and win) the NHRA US Nationals and the Finals at Pomona, California.

Bruce Crower

Bruce Crower is a Californian, whose name keeps cropping up in careers of many racers. Crower was a gifted engineer who designed and made camshafts, blower drives, clutches, transmissions and aerodynamic airfoils. He shared Garlits' Christian faith and interest in innovation.

Bob Taaffe

Bob Taaffe was remarkable in that he first came to Garlits' Automotive Speed Shop in 1959, as a very enthusiastic, hard-working volunteer on race weekends. When Bob was discharged from the Marines, he was employed at the speed shop as an assistant and paid $50 per week, mainly to sweep floors. So keen was Bob to be part of the team that he would attend race meetings just for his keep, as was often the case in motor racing "in them days". Bob grew in expertise to become a Top Fuel dragster tuner, designer and fabricator, remaining with Garlits through thick and thin, for many years. Following a long, winless run, including a DNQ at the 1966 NHRA Springnationals, Taaffe inspired Garlits to build a new car in 72 hours of non-stop work, to compete in a match race at the end of the week. As the new car became increasingly successful, Taaffe's enthusiasm convinced Garlits that they would be a contender at the 1967 NHRA Nationals at Indianapolis. After qualifying a distant 23rd, confirming the possibility of his status as a has-been, Garlits wore down the field to win the event. To celebrate the win, there on the track he shaved off his beard that he had grown as a bet against ever winning again. Taaffe, eventually left Garlits when they lost confidence in each other's strong and loudly-expressed views.

Team Garlits

Connie Swingle

Connie Swingle burst into Don Garlits' life in September 1959. "Swingle", as he preferred to be known, was originally a hotrodder from Biloxi, Oklahoma. Following his discharge from the Air Force he came to Florida to earn a living as a street racer, taking money from "unwitting rubes", as Garlits put it. Upon his unannounced arrival at the workshop, the brash Swingle immediately set to work assisting Ed. He later proved to be the best welder Garlits ever knew, and earned himself a place in the team. Like so many other drag-racing aficionados, Swingle wanted to be a dragster driver. He accomplished this dream with Garlits (leaving from time to time to drive for other dragster owners). During a tempestuous six-year relationship with Garlits (in which, Swingle, by all accounts, seems to be almost as head strong as his boss), he would leave to build cars for others. Swingle was Garlits' savior on more than one occasion, as were other travelling companions who were present in a moment of crisis. Most memorably, as a result of an axle breaking, Swingle extracted Garlits from a tow vehicle that submerged in a roadside canal. As the water reached window level, Swingle pushed his young son, Teddy, out the window with instructions to swim for the bank, while he returned to help Garlits who was trapped in the driver's seat. Just as Garlits was about to go under, with superhuman strength, Swingle forced back the heavy Chrysler engine that had broken the seat mounting. On another similar occasion, Swingle lifted the rear of the tow vehicle off Garlits' head, when it collapsed, while he was underneath locating the jack. Swingle would leave after a big argument, only to return and perform his magic as an engineer/welder/dragster driver. Finally, he succumbed to disease and could no longer work.

Don Cook

Don "Mad Dog" Cook, was a drag-racing perennial from California who was involved in the construction of Swamp Rat dragsters including SR 21, 22, 23.

Ed Garlits

Edward Garlits, Don's younger brother was the first assistant mechanic. They had learned to work together on their parents' farm developing their inherited mechanical aptitude by repairing farm machinery and friends' bicycles. When Ed was discharged from the Marines he joined Don's new enterprise at Don's Garage. There, dragster construction was already well under way with assistance from Dave Phillips, and fellow members of the Strokers Hot Rod Club. The brothers built Ed a gasoline-powered dragster. He successfully ran it until work at the garage and Don's interstate competition took over. (To say nothing of his wife's threat of divorce if he didn't stop.)

Ed Iskenderian

The perennially-smiling "Cam Father" Ed Iskenderian was as much a part of the hot-rodding and drag-racing phenomonon as any individual. An instinctive and methodical engineer whose marketing prowess was even more legendary than his cam-grinding ability, Isky was the great hot-rod entrepaneur. He was trusted by all as an honest broker (as long as you did not include the camshaft advertisment claims). Isky was always on the lookout for the next-up-and-comer for him to promote and encourage in a never-ending quest for more speed and more camshaft sales. As the first president of the now-huge speed industry association, SEMA, Iskenderian is one of the true pillars of the high-performance industry, that could not have developed without him. Isky was quick to see the value in an ambitious young racer from Florida, whose tenacity and marketability made them a good pair. Isky's hospitality extended to home-cooked meals, volunteering as pit crew and parts gofer when things got really desperate.

Emery Cook

Garlits had a picture of Emery Cook on his wall, representing the person he wanted to emulate. Later, it was Emery Cook who, at some cost to himself and at a crucial moment, gave Don the information he needed to become competitive using nitro methane (Cordova, Illinois, in 1957). Not one to forget a favor, Don employed Emery ten years later to work in his new Detroit shop (alongside Setto Postoian), and to drive dragsters and the funny car that was funded by Dodge and built by Connie Swingle. Both Garlits and Cook eventually tired of the cold winters and returned to their home states of Florida and California.

Herb Parkes

Herb Parkes came to Garlits having worked for drag racer, Clayton Harris, (who was also a friend of Art Malone and Connie Swingle). He became part of the Garlits' furniture probably because he was a very smart crew chief and also because he was not intimidated by Garlits' occasional dummy spits. One such story recalls how, in the midst of a big argument with Parkes, Garlits got out of his still-moving car and was run over by the rear wheel. This prompted speculation that Garlits' subsequent ambulance ride was not to treat his injuries, but to prevent any further injuries being inflicted by Parkes. Parkes was not only an outstanding Top Fuel crew chief (in an era when it is they who determine the outcomes of most races more than the driver).

He also owned and maintained IMSA GTP race cars interspersed with drag racing. Following Garlits' amazing NHRA comeback in 1977, Parkes' share of Garlits' prizemoney provided him with a sizable income. This ended when Garlits began experimenting with unconventional cars.

Setto Postoian

An early competitor from Detroit, Setto Postoian, like Don, was ambitious enough to compete nationally. Postoian had no peer as an antagonist. He placed advertisements in drag-racing magazines doubting Garlits' achievements and accusing him of placing substitute driver, Art Malone, in jeopardy. But this was all grist for the drag-racing mill as they were both underdogs against the dominant Californians. Don acknowledged Postoian's role in his competitive career by appointing him as his assistant when he relocated to Detroit, and later including Postoian in the Drag Racing Hall of Fame.

Tommy "TC" Lemons

Tommy Lemons came to Garlits' workshop at Seffner, in 1968, when fellow Okie Connie Swingle, returned to Florida from Christmas holidays in Oklahoma. Tommy, also known as TC, whom Garlits dubbed "Top Cat", took over as crew chief when Bob Taaffe left (soon after Lemons' arrival). TC had come to Florida with his friend Swingle to work with Garlits "for a couple of weeks" with the intention of helping Garlits build cars, and trade labor for a dragster chassis for himself. Apart from racing ventures and the occasional sojourn home to Oklahoma, Lemons spent the rest of his life with Garlits. Forty-three years later he was living in a cabin on the Museum property as part of his retirement benefit that Garlits provided.

Team Garlits

Garlits recalls why Lemons was the most enduring of his many helpers and crew chiefs:

> We were peas right out of the same pod. We were both just a little right of Attila the Hun. He was never afraid to tell me what he thought. A lot of my crew guys were intimidated by me and were afraid to tell me what they thought. TC wasn't afraid to tell me. Back in those early days, it wasn't really a lot of engine work as a crew chief. The engine made whatever power it made, but it was how you engaged the clutch that made all the difference in the world. All of those big races that I lost in the old days was basically because of not enough clutch, and those were usually the races when TC was there to say, "'Old man, we need to put some clutch in this thing."

One of Lemons' favourite stories Garlits now tells against himself, is about the first time they ran the "Front Driver" car.

> The very first day we took it over to Tampa Dragway—not to make any runs, just to start it and see how everything looked—we unloaded it, and we stood there—me, Tommy, and Swingle—and I gave this little speech. I said, "Boys, you're looking at the safest Top Fuel dragster that's ever been built... and Swingle, for this first test, you need to drive it." Tommy probably told that story hundreds of times.

Typical of this relationship, was Lemons' technical analysis of each run Garlits completed. On one occasion when Lemons arrived at the top end of the track after a run, Garlits asked, "Well, how did that run look?". TC answered, "I'm not sure. Which lane were you in?". On another occasion, someone had made a T shirt that quoted one of Lemons' sayings: "I didn't want to tell my momma that I spent 20 years in drag racing, so I told her I was in prison". "Don't let 'the Old Man' see these; he'll be sellin' 'em!" said Lemons. Before long, as he predicted, they were on sale in the Garlits Museum gift shop and are still one of their bestsellers. (I can attest to the attention these T shirts still draw as I wore one to the NHRA Mello Yellow event in Atlanta, 2014. Many people stopped me to read the caption and ask where I got the shirt.) TC Lemons finally passed away while still resident at the Garlits' property. According to Phil Burgess, who published several of these anecdotes on the NHRA website, Lemons' memorial service honoured him with the last laugh, as his life was celebrated by the retelling of TC Lemons stories. Burgess recalls,

> TC, an ornery little guy from Texas/Oklahoma, had touched so many in the drag-racing community. This was no more apparent than at the memorial service where it was standing-room-only, packed with numerous friends and fans that TC had touched with his quick wit and dead-pan delivery. In fact, TC would have appreciated this service, because, instead of being filled with sorrow, there was laughter and more laughter as Garlits, Pat Dakin, Jim Walther, Donna Garlits and others told tale after tale about the adventures or misadventures of Tommy TC Lemons.

Lonnie Curley

Lonnie Curley was an African-American man from Green Valley, Texas, who had commissioned Garlits to build a 392 Hemi for his Ford truck. Whenever Garlits ran in Texas, Lonnie was on the team. He was one of many helpers without whom Garlits could not have operated in the early days (or the later days, for that matter). Curley was perhaps not a great engineer, tuner or tireless worker like other Garlits' supporters. But he represents the legions of young men for whom Garlits was a hero (the difference in his case being, his participation was not imaginary).

Tim Bucher

Crew members' stories about Garlits abound. One of the best came from Tim Bucher.[60]

> At the 1985 Grandnational Molson, I remember not liking the intensity of Don during the event. I thought he was being kind of a jerk during the whole weekend. I kept to myself as much as possible, tried to do my job as best as I could. After winning the final round, I remember getting to the end of the track; I walked past Don just trying to do my job right, getting the car ready to tow back to the pits. Don ignored everybody else, stopped me, gave me a big hug, and told me, "That was for your dad". From that point on, I looked at "Big Daddy" differently.... After losing in the first round of the Brainerd event, it was just the three of us towing out of the track. Herb was driving the truck, Don was in the front passenger seat, and me in the back seat. It was a disappointing loss. At a quiet moment, I felt comfortable enough to ask, "So, who do you want to win this event?" I'll never forget what happened next. Don turned around to look at me, said nothing, then turned back around. We drove

---

[60] "...the middle son of late, great, Chevy Top Fuel racer Jim Bucher....the Bucher boys had been part of the effort to help Garlits ready Swamp Rat 34 for the 2001 Indy event...also...'After I graduated from college, was engaged to be married, thought I had to give this racing thing a shot. I got hired by Don after the Springnationals in Columbus 1985. I traveled with Herb Parks for the summer, was with the team long enough to win four national events that year. Here [is one] of my

in silence for quite a while. I wondered what was so wrong with what I said. Herb later told me, "If Don doesn't win, he doesn't want anyone to win". Wow, I've never been around someone so intense and so driven to succeed as "Big Daddy."

Chapter 10 The Swamp Rat Dynasty

"No man has power over the wind to contain it; so no one has power over the day of his death. As no one is discharged in time of war, so wickedness will not release those who practise it."
– Eccles 8:8

A Dynasty of Power

To have power at your disposal is a very attractive idea. To have a dynasty of power—lordship/domination—is doubly attractive. The word "dynasty" comes from the Greek word *dunamis*, meaning, to be able. It is also the root of "dynamite". To use power for good is the challenge for all humanity. Power is an addictive enabler. It causes human beings to indulge themselves in it. If we could question Pol Pot, Karl Marx or Adolf Hitler about their motives regarding ambition for power, it is unlikely they would respond, "to kill millions". Instead, their comeback would, no doubt, comprise something of "promoting the cause to save the world". But as we know, the more power they got, the more they wanted. Lord Acton's well-known statement regarding power confirms what our experience tells us, "Power tends to corrupt, and absolute power corrupts absolutely."

Political power comes out of the barrel of a gun. – Chairman Mao Zedong

From a drag racer's point of view, *having* too much power is never the problem. *Using* too much power is. As we have seen, drag racing has always been the art of balancing power with traction. Usually the competitor who "bogs down" or goes "up in smoke" loses. The above text from Ecclesiastes reminds us that our use of power is always limited. It cannot contain the wind or be used to circumvent death. And while we are limited in our personal use of power, we can still abuse it, as implied by the Teacher's use of the word "wickedness". Abuse of any power, such as in personal conflict or war, brings unintended consequences. *Its chickens come home to roost.* Garlits would maintain, as he did at the Rat Roast, that he not only loved the sport he dominated, he also loved the people—both supporters and competitors. This is quite the opposite to the abuse of power often seen in sports, politics, business, and family relationships.

During their second tour of Britain in 1976, Don and Pat visited the National Motor Museum (originally known as the Montagu Motor Museum) in the village of Beaulieu, set in the heart of the New Forest, Hampshire. This made a lasting impression on the pair. They decided, at Pat's suggestion, to open their own Museum of Drag Racing, on their property at Seffner, to display Don's many personal cars, dragsters and cars of yesteryear. The museum was later relocated to Ocala where it can be seen from Interstate Highway 75, and benefits from greater exposure to passing tourist traffic. The museum has become the focus of Don Garlits' empire with a magnificent collection of race cars narrating the evolution of the sport, plus hot rods, antique cars, engines, machinery and other cool stuff that any motor head would want to see and should have on their bucket list. This complex also includes the museum workshops where cars are restored for exhibition, and Don's own workshop and private collection of cars, machinery, old engines/parts, and his current (pun intended) electric dragster. Garlits also created the International Drag Racing Hall of Fame to recognise the greater and the lesser heroes of drag racing. These are memorialised in ceramic tiles in the path outside the museum. Garlits has ceded the title of the museum property

The Swamp Rat Dynasty

to the State of Florida, ensuring that it remains a car museum in perpetuity.

Don Garlits was the first successful professional drag racer. He was the first to officially record the 170, 180, 200, 240, 250, and 270 mph marks in the quarter mile; he was also the first to top 200 in the 1/8 mile. In May, 2014, at age 82, Garlits set a speed record of 184 mph in an EV dragster—a battery-powered, electric vehicle. He has won ten American Hot Rod Association Championships, four International Hot Rod Association Championships, and three National Hot Rod Association Championships for a total of 17 World Championships. At age 54 he won his last Championship. Don Garlits has won a total of 144 national events.

On October 20, 1987, his Top Fuel dragster, Swamp Rat 30 was enshrined in the National Museum of American History, a branch of The Smithsonian Museum in Washington DC. To celebrate the occasion Garlits delighted the crowd by firing up the dragster. He was a great performer and safety innovator. Not only did he design, build, tow, maintain, drive and promote his own cars, he was an early adopter of a full-body, fire-resistant suit, complete with socks and gloves. He is perhaps best known for creating a safety revolution in the sport by making the rear-engine dragster competitive.

Swamp Rat Dynasty

SR#	Year Built	Car Design and Engine Features	Speed (mph), ET (seconds) and Accomplishments
1	1956	Chrysler Hemi engine running carburettors with nitro, Chevrolet chassis rails	176.40 @ 8.76 at Brooksville, won Bakersfield unsupercharged, won Kingdon with supercharger fitted
1B	1959	supercharged nitro Hemi, chassis modified for Art Malone	won Riverside, California challenge with Art Malone driving, ran 204.54 @ 8.23 with Garlits driving
3	1960	chrome moly frame	Connie Swingle driving, ran 198.22 @ 7.88

Don Garlits. The Enigmatic Hero

4	1962	Dodge 413 Wedge on gasoline, built for 1962 US Gas and Fuel meeting	205.00, finished second
5	1962	Nitro Hemi, several wheel base variations, wing by Bruce Crower	
6	1963	several variants, originally painted red, repainted black after no success, built by Garlits and Bob Taffe	Art Malone 201.34 @ 7.78, Garlits drove UK tour 197.00 to set British land speed record, won Bakersfield 1965
7A 7B	1963	built by Connie Swingle, Bob Taffe and Garlits	Swingle campaigned separately from Garlits design became the basis for several customer cars sold Swingle's car so Swingle left for 12 months
8	1963-5	built for the 426 Dodge Hemi by Connie Swingle and Taffe with torsion bar suspension by Bruce Crower	Swingle returned initially to drive car no wins for 12 months beaten 23 straight by Chris Karamesines in match races
9		built by Emery Cook as a Dodge Dart funny car on a dragster chassis	first funny car to run 200
10		built in Troy Michigan by Emery Cook from SR #8 with 176" wheelbase	driven by Emery Cook while Garlits finished his new house at Seffner
11	1967	built by Bob Taffe and Don Garlits in 72 hours	Garlits, after a win drought, agreed not to shave until the car became a winner which it did at the 1967 NHRA Nationals
12A 12B	1968	built by Bob Taffe, Garlits and Jim Marrone with short 137" wheelbase	12A a failure and replaced with 12B with 215" wheelbase won 1968 Spring Nationals at Englishtown and at the Nationals at Indy ran 240 12A was recreated in 2007 by Garlits and Jim Hunnewell with a current model 392 Chrysler Hemi engine

The Swamp Rat Dynasty

13	1969	built to replace damaged 12B, fitted with two-speed transmission	won Smokers G&F Championship transmission exploded at Long Beach sold to TC Lemons Garlits drove for percentage of winnings.
14	1970	prototype rear-engine car by Lemons, Swingle and Garlits	abandoned after 3 months testing reactivated with Pat's encouragement ran 240 @ 6.21 at Indy.
15	1970	built as front-engine alternative to SR 14	sold to Goodyear as display
16	1972	evolution from SR 14	wing collapsed at 1972 Gatornationals
17	1972	streamliner with body by Jocko	negative lift limited speed to 180 disproving streamliner advantage for dragsters
18	1973	180", short, wheelbase car built by Swingle and Garlits	no wins
19	1974	built by Garlits, Swingle and Gary Werner	Swingle quit for having to train Werner car ran 247 @ 5.78 car sold to Graham Withers in Australia
20A 20B	1975	display car built by Glen Blakely, 20B sold to customer who then sold it to Art Malone	built for Bill Harrah's car collection in Reno, Nevada
21	1975	built by Garlits and Gary Werner for "Jungle Jim" Lieberman, sold to Santa Pod in U.K.	1975 NHRA Winternationals winner 1974 NHRA World Champion British Land Speed record, 232
22	1975	built by Don Cook, TC Lemons and Garlits	set record 260.69 @ 6.63 that stood for seven years brought out of retirement to win 1977 Gatornationals
23	1976-7	built by Glen Blakely, fitted with Donovan engine, Ron Barrow crew chief	runner up in 1977 NHRA Winternationals and Bakersfield
24	1977-9	built by Don Cook and Garlits, painted blue with crucifix, U.S. Navy withdrew support, car rebuilt several times	ran for 2 years with no sponsor won 24 of 30 national events and $600,000 Herb Parkes crew chief TC Lemons retired

Don Garlits. The Enigmatic Hero

#	Year	Description	Notes
25	1979-80	built by Lester Guillory on ground effects concepts, car too heavy and inflexible, lost Mello Yellow sponsorship because of cross on car	DNQ 1980 NHRA Winternationals became known as the Kendall Kable Kar when the diagonals were cut out and had to be strengthened by cables and turn buckles
26	1980-4	built by Garlits and Bob Taffe in Seffner, not eligible for NHRA events, ran AHRA events only until modified in 1983 AKA "The Black Car"	in the trailer for the Howard Franklin Bridge episode Herb Parkes left Art Malone funded 1984 come back to win US Nationals and NHRA Finals at Pomona Bob Taffe left when he thought Garlits had lost his ability to win Ed Garlits and sons became team
27	1983	Sidewinder	ran only 6.30 against 5.86 with same engine in another car due to 27% power loss in transmission
28A 28B	1983	high gear only design was too advanced for power available, converted to gas turbine, Richard Hogan Crew Chief	plagued with tire shake both configurations unsuccessful
29	1985	Garlits built at Ocala Museum workshop, Herb Parkes returns	crashed first time out won 1984 National Finals at Pomona ran 268.01 rebuilt—very successful car
30	1986-7	built by Garlits and Herb Parks	blew over and set low ET for the meeting 215.51 @ 5.51 upside down, backwards and on fire displayed in the Smithsonian
31	1987	built by Garlits and Mark Buchanan	destroyed at Spokane Washington
32	1991-2	built by Murf McKinney to break 300 mph, mono wing	DNQ at NHRA Atlanta due to lack of finance ran 299.30 driven by Bruce Larson
33	2001	Bonneville streamliner built by Rich Venga, powered by a supercharged flathead V8	ran 221
34	1994-2003	built in 1993 by Murf McKinney, later stored until 2001, sponsored	driven by Bruce Larson loaned car to Richard Langston ran 323.04 @ 4.76 last ran at Indy in 2002 at 310.81 when

200

The Swamp Rat Dynasty

		by Summit Racing Equipment	Pat said "no more" driven by Garlits DNQ for NHRA Indianapolis
2001 Garlits drove car owned by Gary Clapshaw at Indianapolis to run 4.72, 303.37 lost to Mike Dunn in the first round				

			Garlits' last race
35-36	2008-11	Dodge Drag Pak Challengers	ran several NHRA events
37	2014	electric dragster built by Shawn Lawless	ran 186 in 2014
38	2019	electric dragster built by Shawn Lawless	ran 189.03 looking for 200

Swamp Rat 30 blew over and set low ET for the meeting 215.51 mph @ 5.51, upside down, backwards and on fire! The Dragster is now displayed in the Smithsonian Museum (GARLITS COLLECTION).

The Swamp Rat 26 NHRA Comeback

Swamp Rat 26, built by Don Garlits at Seffner, was immediately successful. But Garlits had decided not to run the National Hot Rod Association National Championship events due to a change of rules that required he redesign his new car. As an alternative, Garlits was intending to run second-string, American Hot Rod Association events, to which Herb Adams protested and resigned. Adams could predict another financially-lean year. As 1981 unfolded, Adams' prediction was realized; (other than wins at the AHRA Winter Nationals, Snowbird Nationals and some minor match race victories with Don's brother Ed and his sons as the crew). The year further worsened with the simultaneous relocation of Garlits' Museum of Drag Racing (from Seffner, Florida, to Ocala about 100 miles north), and the construction of a new home. For three years Garlits was diverted with new projects and the museum. He experimented with SR 27, a Chrysler Hemi "sidewinder", SR 28A, another Hemi without a transmission, and SR 28B, a gas-turbine-powered car, all of which were unsuccessful. In 1983, SR 26 was rushed back into service for a series of meetings in California, where the sidewinder had destroyed itself due to tire shake. Being without a car and contracted to compete in the AHRA Winter Nationals in Arizona, Garlits called some friends in Florida to pick up SR 26 from Seffner. They drove to Arizona where the mechanicals out of the sidewinder were installed at a Ramada Inn car park, in Tucson. Garlits then modified the chassis to allow installation of the reverser, to make the car NHRA-legal. But Garlits had lost his way. While he experimented with innovations to reduce cost and to create a competitive advantage, the competition caught up and passed him by.

Apart from the occasional foray into AHRA events and being beaten regularly by Shirley Muldowney in match races, Garlits was out of mainstream racing for four years. That was, until in 1984, when Art Malone came to visit the museum. Malone, who had previously driven both Garlits' and his own dragsters, proposed that he and Don go to the NHRA US Nationals, in September. Don agreed, thinking that they would attend as spectators. But this was not what Malone had in mind. When Malone asked what it would take to compete, Garlits listed the modifications to the car, plus engine and transmission upgrades that were required, and the return of Herb Adams, (for which Malone agreed to pay). Arrival of the Garlits team at the Nationals in Indianapolis was not treated seriously by the NHRA. They were parked in the wilderness of the pit area and greeted with derision, to the amusement of competitors and onlookers, who enjoyed the humiliation of the old dinosaur. Bowed, but not beaten, and still lacking the big money of his competitors who had taken drag racing into a new era of professionalism and cost, Garlits won each round. He despatched the current hot dogs with reduced times and increased speed with each run, until he won his first, major, NHRA event in four years. Don Garlits was back with a vengeance... back, with all of the motivation he ever had to keep going, to find a sponsor, and to re-establish himself at the top of the sport by getting through to the semi-finals at the season-end event at Pomona, California.

Many of his contemporaries have gone on to fulfil their competitive urges with careers in business. But Don Garlits is still a racer, setting records in Swamp Rat 38, his latest, electric, dragster iteration. Don Garlits is still fulfilling boyhood dreams that so many of us share. No wonder, to so many, he remains a hero.

Chapter 11 Persistence Wins

*"Now all has been heard; here is the conclusion of the matter:
Fear God and keep his commandments for this is the duty of
all mankind."*
– Eccles 12:13

Towards Transformation

Don Garlits realised early in his racing career that he could make a living from his sport. His ability to succeed in enterprise can be attributed to his unique character and life circumstances combined with the insights and abilities he gained in the most exclusive of all schools—the school of hard knocks. His drag racing career was turbulent, to say the least, but he was unwavering and persistent in working toward his goal. On the surface, it may seem that Garlits was all about the racing. But there were other dimensions to his experience that he claims to be unexpected gifts—*links in the supernatural chain*.[61] From the beginning, Garlits marched to a syncopated beat of a different drummer. This was a reflection of his father, Edward, whose esoteric motivation was seemingly different for its own sake. Edward, for all his brilliance, often defined himself against social norms, exemplified by his atheism and nudism. Don

---

[61] A concept of spirituality learned from his mother.

rejected some aspects of his father's attitudes, but took on alternative, contrary views with equal passion. Fortunately for Don, most of them were beneficial and life-giving. Most unusual and distinctive of these, from a drag racer's point of view, was his embryonic Christian faith that frequently drove him to his knees and to God, begging: "Please help me, Father". Certainly, this is the missing link in any supernatural chain.

Drag racing is a brutal sport. For Garlits it was not just the acceleration, the speed, the accidents or the even more brutal parachute deceleration (that caused him to eventually suffer from detached retina, effectively ending his competitive career). There was other savagery: the competitors' taunts, the media, and the crowd that one day would acclaim him "King of Dragsters" and the next day, "Don Garbage". (Name calling had opposite to the intended effect, only making Garlits more resolved to dominate the sport.) Track announcer Bernie Partridge, called him "Big Daddy", and that name stuck. It stuck because it reflected the unassailable position Garlits had created in the first decade of drag racing and maintained for the next 30-plus years. Expounding one of his father's theories, Garlits reiterates: "To test any idea or thing, take it to its logical conclusion and see if the idea is still good". Garlits uses this argument to show that drag racing must be a good thing, because it has endured. I suggest, however, that there is a much better example than drag racing to prove the theory of what is truly good. What Don Garlits has become, and what all good men and women persist in taking to the logical conclusion—*this* is truly valuable. The essence of *The Good Life* is persistence and hope. "For everything that was written in the past was written to teach us, so that through the endurance taught in the Scriptures and the encouragement they provide we might have hope."[62] Garlits is still Big Daddy, not just for his drag-racing accomplishments, but for persisting to be the enigmatic hero that he is.

Persistence

In 1941, when Winston Churchill was invited to speak at his old school, Harrow, Churchill stood before the students and said, "To be successful in your life and business, never, ever, ever, ever, ever, ever, ever, give up. Never give up. Never give up. Never give up. The pessimist sees the problems in every opportunity. Whereas the optimist sees the opportunity in every problem. Never give in, never give in, never; never; never; never—in nothing, great or small, large or petty—never give in except to convictions of honour and good sense". Albert Einstein on the other hand, asserted that continuing to do the same thing and expect a different result, is a sign of madness. Where is the crucial line between persisting with what is good and flogging a dead horse? At what point do we review the reality of our lives and ask, *did our goals fulfil our hopes, or did our hopes fail us?*

My use of the term persistence is similar to the more fashionable term *sustainability*. That is, *to purposefully do what gets the best results in the long term; to endure, maintain or conserve what is objectively beneficial for the individual and the common good.* Persistence is not austere and unambitious. It does, however, require a goal and a process of review to make sure we are going where we want to go. Given that we cannot possibly anticipate all future challenges, it stands to reason we can at least set realistic goals for the future by learning from our past. Which goals

---

[62] Rom 15:4.

will endure? Which of our passions are the madness and vanity that we should avoid if we are to find satisfaction in life? Listen to the Teacher: "Remember your Creator in the days of your youth, before the days of trouble come and the years approach when you will say, 'I find no pleasure in them'".[63]

Don Garlits was not exactly following good advice when he started street racing and working on cars, but his wise stepfather Alex, knew enough to guide the energetic young man to follow his passion and to quit his bookkeeping job. Was this good advice? Were there other higher callings Garlits could have pursued than drag racing? Did Garlits make good choices for himself? In my view, these questions are irrelevant because they don't take reality and the force of youthful, human passion into account. Even if we do pursue an obviously-harmful path in full view of the alternatives, at least we are seeking our own goals, and, on reflection, can learn from experience, should we be so wise. It is, however, the duration that counts.

The candidates Jesus chose as friends and disciples were among the most unlikely and most hated in society: tax collectors, smelly fisherman, prostitutes, religious bigots and other untrustworthy misfits. The one shared characteristic? When they were invited to follow Jesus, they persisted (with some exceptions that illustrate the point perfectly) because they were irresistibly attracted to Jesus and his New Kingdom. Jesus warned his disciples that once they began to follow him, their entire mission was dependent on persistence. "But he that shall endure unto the end, the same shall be saved."[64] Fortunately for us, God's gift of grace does excuse us from achieving the goal of perfection because it is beyond us. But persistence counts

---
[63] Eccles 12:1.
[64] Matt 24:13, KJV.

for more than any other aspect of achievement. Conduct a little self-analysis by looking back over your own life to see what you have continued to do for the longest time. When all the words have been said and all deeds done, what remains is the reality of your life. What do you see when you conduct this review? According to Jesus, the quality of life is objectively measured by the quality of relationships, including our enemies. Again, Paul confirms the true goal of endurance when he says, "And now these three remain: faith, hope and love. But the greatest of these is love".[65]

Learning to Love

Of the human characteristics faith, hope and love, love is the greatest, because when it is taken to its logical conclusion, when it persists, it always seeks accountability to God and the good of others. In essence, this was Jesus' message and example. A good life is contained in and fulfilled by the greatest command to: "love the Lord your God, with all your heart, mind, soul and strength and your neighbour as yourself". This is the moral code we know as the *Golden Rule* that appears in different forms in many philosophical traditions. It is a profound statement worthy only of God incarnate who was prepared to apply it to himself—to "turn the other cheek" and "love your enemies", even at the hands of those who unjustly killed him.

Despite its apparent simplicity and the lip service it has been given by many philosophers, the Golden Rule is often not a conscious discipline even among Christians. Most attempts to apply it are so confronting to our self-importance, that we excuse ourselves and reject it out of hand. Perversely, 2000

---

[65] 1 Cor 13:13.

years of Christian history has taught us religious language so well that we can make its words mean the opposite of what was intended. For this reason, it seems necessary for practical purposes, to invert the command in order to proceed. That is, we should consciously love ourselves before we can learn to love others or love God.[66] To love ourselves, means simply and reasonably, to desire and work toward the best and most satisfying result in life. Philosopher, Dallas Willard calls this the good life.[67] This is not the travel-brochure "good life". Willard uses the term in the same way that Jesus does in the Sermon on the Mount. Jesus pronounces, "blessed are you who mourn...who are weak...who are persecuted for my sake..."[68] Jesus espouses that when we act against our natural instincts, in obedience to God, there is both an advantage and a price to pay. The advantage? We discover what we were intended to be–fully human. The cost? A crushed ego. The price must be paid.

Garlits' many abilities as a racer are well known. His spiritual competencies remain less so, but to those who know him personally, they are very distinctive. In fact, they are striking in contrast to his natural instincts. Mostly, they are relational qualities, as demonstrated at the Rat Roast, both by what others said about him, and by his own behavior on the night—behavior such as his self-deprecating sense of humor; his words "I'm sorry", "I was wrong", "I apologise"; and his unstated recognition that the contest between drag racers was not important enough to bear grudges that would prevent him from enjoying friendships. Garlits' declaration of his love for Ed Iskenderian is very telling. Though it could be easily mistaken for nostalgia,

---

[66] *How Good is the Golden Rule*, Warren Mills, Freedom Publishing Books.
[67] Dallas Willard, *The Divine Conspiracy*, (Harper One), 98.
[68] Matt 5.

it is rather, the sentiment behind the cross and the words he painted on his car: God is pursuing the highest good for himself and for his creation.

If we are not guided by love we become deluded, impoverished souls, hating what we are but blind to a better path. To make no progress toward sustainable life goals, we run the risk as we get older, of becoming more and more inflexible and bitter about the cards that life has dealt us. Alternatively, we become increasingly appreciative, thankful, grateful and graceful as we age. We learn about ourselves and others as we go, and see God's grace manifest in us and particularly in our relationships. Such is the power of love.

The Good Life is Passionate

Passion is the most powerful of all human instincts that impel men and women. That the Bible condemns "soulish" passion is a common but ill-informed misconception. Certainly, some passions must be restrained, but genuine love is the one passion that needs no restraint. Scripture uses different language for what we understand to be the source of all emotion. Solomon repeatedly uses the term "in my heart", speaking to the passions of his soul that were not satisfied until he recognised his need for God. Jacques Ellul asserts that Ecclesiastes' statement, "God has placed eternity in the hearts of men", is a passionate yearning for the mystery of God within us both now and beyond time and space.[69] And passion it must remain, because we cannot possibly know what lies beyond. Only God can answer questions of eternity. *To understand the wind is pointless vanity*, says King Solomon. However, since *God has placed*

---

[69] *Reason for Being*, Jacques Ellul, Erdmans

eternity in our hearts we can, like Solomon, reconcile to allowing God to fill the void in our hearts and investing our passions in Him. This squares with the message of Jesus in the beatitudes of Matthew 5, "that those who hunger and thirst after righteousness will be filled".

The good life is my personal experience. The good life is Jesus' promise of abundant life that millions throughout history have experienced. They are people you know, like your mom and dad, your uncle and aunt, your neighbours and maybe your enemies. I admit that this is what I desire. I want the good life to be a reality, and it is.

Satisfaction and Fulfilment

When our souls find no rest, it is because we are not fulfilling our intended creative purpose.

This sceptical, post-modern age has produced an unprecedented crisis of meaning in the Western world, especially among young men. Despite my age, I can personally relate to some of the reasons why. The rise of feminism, for example, has displaced men from many of their privileged roles in society. Feminism is but one factor in the loss of a comprehensive, male worldview in which power, education, wealth and sexual entitlement were normal. The underlying problem, in my opinion, is not just about status and power, but healthy relationships; with ourselves, each other, and ultimately with God. An encroaching unbelief in God has fulfilled philosopher Friedrich Nietzsche's declaration, that God is dead. We have killed him, you and I.[70] Attraction to an alpha-male like Don Garlits is a mistaken solution to this crisis because there is far more to his

---

[70] *Thus Spake Zarathrustra*, Friedrich Nietzsche.

maleness than meets the eye. In particular, Don's declaration and testimony to the living, loving God.

Meanwhile, Don Garlits, The Teacher and the sages of history maintain that God is frustratingly unknowable. Despite all the knowledge available to us, God remains spirit; an essence as elusive as vapor or smoke. Apart from when God has revealed Himself clearly, such as to Moses on the mountain, God is by definition, knowable only as the ultimate cause of all causes and the numinous power behind all power. French theologian Blaise Pascal posits that all humans bet their lives on God either existing or not. ("Eternity in our hearts", as Solomon would say.) Given the possibility that God does exist, and assuming the infinite gain or loss associated with belief or unbelief in God, a rational person should live as though God exists and seek to believe in God. If God does not exist, such a person will have only a small loss of vain pleasure. Soul is the aspect of human need that is fully satisfied only by God. To be a *strong soul*, is to be satisfied in God...and begin the transformation of becoming more like Him.

In 1984 Garlits wrote,

> If it had ended today, I would be satisfied. My life has been full and rich. I would still be able to reflect on all those grand moments during my drag racing-career. I've done more than most men dream of doing in one lifetime. But I would be willing to have everything erased if those 'things' meant never knowing the love of God. Even today, sometimes I wonder how He could really care about me. I'm still driven. I'll probably always be hard-headed. I'll undoubtedly continue to put my life on the line more than I should. I'm still

brash and prone to exhibit my volatile temper, and there's that brash mouth. But He keeps on loving me.[71]

The White Throne

Don's answers to deep questions about life are not complex, philosophical or theological statements. His attitudes have been largely and profoundly shaped by life experiences; by allowing his passions to both put him in harm's way, and be deeply influenced by his devoted wife. Some of Don's attitudes reflect transformation, some reflect further need of transformation (as do ours). His sensibilities and perspective are as enigmatic as he is. They are at the same time simple and complex, divinely inspired yet ruggedly imperfect. There are still some subjects that he likes to advocate—issues not necessarily fully-thought-through, for which he has yet to apologise.

During the two days we were at Ocala to meet Don, he had gone from talking about "your book", to "MY BOOK", which I accepted as a compliment. As we left, Don took my shoulders, and said with tears, "When we walk up to the white throne of Jesus[72] there will be crowds of souls on either side, looking on, cheering. If just one of them is there as a result of your book it will have been all worthwhile". My goose bumps signalled the end of an incredible two days. We embraced and shared a moment of manly passion.

---

[71] Don Garlits, *Close Calls*.
[72] This he had earlier described in great detail as being made from solid wood, as seen in a vision he had experienced.

Persistence Wins

The difficult relationship Don had with his father Edward was possibly due to Edward's many esoteric and loudly-proclaimed atheistic beliefs. When his parents divorced, Edward remained on a farm property at Seffner (that Don later inherited), running a small welding and engineering business. Edward's name does not crop up much in Don's several autobiographical books, other than to say that he borrowed money from his dad from time to time. While Don and Pat were living in Detroit, Edward was critically injured. (A drunk crashed head-on into Edward's car, hospitalising him, and causing Don to urgently visit his father in hospital.) Don recounts this episode in his book, *Close Calls*, as being a crisis in their relationship. With remorse, Don admits he was afraid to discuss his Dad's mortality and need for salvation. When the news came, a week after Don had returned to Detroit, that his father had passed away, He was grief stricken. Compounding the grief was his shame at not broaching Edward's readiness to meet his Maker.

Years later, Don was talking with a Seffner realtor, Mr Moore. Moore had befriended Edward and visited him many times (including when Edward was in hospital just before he died) to discuss atheism and other matters. To Don's surprise, Mr Moore mentioned a conversation he had with Edward in hospital, when he enquired about some beautiful flowers by his bedside. Edward explained that the flowers were from his "brothers and sisters" at the local Baptist church. (Don's brother Ed, had encouraged them to visit his father.) This news astounded the realtor who remarked, "I thought you were an atheist". To this Edward replied, "I used to think that way, but ever since I've been in hospital and had to lie here, I've had time to weigh everything back and forth. I've been reading the Bible some, and I have realized how wrong I've been all these years.

Don Garlits. The Enigmatic Hero

I know that the Lord did do just as it says, and I've accepted Him". "The next day, he was dead", Mr Moore concluded.

Garlits recalls that he was overcome with emotion to realise that God cared enough to "reach past me into my father's life, before it was too late". Don's fondest hope for his father was fulfilled, despite his reticence to confront his and his father's fears. As Edward Garlits faced the unknown at the end of his life, so we must face ours. If we acknowledge the reality that "God has placed eternity in our hearts", then we should agree with the Teacher's conclusion when he says, "Now that all is said and done, here is the end of the matter, Fear God, and keep his commandments, for that is the whole duty of man".[73] Regardless of what we have achieved in life in absolute terms, we are ultimately assessed for what we have done with what we were given. We are each accountable for ourselves, to the One who made us and loves us.

> This is what the Lord says—
> your Redeemer, the Holy One of Israel:
> "I am the Lord your God,
> who teaches you what is best for you,
> who directs you in the way you should go.
> If only you had paid attention to my commands,
> your peace would have been like a river,
> your well-being like the waves of the sea.
> Your descendants would have been like the sand,
> your children like its numberless grains;
> their name would never be blotted out
> nor destroyed from before me." – Isa 48:17-19

---

[73] Eccles 12:13.

(GARLITS COLLECTION).

Chapter 12 Alter Ego

"Remember your Creator in the days of your youth, before the days of trouble come and the years approach when you will say, 'I find no pleasure in them'"
– Eccles 12:1

The Siren Call

   Do you recall when you first heard the sound of a racing engine? Was it calling you, like the mythical virgin Peisinoe who called sailors to their doom on the rocks of their desire? I have many childhood memories of this experience and later, when traveling in Europe with my wife Elaine, before we had a family. She wanted to see the castles that represented the history she so avidly read. I made a bee-line to visit the Formula 1 Grand Prix events at Brands Hatch, located in Kent, England; then to the German Grand Prix at Nurburgring, in the Eiffel mountains, south of Cologne; and to Monza, Italy, to witness what I had dreamed of all my life. Happily, we were more or less able to combine the two interests. As we approached Brands Hatch, we could hear the ascending scream, the "Pop...Pop" descent of Ford DFV and the more mellow, basso profundo of Ferrari Formula 1 racing engines that were already on the track for practice. My barely-suppressed anxieties rose while we were stuck in traffic as, despite my urgings, we had not left London in time to catch all the action. Later, in Italy, at the Monza Autodromo, we camped within the race track so I could listen to cars competing in local events at all hours of the day and night. Four years earlier, while honeymooning on the Queensland Gold Coast, I took my new wife to the drag races at the Surfers Paradise International Raceway, to watch American drag racer Steve Carbone, race his "Soapy Sales" Top Fuel dragster against local cars. After all these years, Elaine, as she reads these words, has only just begun to realise why I waxed lyrical about the ground-shaking noise and the nitro fumes burning our eyes.

As I describe the intersection of my experience, ambition, motivation, vocation, religion and spirituality, it is clear, and I confess to having-motor racing heroes as alter-egos. Having been aware of Don Garlits as a motor-racing hero since my teenage years, I was interested to know why he displayed the cross and *God is Love*, on his dragster. I tell this story because both Don Garlits and I claim to have found that life is very satisfying—life with faith, hope and love; with good relationships, and a sense of peace and joy.

What Counts for Success?

It could be that I have embarked upon this book as a supreme effort to vindicate my otherwise-pathetic life. Not so. Because, in spite of my not being wealthy or particularly successful in business or any other of the usual measures of worldly success, I have achieved what I set out to do. I am the husband of my first love, the father of three adult children that I love and who, with their partners, seem to love me, plus four grandchildren, who are the best evidence I have ever seen of God's grace made manifest in my life, or for that matter, any other life I have seen. I know people who have been very successful in business, who are wealthy and powerful, but the most successful of them say the same thing as I do. Their greatest success and pleasure is in their family. Their creative and responsible work is important, but it does not compare with loving and being loved by those to whom they have committed their lives.

I became most aware of God's grace when my first grandchild, Chase, was born and when he started to relate to me watching steam trains on YouTube. Since Chase, Hamish, Taylor and Sara were born I have become more aware of God's grace in every aspect of my life. It is trite to say that I am blessed. I could not imagine being any more blessed, or fortunate than I am. My life is far from perfect, but God has been very good to me and I am very proud to say that I am a son of the Most High. My Christian Brethren heritage emphasised a protestant doctrine known as "the priesthood of all believers" (also shared by some protestant, evangelical traditions). This idea is based on 1 Peter 2:9, "...for you are a chosen people. You are royal priests, a holy nation, God's very own possession. As a result, you can show others the goodness of God, for he called you out of the darkness into his wonderful light."

As a theologian I am unqualified. But I write as an opinionated hotrodder, on good authority from the great theologian Karl Bath, who declared that, "all believers must be theologians". As we have seen, hotrodders are amateurs who attempt to make a machine of mundane origins perform like a thoroughbred and so much the better if the contradiction is also visual. My qualification as a hot rod theologian is that I think an old, broken down mechanic can respond to Divine inspiration and effectively flourish.

Don Garlits. The Enigmatic Hero

In 1956, as a 10-year-old, I watched Murray Carter, a local panel beater with an oxy torch and a plumb bob in hand. From the home we shared with my grandmother, I could see him building his Chevrolet Corvette V8 special sports-racer chassis in Suhr's Bus Depot. Carter was a true pioneer of racing-car design in the Australian tradition of home-built specials. Having previously raced an XK 120 Jaguar and wanting something better, he designed and built the car in his spare time, between maintaining bus bodies. Carter created the tubular steel frame to his own design with fully-independent suspension patterned on Holden parts, intending to use a 134-cubic-inch, "grey" Holden engine—a scaled-down version of the overhead valve Chevrolet six-cylinder "stove bolt". When he heard that he could buy a Chevrolet 283-cubic-inch Corvette V8 from Boyanton Motors (the local Holden dealer), Carter bought one, along with a "Muncie" four-speed gearbox, to create his record-breaking "Corvette special". The unpainted, hand-made, aluminium body went through several evolutions until it finally became the well-balanced shape of a contemporary masterpiece.

This is my earliest memory of an encounter with a racing car, that I replicated almost 50 years later, by building my own sports racing car, using the same methods as I had seen Murray Carter use. (About 30 years later, when Carter had become a motor-racing identity competing in the Australian Touring Car Championship in his Ford Falcon V8, I mentioned that my memory had motivated me to a career as a mechanic and aspiring race car builder. His amused but serious reply was to warn me, from experience, about the perils of being seduced by racing cars.) In nearby Brewers Road, Bentleigh, neighbours Ray Tucker and the Curtis brothers, built less-sophisticated,

Alter Ego

Ford V8 speedway jalopies and hot rods in the streets and driveways of their parents' homes. The presence of these cars in the street always had a slightly sinister feel. This impression was confirmed and burned into my memory when Ray Tucker, with Gary Curtis riding as passenger, pulled up alongside my push bike at the intersection of Brewers and Jasper Roads, with the loping *thrump* and noisy tappets of a multi-carburetted, full race sidevalve V8 engine in his channelled 1935 Ford coupe hot rod. To my delight, and perhaps for my benefit, Tucker performed the most awe-inspiring, smoking-tire burn-out ever seen by an impressionable young boy. From my family home, I could hear the sound of racing engines on Jack Wilson's dynamometer about a kilometre away. This was the siren call that led me and my schoolmate, Allan Coombs (aka "Coombsie"), to peer down the driveway of his workshop, before we worked up the courage to venture further to source the noise. Far from us founding on the rocks, Jack took pity and invited us in to watch engines being tested and cars being built for the road racing greats of the 1960s era, including Norm Beechy's early and late-model Holdens, his 409 Chev Impala, and later, his black 350-cubic-inch Chevy Nova coupe. Wilson's garage was also home to Len Lukey's stable of cars, including a Cooper Bristol open wheel racing car and his big red 406-cubic-inch V8 Ford Galaxie sedan. Before race meetings, the Cooper Bristol would be towed around the block (including our street) on the end of a rope, to bed-in new brake linings. Nearby, Max De Jersey worked in his family engineering business and after hours built Australia's first drag race cars. Around the corner from Coombsie's house, in his backyard garage, Lloyd Pedrick, a mechanic who had previously worked at Suhr's Bus Depot, built and tuned racing engines for his own and his customers' speed boats. Lloyd was always ready to stop work and have a smoke while he talked racing-car talk to teen-aged boys, perhaps in the hope that we might become customers (which we ultimately did). Directly across the road from our house lived Bob McKinnon, a service station owner who had rebuilt a Vauxhall E-type 30-98, that in 1923, was the fastest car in Britain. Fervent pestering convinced Bob to start up the Vauxhall and to take us for a concessionary 100-mph ride down Brewers Road in his Mk 7 Jaguar sedan. Next door to Bob, lived Bruce Heymanson, founder of Eurovox Car Radios, who also took us for hair-raising rides in his hotted-up 1954 FJ Holden. Across the street from Bruce, was a guy with a modified bug-eye Austin Healey Sprite, who used the intersection outside our house to practice his high-speed cornering techniques. And next to him was Noel Penrice, who had a collection of English car magazines, the aroma of which remains in my olfactory archive. What hope did I have? I had entered the dark world of high-compression pistons, and I was hooked.

Guilty Pleasure

As a 12-year-old on a family holiday in Sydney, I was given an allowance of five shillings, all of which I spent on a *Hot Rod* magazine. I still get the same guilty, pleasurable feeling today when I make a similar purchase of the British MotorSport magazine (I now subscribe to *Hot Rod* online) to feed my car addiction. According to Sigmund Freud, there is an unconscious, impulsive, childlike portion of the psyche that operates on the "pleasure principle" which is the origin of our basic impulses and instinctual drives that he called the id. The id is the source of our primary motivations and our energy, constrained only by our moral sense, that he called the superego. Both forces

Alter Ego

combine to become our ego, which moderates the two competing forces. Freud compared the relationship between the superego and the id to that of a charioteer and his horses. The horses provide the energy and drive (id), while the charioteer provides direction (superego). Brighton Technical School taught us the basics of academic essentials plus the far more useful skills of sheet metal work, machine shop practice and carpentry. *Hot Rod* magazine became the source of everything really important and worth learning. Visits to the library left me bringing home the same hot rod books and magazines each visit, most of them published in California. So, Freud's theory of the ego seems to be true in my experience. My school reports from 1962 say that I was "a keen responsible lad" who topped my class level. I assume that meant that my superego had already kicked in to restrain some of the things that I envisaged. My sense of responsibility tempered my imagination, which was active to the extent that my grandmother called me a liar, (which was true). Regardless of Freud's theories and whatever our sources of motivation, we are creatures of our time and place. And there we create a mental list of priorities that we look to accomplish as freedom allows. Not that I thought of myself as capable of high achievement. Proficient at building billy-carts with Coombsie perhaps, but not a disciplined student by any stretch of the imagination. Coombsie's dad, Russ, occasionally took us boys to Tracy's Speedway to see the action on Saturday night. He also built a speedboat in his garage at home to be used for circuit racing in Albert Park Lake, where the Melbourne F1 Grand Prix is now held each March. The boat was powered by a highly-modified, Ford Falcon engine that was dyno-tuned by Jack Wilson. Wilson, who was killed by his exploded dynamometer when testing a racing engine, produced a son, Craig Wilson, who was a small child when his father died. (I am fascinated that Craig went from being a motor mechanic, to being a leader in several motor racing and engineering businesses; he is now the head of the world-leading, UK engineering business, Williams Advanced Engineering [one of the stable of companies created by the Formula One owner, Frank Williams]. I am further intrigued that the guy who first employed Craig as a mechanic was Dave Bennett, who sold Murray Carter his Chev Corvette engine when was the parts manager at Boyanton Motors where my dad worked.)

My family regime of church on Sunday provided a restraining force that meant attendance at the car or boat races was a clandestine event, until I went to work for PBR, where attending race meetings was part of the job. (PBR was part of the Repco group that built Jack Brabham's F1 World Championship winning V8 engines.) I admit that childish passions should not intrude into adulthood, which it did and still does (thankfully less so as the years go by). My attitude toward Bible interpretation was acquired during my early teenage years from a dentist, John Messer. John was leading a youth Bible study in which he asked, "How should we resolve apparent contradictions in our literal understanding of scripture?" John's answer was, "Keep reading...", looking for unity and consistency in the major themes of scriptural Divine revelation. I have taken this advice ever since, as I have continued to read scripture erratically, to my immense comfort and understanding of paradox and irony (with which I find scripture to be heavily-punctuated) and to stimulate my understanding of history and reality. This position allows me, in good conscience, to not always defend a literal view of revelation that I do not understand. I am happy to wait a long time until my mind catches up with my experience. A good example of this has been the difference between the *letter of the law* and the *spirit of the law*. I am inspired in a dynamic relationship with Jesus, the Living Word, as he gives meaning to the words on a page.

Yours truly as a cool, jazz, bass cat during the late 1960s and with my beautiful Elaine, the love of my life (MILLS FAMILY COLLECTION).

European Adventure

Our European adventure in 1974, was our usual combination of sacred and profane interests. We visited castles, museums and race tracks, but we also went to sit at the feet of the great Christian theologian/writer/teacher Francis Schaeffer, who had written several impenetrable books that young Christians often carried around with them. He did make a big impression in person though, as did tapes by Os Guinness that we listened to and discussed during our stay. Schaeffer's wife,

Don Garlits. The Enigmatic Hero

When I announced that my first car was to be a Model A Ford Tudor, my dad insisted that it should be a far more-practical machine; an MG TC powered by a 2.0-litre Triumph sports car engine—a hot rod with an English pedigree. This car gave me plenty of experience with engine rebuilds, broken gearboxes, clutches, differentials, and axles. It was great fun teaching Elaine to drive. She thought every start had to be a burn-out (MILLS FAMILY COLLECTION).

Edith, had written a thoroughly understandable book called L'Abri, about the center and the work they had established in the village of Hu'emoz, in the Swiss Alps. We turned up in our MG GT fastback only to find no room in the village for camping or accommodation. So, we camped on a farm up the mountain. Years later, I am still coming to grips with Schaeffer's writings, which still seem very important to repeatedly ponder.

Some are born great, some achieve greatness, and some have greatness thrust upon them. – William Shakespeare

Greatness, however we may judge it, is never just nature or nurture. It is a constant mix of both that diminishes or enhances natural attributes and creates new abilities born of opportunity

Alter Ego

A much younger and thinner 19-year-old at work in PBR Experimental department doing what I have always loved to do—design and construct things, usually with an automotive theme (MILLS FAMILY COLLECTION).

and encounter. My experience is, that our instinctive drives are sparked by our senses of sight, smell, sound, creating and imagined world that we either occupy or wish to occupy. Most of us though, have other priorities or perhaps, if we miss the cut when greatness is handed out, we live vicariously through our heroes—imagined or real. We may think of ourselves as lemmings rushing to our destruction as helpless dupes of our own desires, lured by Satan. But to the contrary, theologian Walter Wink, describes our compulsions as essential elements of our humanity—aspects of our souls that need to become conscious and redeemed if possible. (Otherwise, our compulsion is indeed, dark and evil.) "Transformation comes not through denial and repression of our evil, but by naming it, owning it and lifting it up to God. To face our own evil as courageously as we can; to love it into the light; to release the energy formerly devoted to restraining it; and to use the energy for the service of life."[74]

Alter Ego

Living vicariously through our heroes, who do what we dream of, creates our alter egos—the self we wish for. Whether this is healthy or not cannot be resolved in these flimsy pages, but we can observe the effect that Don Garlits had upon me. We have alter-egos because we don't have the opportunity or the ability to become what we idolise. This is both regrettable, if we pull back from an achievable challenge, and understandable, if other realities stand in our way.

---

[74] Walter Wink, *Unmasking the Powers*, 40.

Alter Ego

My projects have usually incorporated my current responsibilities (in this case, my 3-year-old son Brock) with some automotive theme. This is a very elaborate billy-cart with a high wing designed for pushing up hills before a hair-raising, gravity-powered, down-hill trip to follow. I later fitted a two-stroke engine for Brock to drive the car to his first day at kindergarten (MILLS FAMILY COLLECTION).

Regrets, I've had a Few.........

At age 68 (now 73) my inclination is to say, "Regrets, I've had a few...", but they are nothing by comparison to the fullness and joy of life I have experienced. To put it more poetically, *le joie de vivre sentiment exaltant ressenti par toute la conscience*, which is to say in Australian, "No worries mate". I have been self-employed for most of my last 30 years. At one stage I bought a business from PBR, renaming it "Warren Mills Friction Dynamics", to reflect the products and services related to brakes and clutches that I supplied to everyday customers, and to the motor-racing fraternity. But I suffered anxiety with my self-image as a mechanic. I wanted to be something that, in my mind's eye, was unclear. In the second part of my working life I have become a trainer and consultant to the automotive service industry, specialising in developing and providing management systems for quality, environment and safety. Today, I continue to provide services to farm-machinery dealers, as, unaccountably, I continue to love tractors and machinery. At some stages I have been quite financially successful, at other times not so. My conclusion is, that I have not been sufficiently interested in business, or sufficiently good at it for that matter, to make it my life's work. Looking back, I see that I have actually been a student of ideas, with a bit of an entrepreneurial streak. I am also a trainer whose job is to explain difficult concepts to successful people, which is what I am doing as I write these words.

Success is the achievement of what we have set out to do or to become. My successes have been small in number, but they have been very satisfying. My automotive and spiritual compulsions have been strong enough, that they are still compulsions. This is why, 30 years after first envisaging the title of this book, I am now writing it. Whether this results in anything more than my pleasure remains to be seen, although just the act of writing has its own satisfaction. Of far greater importance, though, is the peak experience of my life—my love for my wife Elaine. This this is the most powerful, most energizing force I could ever imagine. It almost seems too mundane to make this statement, but try as I might, I cannot imagine any achievement worth exchanging for what I have enjoyed with her. I recently read that the actor, Shirley Temple Black died at the age of 85. Outrageously successful as a child, she retired from movies at age 21 to marry. She later became involved in politics with several diplomatic postings, including US Ambassador to Czechoslovakia during the collapse of the USSR, in 1989. Despite all the successes of her life, Temple rated her family life with her late husband of 50 years, John Black, as her greatest accomplishment. She is on record to say, "My role as a wife, mother, and grandmother is the greatest thing. True love, there is nothing like it". My heroes have lives that I would not and could not want to live, nor would I want to exchange my life for theirs. Relationships are many and varied, relating to circumstances, time and place; the work we have done, where we have lived, the people we have met, the friends we have made. But as Elaine keeps reminding me; as we began with just the two of us, so we live life now; just two people, sharing hopes, interests, a house and family...and some regrets, but not many.

Love is Risky

Having tasted love, I know that it is good. Like a beautiful flower, I need to gaze at its beauty. Enjoy but not possess it. Because love is fragile and easy to destroy. I am painfully aware, from the experience of many friends and family, that an investment in love is risky. But, knowing what love is and what it can become, the risk is worth taking if we can protect, rather than possess the object of our desire. Lovers' anticipation and early hopes for the delights of relationship are quickly brought into sharp focus by the realities of life. Each incident beyond the early blush of romance is a crisis, although it may seem insignificant at the time. Each crisis is an opportunity to learn, (to crash or crash through), especially if we are insensitive brutes, as many are in our early years. Each breakthrough, each step gained, each crisis overcome, is a brick in the wall of life that takes a lifetime to build. I agree with Shirley Temple Black that there is nothing better in life than love that endures. I believe that true love lasts forever and leaves no regrets. Many of my generation have squandered their freedom for what they imagined to be a *new experience,* or *to understand myself or to be understood and appreciated for being myself,* or *to escape the oppressive rules of society,* particularly the judgements of those with religious inclinations. God's rules are not intended to harm us, or to spoil our fun. Nor are they to make us judgemental, ever. They are like the maps that a ship's captain slavishly uses to keep his vessel and crew off the rocks of destruction. The captain's ship is his kingdom, for which he is responsible. I am the captain of my ship. I am the master (for the most part), of my destiny. This has been my great fear; knowing what the good life is, that I could run aground.

I find it hard to conceive a more vain or meaningless statement than, "I'm here for a good time, not a long time". This implies that a brilliant but momentary flash of light is better than a small, steady, illuminating glow. The nature of love is that it takes a long time of learning and trusting to be experienced, as against hoped-for. Love based only on hope, comes with no guarantee. Its risk requires the same input from the other person, as from the instigator. When given freely, love endures for successive generations, perhaps for eternity. When not given freely, its consequences are felt immediately and into successive generations. Consider the benefits of love: encouragement, enjoyment, trust, sexual pleasure, and meaning given to the cycles of meaninglessness. Opposite to love is indifference, (not hate, as there is some passion and energy in hatred). Indifference is despair personified. Vacant eyes. Morbid gloom. Pointless, merciless, graceless desperation. Anathema. What are the alternatives to love? Perhaps power. If so, for what purpose? Maybe money. Can you ever have enough? How about status. I am sure the pigeons will be pleased if you become a statue. Sex for pleasure? Please, it was good while it lasted, but we are talking about things that have some hope of enduring. Work, comfort, leisure? Solomon didn't think so.

"You Wouldn't Be Dead For Quids"

"Quids" is an old, Australian expression for money. Roughly translated, it asks the rhetorical question, "What could be better than this?" Or, in this case, "What could possibly be better than your own kids?". The answer is, "Their kids, of course!". This joy was predicted by Solomon when he said, "When two lie down together, they become three.", and then, "A cord of three is better than a cord of two".[75] Wise man, that Solomon.

Does Racing Improve the Breed?

Motor racing is an intensely selfish sport. It is often justified, perhaps disingenuously, by the saying, "racing improves the breed", that is, *evolution of the common good is achieved by competition*. A study of acceleration and competition would prove the point—drag racing being the obvious choice of subject. My thesis is that motor racing does not need some sort of high moral value to be worth doing. Providing it proves beneficial rather than harms the common good, then it is justified on the basis that men and women are highly motivated to do it.[76]

---

[75] Ecclesiastes 4:11,12.
[76] In the same light, my wife accuses me of being inclined to take on difficult

Grandsons are always going to be spoilt by grandfathers, aren't they? This car is very advanced with two battery-powered electric motors; regenerative, dynamic braking; aluminium chassis and body; with wash tub aerodynamics (MILLS FAMILY COLLECTION).

The Promise

The prophet Isaiah makes God's promise to Abraham very clear: God, who created us, knows what is best for His own creation and teaches us with his commands (if we will would only listen). It is clear from this text that we have a choice. If we choose not to accept the Lord's commands and teaching then we deprive ourselves of righteousness, peace and joy. Joy, in this case, is what we experience as the result of our offspring being numerous—each one bearing their heritage that will never be destroyed. While it is true that this promise is made to the

---

tasks with limited prospects of reward, so I have told her that I am trying to prove her right.

Alter Ego

nation of Israel, it also has a very practical application to each of us. My friend Wally Beattie, says that grandchildren are our reward for not strangling our own children during their teenage years. This is a slightly different appreciation of the promise made by God to Abraham. Speaking for myself, the promise of offspring being a blessing had to be experienced to be fully appreciated. The birth of my first grandchild, Chase, was a greatly-anticipated occasion. Following the years of parental despair and angst while enduring our children's teenage years, it was truly amazing to see the three of them become adults, partners, wives and husband...and then parents. Our amazement was that they had become lovely, responsible people who had now reproduced themselves. It is not just the miracle of birth that is breathtaking. It is that the new creation of my flesh and blood has just smiled at me for the first time. When Chase began to crawl, he would come to my office to help me bash the computer keys. To divert him, I found a YouTube clip of a popular, narrow-gauge steam train called Puffing Billy, that runs in the Dandenong Ranges, near Melbourne. Chase soon became obsessed with Puffing Billy, especially after he and I spotted a bigger version from our 13th floor window, seemingly for his benefit. Elaine and I followed up these sightings over the next few months by taking Chase to the nearby Southern Cross Station, to see the trains, and to Belgrave, in the Dandenong Ranges, to ride in Puffing Billy.

What a joy! Our lives were transformed by an 18-month-old, who became the one person we wanted to spend time with. The subsequent arrival of Hamish, Taylor, Sara, Josephine and Ella has meant that our joy has been multiplied by six. This was a revelation for which only Wally Beattie had prepared me. Our experience of grandparent-hood is, amongst many other things, a vindication of every aspect of the faith, hope and love that we invested for our children. Of course, there are many satisfactory alternatives for those who are not married or who have no kids of their own, but for me (and Wally), being a grandparent is easily the most fantastic experience of my married life.

Weird Science

The words of truth are always paradoxical. – Lao Tzu

Blessed are the poor in spirit. – Jesus

I have for many years been interested in paradox, mainly because it is how Jesus often spoke. It is interesting to me that philosophers often use the same language (or at least they do when they are really trying to explain things, rather than trying to make themselves appear clever). It is even more interesting to learn that much of scientific discovery is also paradoxical, such as light being both particles and waves. Many discoveries of science are counter-intuitive to the extent that Albert Einstein initially rejected the concepts of quantum mechanics, with his statement, "God don't play dice". Paradox seems to me, to be an inherent characteristic of the Divine mind, as His ways are not our ways. His ways are only able to be received by faith; faith in his goodness, his kindness, his grace and his mercy. This is an unacceptable obstacle for many people who reject the possibility of one, seemingly capricious God, who is the Supreme Authority to whom we are all accountable. People much prefer to be accountable only to themselves, or some, lesser deity.

Who Inspired You?

Writing this chapter has made me aware of the incredibly rich legacy I have inherited from my parents, encouragers and

Alter Ego

alter egos. I wonder whose alter egos we will leave behind for the next generation? Will they be filled with hopeful, passionate, life-giving motivation? Or will our legacy be more rules? (As we are being told the environment heats up, so principles and inspiration appear to have dried up.) Will it be prophecy or pornography? Hope or hatred? Destiny or despair? I hope our legacy will be more of Winston Churchill than of Adolf Hitler; more Bill Gates than Mark Zuckerberg; more Don Garlits than Lance Armstrong; more Jesus than Peter Singer.

Who put the bomp in the bomp bah bomp bah bomp?
Who put the ram in the rama lama ding dong?
Who put the bop in the bop shoo bop shoo bop?
Who put the dip in the dip da dip da dip?

Who was that man? I'd like to shake his hand
He made my baby fall in love with me

When my baby heard bomp bah bah bomp bah bomp bah bomp bomp
Every word went straight into her heart
And when she heard them singing rama lama lama lama lama ding dong
She said we'd never have to part

Well, who put the bomp in the bomp bah bomp bah bomp?
Who put the ram in the rama lama ding dong?
Who put the bop in the bop shoo bop shoo bop?
Who put the dip in the dip da dip da dip?

Who was that man? I'd like to shake his hand
He made my baby fall in love with me

> – "Who Put The Bop In The Bop Shoo Bop". MetroLyrics.
> I think I know who did it. It was God.

Chapter 13 The Final Chapter

"Whatever your hand finds to do, do it with all your might, for in the realm of the dead, where you are going, there is neither working nor planning nor knowledge nor wisdom."
– Eccles 9:10

Garlits' Vision

Workshops are noisy places. Especially when a new project such as building a dragster is in full swing. It is a cacophony to the senses; voices over the background of cutting, grinding, banging and welding; often with the added, dramatic effects of smoke and fire, bright flashes of light and the smell of paint and oil. There is another contrasting time that workers savor—when work is done for the day, or the next morning before work recommences. The craftsman can be alone with his thoughts, to inspect what has been accomplished with secret pride and anticipation of the next stage of work, when the creation takes its final shape, ready for action.

Garlits was alone, looking at his new car (this time painted blue, not black) in anticipation of a sponsorship deal with the Navy. He recalls, "The idea of displaying the cross on my dragster came to me when I was alone in the workshop one night after the new car had been freshly painted. I was looking at it and all of a sudden I just envisioned a cross on the cowl, ... it would be a good way to give God recognition for all the times...[my] life had been spared..."[77] This was an act of unconventional brilliance, the sort of alternative thinking for which Garlits was famous. An innovation, not of technical genius inherited from his father, nor of gritty determination against all odds. In fact, it was more likely inspired by his devoted life partner. Garlits' cross was an exposé of his previously-unseen advantage, a revelation of his growing passion for the arcane and numinous reality beyond himself. This was Garlits at his Swamp-Rat-best, declaring the significance of another dimension seemingly at odds with his sport. On the one hand, this was the consummate racer of the Wile E. Coyote school, looking to out-run the Roadrunner with whatever dastardly contraption he could dream up. On the other hand, this is a devotee following Jesus' mysterious challenge, to "be as wise as a serpent and as harmless as a dove".[78] This was Garlits on the cusp of an intuitive moment of inspiration, when he would make a decision that would change his life in ways he could not anticipate. Don had been in this place before. Sometimes he seemed to be on the outside of his life looking in on an unfolding catastrophe over which he had no control. On other occasions, he would be making decisions with far-reaching personal and financial impact on the family's security. (Such as the time he and Pat discovered the future site for the museum—for sale at exactly the amount of cash they had available. Or when Pat gave him a leather jacket to wear instead of a T shirt, just before the supercharger exploded and engulfed him in flame.) Sometimes there are moments of inspired revelation when we see on another level, not just to gain an advantage for ourselves. This is the world of faith, the substance of what we hope is true.

---

[77] Chapter 7.
[78] Matt 10:6.

The Final Chapter

"GOD IS LOVE" and the cross painted on America's top dragster are, at the very least, a clash of cultures if not a contradiction. They beg the age-old question, "What has Athens to do with Jerusalem?"[79] Or a more cynical version of the question, "What has the swaggering, machismo, risk-taking world of drag racing got to do with a weak religion whose god was killed off by a mob?".[80] Significantly, Jesus resolved the secular/spiritual divide. He acknowledged both when he told his disciples, "...give to Caesar what is Caesar's, and to God what is God's."[81] This was not just an accommodation to worldly power. It was Jesus' insistence that there are two realms—one earthly and secular, limited to time and space and another spiritual and eternal—both significant and essential to human flourishing. This was a radical departure from earlier Greek and Hebrew theologies which sought to ascribe legitimacy to God alone. Or to the material age in which we now live, where the only reliable and authoritative things are those that can be measured and manipulated by people. To his disciples' surprise, Jesus stated plainly that secular and spiritual realms overlap and co-exist. We continue to live in the overlap between these two kingdoms—the Kingdom of God (which is both *now and not yet*, where God's sovereignty is represented by the statement, *God is love*), and the secular world (represented by the cross which symbolizes the limited power governments have, to kill those that threaten them). Don Garlits was acknowledging

---

[79] Tertullian of Carthage, Wikipedia.
[80] The contrast between Athens and Jerusalem prefigures the chasm between science and religion, or the secular world of political solutions and an idealized, spiritual world. Many modern children of the enlightenment have dispensed with Jerusalem altogether, claiming to have no need for Richard Dawkins' "imaginary friends".
[81] Lk 20:25.

his own solution to this dilemma (within the limits of human experience), by declaring his ultimate accountability to God. This was no illusion of his imagination as he had experienced both in the same moment. He had endured the awful reality of an inferno of hell in his face at 170 mph and the mocking demons of excruciating pain in every nerve of his body for days on end. Despite, or indeed, because of these events, he trusted in God, because his spiritual encounters were as real as any other experience of his life.

Once again, Garlits was breaking new ground, as far as motor racing was concerned. Previously only a small number of sportsmen (including Ab Jenkins with his Mormon Meteor, Bonneville land speed racer and the champion British runner, Eric Liddell, who refused to race on Sunday), had publicly integrated spirituality with their career. Such an audacious declaration of faith required an explanation. But Garlits was secretive as usual. Competitors speculated that this was just another Garlits' ruse to create attention. Shirley Muldowney scoffed, "I guess Garlits is looking for the big sponsor in the sky". This was, perhaps, ironically true, as the US Navy immediately reneged on a sponsorship agreement unless he remove the offending words and motif. (Garlits refused their demand and went on to win more than $600,000 prize money with this car.) Although many decried his mixing religion with sports, they had no idea how deep and complex was his motivation.

The Power of Love

It is love that believes in the resurrection. – Ludwig Wittgenstein

As we have seen, drag racing is the science of harnessing power. An engine converts chemical energy from fuel into heat and then into power. Power is a function of torque and engine speed, which must be controlled to not exceed the adhesion available between the tire and the road as it converts power to kinetic energy (measured by the acceleration and speed achieved over a distance). This is a balancing act of many elements including technology, cost, safety, reliability and the repeatability required to win races. More power alone is useless, unless it can be harnessed within these restraints. This is true of every form of power. It must be harnessed to be useful. All human uses of power must be restrained and moderated by love for which there is no limit. Love re-directs our use of power back toward others so that it is not selfishly misused. Even so, we must define love in terms of its highest form—God's agape love—because we know that unrestrained self-love is not love at all.

Garlits has been driven to his knees many times since becoming a Christian in his teenage years. His prayers were sometimes for an opportunity or a competitive advantage. But now they are increasingly expressions of gratitude. Garlits became more conscious of insights, of many successes, and of narrow escapes he had experienced.[82] This time, however, Garlits' public reveal went beyond thankfulness or rat-cunning. Together, the words and the cross signify profound insights into the Judeo-Christian faith that set it apart from all other creeds and religious claims. In their Biblical context, they proclaim God's overwhelming love that required his surrender on a cross for our salvation for the sake of him being reconciled with his own creation.[83] This unprecedented act of God's love was fulfilled, when three days later, Jesus was resurrected.

---

[82] Don Garlits, *Close Calls*.
[83] Jn 3:16.

This launched the new, life-transforming, cosmic reality for the whole of creation. It is now possible for all humanity to be reintroduced to their maker. Desiring the highest good for us, who are made in his image, God made this life-transforming power of his resurrection available as a free gift of love. Our acceptance of this gift is expressed as an act of faith in a mysterious symbiotic relationship that becomes: *Christ in you, the hope of glory.*[84] This fulfills the secret of the ages unprecedented in human imagination, theology, or experience. And it is this stupendous, improbable truth that Garlits chose to publicly affirm.

Drag-racer Theology

Simple workmen have been able to convince of error those great men that are called 'philosophers'. It was...these unlearned men...who were most ready to believe what they saw with their eyes and touched with their hands. – Blaise Pascal

This is a story about the tension between spiritual and secular kingdoms in the lives of ordinary people. A story about resolving apparently conflicting motivations in everyday life—a challenge that has defeated many great minds. Even gurus in philosophy and religion struggle with life and its contradictions, though they might maintain a professional façade. Neither brains nor sentiment provide a solution. What is required is simple faith. When fully-formed, faith is a passionate belief that God will redeem us. Faith is the hope that God rewards those who seek him. Faith hopes not just intellectually or emotionally, but with a commitment of the whole

---

[84] Col 1:27.

The Final Chapter

self—body, soul and spirit—to walk a path where thoughts, words and deeds are aligned with truth and human passion.[85] This is a picture of an integrated person, like Don Garlits, who gambles his life on hope in God—God who loves him enough to die for him. The text from Ecclesiastes at the head of this chapter is restated by Paul in Colossians 3:23, *Whatever you do, work at it with all your heart, as working for the Lord, not for human masters.* Perhaps Garlits had heard a preacher telling of God's delight with diversity within his creation, but I doubt it. He was usually too busy racing for such abstractions. More likely is, that Pat considered these verses about God's delight in human skill (women are often better at such profound insights) to then encourage Don's passion for creativity, power and competition. Regardless, Garlits did what he did for his own reasons, needing no further confirmation other than Pat's encouragement.

Don Garlits is not my hero because he is a great theologian. To me, he is a hero because he is a racer who expressed life's dilemma writ large on his dragster. What a perfect canvas on which to display the apparent dissonance between sacred and profane. It can be hard to identify with conventional spiritual heroes and their saintly reputations. Take Saint Patrick who drove the snakes out of Ireland, or Dietrich Bonhoeffer, the theologian who resisted Adolf Hitler only to be executed by him. Martin Luther, Billy Graham, Mother Theresa—all rare and sacrosanct—these saints do not relate easily to young men and woman consumed with a material world. Garlits, however, *is* relatable. His unpretentious beginning as a poor farm boy from a broken home is a story commonplace to many. He had no deeply-religious education. But he was willing to take life

---

[85] Heb 11.

by the neck and strangle the deepest possible meaning and satisfaction out of every situation that came his way.

Hero-worship, under the guise of mimetic theory, was popularized by a French Roman Catholic academic, Rene Girard, to become known as the ethical system of mimetic desire. Girard believed that *human development occurs initially through a process of observational mimicry, where the infant develops desire through a process of learning to copy adult behaviour, fundamentally linking acquisition of identity, knowledge and material wealth to the development of a desire to have something others possess.*[86] Desire, reinforced by our rational will and personal attitudes, is a powerful force at the heart of all human motivation. It is strongest when it involves our most basic physiological and instinctive drives such as food, drink, sleep, relationship and sex. Christian faith seeks to simplify and channel our motivations and desires into areas that are life-giving, rather than life-depriving. In fact, the Bible's ethical standards are predominantly about the benefits of controlling our desires to ensure that we are not totally selfish. The outcome of this is a transformation from selfishness to a fulfilling life of engagement with others, for our common good. Christianity is often misrepresented as a long list of *thou shalt not* instructions designed to spoil the fun we could otherwise enjoy. On the contrary, the Christian message properly understood, calls us to "hunger and thirst for righteousness"; to pursue right relationships with God and our neighbours for the mutual benefit of enjoyment, adventure, discovery, excitement and achievement.[87] It is here that I see the life of Don Garlits gain some focus of heroic proportions.

---

[86] Wikipedia.
[87] Matt 5:6.

The Final Chapter

"I'm Not Who You Think I am"

Garlits is an enigmatic pragmatist who is always busy with his next project. Even today he is attempting to set the world record for electric dragsters, travelling to nostalgic cackle fests (where old dragsters are lined up, stationary, with flames leaping out the exhaust pipes), promoting the sport, collecting guns and studying alien life, while being a proud American who lives life to the full. Initially, it was Pat's influence that converted her new boyfriend from outlaw-street-racer, to family-man, touring-Top-Fuel-dragster. Later, as an established champion with a business to run, Don was motivated by the need to keep the wheels turning and the money coming in. Common to champions was his competitive bent. He needed to excel. To prove he could out-think, out-engineer, out-work, out-drive, out-smart and out-last his opponents. Circumstances and opportunity combined with breeding and primal instincts that led him to fulfil what seemed to be a destiny, a calling, and a title, confirmed by the name Big Daddy.

Early in my correspondence with him, Garlits' lack of pretension took me by surprise. He refused any suggestion from me that he was any sort of spiritual hero. As if to prove his point, when we first met at his museum in Ocala, his first order of business was to burst my bubble with a full-frontal attack reserved for sycophants, like me. Religious people who wear our religion too seriously, need to be brought back to reality and to be reminded that we are all sinners in need of a savior.[88]

---

[88] This is a tough lesson that has taken me many years to learn: that we humans are fatally flawed and victims of our own sins (what Calvinists call Total Depravity, in overstating the case). As a foil, we instinctively justify ourselves to protect our credibility at all costs, especially when confronted by other mere mortals, whose sins are all too obvious. Even when reminded of

...humans are not called to a cool, detached appraisal of the world, nor to a self-indulgent grasping of it, but to a delighted exploration, in which respect and enjoyment go together. – N.T. Wright[89]

Garlits had enough knowledge of the Bible to accept its promise that *God rewards those who seek him*. He put the cross on his car because his childhood faith spawned the possibility that the Bible is true. When he accepted it without question and applied it, he found it to be reliable, leading him to take the risk time and again, to trust God at his word. One of these risks was to choose Pat Beiger as his girlfriend. When I interviewed him, he was raw with emotion. Pat had passed away a couple of years earlier. He spoke of her last days, then reminisced back to the time they first met. "She was a good Christian girl from a good family," Don said. "No sex, or anything like that," he added, (in contrast to girls who would perform favours to be popular). He frankly admits to transgression and strain in their marriage when women would offer themselves to him while he was away for weeks at a time. But more notably, he knows that his experience of righteousness is irreplaceable. He asked Pat and God for their forgiveness, which was freely given. While he does not celebrate his imperfections (nor should we) he does seem to subscribe to Martin Luther's suggestion to; "Sin boldly, and love Christ all the more". This is refreshing in a world of

---

our status before God, we naturally think, *yes, there is much wrong with thee, but not so much with me*. Then, we are reminded that *...we are forgiven, by God, according to how we forgive others*. (Matt 6:9). I believe that this oft-ignored insight is a major thrust of the teachings of Jesus and the basis for our relationship with God. Before we can begin to help others, we must confess our own need for God's help to overcome our own self-righteousness narcissism into a life-long, self-aware process of transformation. *How Good is the Golden Rule*, Warren Mills, (Freedom Publishing).

[89] *Loving to Know, First Things*, (February 2020).

self-righteous virtue where high ideals are often confused with reality. As a couple, Don and Pat's faith was not just a matter of going to church for its religious form and ritual. It was a non-conformist, authentic exploration of applying confidence in God with daily life. Nor does Garlits' concept of God reside in the magnificence of cathedrals or in the study of ancient books. He engages with the real world of time and space. God is in the smoke and fire of the dragstrip. Garlits' faith is deeply undergirded with an encounter of the eternal, all-powerful, intelligent, personal being that brought about creation for his and our shared pleasure. I'm not sure if God delights in the pleasure and excitement of drag racing, but I do know that he loves people who love drag racing.

Who Says So?

"I've won the world championship for the National Hot Rod Association three times, but I could not get by one single day without Jesus Christ in my life!" – Don Garlits.

"I try to make Christian principles a working part of my life, and the better job I do, the richer, fuller, and more satisfying my life becomes. God has made our success possible, and we want to be an example of a life committed to Him." – Drag racer, Eddie Hill.

"I surrendered my life to Christ at the early age of 10 and have since experienced the joy of the Christian walk. My goal in every endeavor of my life is to allow Jesus Christ to be seen through me." – Drag bike legend, David Schultz.

"Knowing Christ as my Lord and Savior and that He paid for my sins is overwhelming and assuring. Because Jesus Christ is my Lord, my strength, and my counsel, I can know the love and grace of God, and the purpose for my life." – five-time IMSA Champion road racer, Al Holbert.

"My life has been filled with too many coincidences for me not to consider God. Becoming a Christian has been a gradual, never-ending process. I could never make it to Heaven if the admission price had not already been paid by Christ." – Canadian drag racer and school owner, Frank Hawley.

"Ayrton Senna's ability and record as a champion are not a matter for debate, but his methods and his relationship with God sometimes were; "I try to pray and to talk to Him please to show me the way of life, to give me some sign, some light some understanding. Opening the Bible, He is immediately there, giving me, talking to me about what I was asking, giving me the understanding.""

"Likewise, Formula 1 champion Lewis Hamilton is unembarrassed about his mixing Christian faith with his competitiveness and his glamorous lifestyle. Ahead of the Formula 1 season in 2012, he told the BBC; "You have to remain hopeful, you have to believe there is a plan. I believe God has a plan for me. I don't know what it is." Asked if he felt God's plan included staying at McLaren, Hamilton laughed and said, "I don't know. I ask him every day and he has not told me yet. You'll know when I do." – Quoted in an article in Australian motorsport newspaper," *Auto Action*, date unknown.

"As I've got older and matured for sure I'm somebody who has been blessed by an immense amount of good fortune and I spend more of my time thanking God than I do asking for God's help." – F1 champion, Jackie Stewart.

The Final Chapter

"Anything worth doing requires faith." – Eight time NHRA Top Fuel champion, Tony Schumacher.[90]

Is Don Garlits Someone We Should Emulate?

The irony of Christian faith is that progress is never measured by the sacrifices that we make or what we have to give. It is never determined by how important, religious, wealthy, clever or how successful we are. On the contrary, our success may make progress as a Christian less likely and more difficult. The "better job" that Eddie Hill mentions is the same thing that Al Holbert refers to when he speaks of "knowing the love and grace of God", and Frank Hawley's "never ending process, where the admission price has already been paid". Progress along the supernatural chain is always and exclusively about how much we are willing to receive as a free gift of God. It is how weak we realize our own souls are, that enables us to add link to link, to following Jesus. Becoming a strong soul is a journey that commences and ends with an admission of need. And some of these needs may not be realized, regardless of how long we live.

..Jesus was a prophet who came into the world not to confirm the mighty in their seats but to exalt the humble and the meek... – Arnold Toynbee

A Foretaste of Paradise

The idea that we come to resemble the object of our worship, is deeply-embedded in the teachings of Jesus. In particular,

Jesus' commands that we love God to the exclusion of all other gods, and that we "hunger and thirst for righteousness".[91] As I reflect on how heroes like Don Garlits have influenced me, I wonder, were my choices well-made? Am I deluding myself? Am I dealing with reality or just my imagination? Could I have chosen better than I did? It is wishful thinking to try to be wise in hindsight. But a time comes in each of our stories when we begin to write the final chapter; when we reap what we have sown; when the fallout of our choices overshadows the opportunity to make alternative choices. This reflective event is bound not chronologically so much as by opportunity and choice. The inputs that have shaped us come to fruition as outputs that cannot easily be changed. In my case, this moment of realization was the birth of our first grandchild, when I was 64. This happy event roughly coincided with a series of reverses in my business. I no longer had the energy to recover the losses incurred. Not that this was all bad. I was happy to slowly reduce the scale of work, to maintain existing customers, and enjoy using the car I had built. A grandchild ushered us into a new era of unanticipated pleasure when, for hours, Elaine and I would gaze at him on Facetime, then drive the 40 km to pick him up for overnight stays. Such a watershed required some reflection, especially to explain my new enthusiasm to friends who had not yet shared this experience. Above all, I had a new appreciation for the fruit of enduring, intimate relationships. What began out of ordinary passion between Elaine and me was now fulfilled. Before we had children, we were a couple of random people who decided to share the adventure of life. The birth of our children strengthened this bond because they were flesh of our shared flesh. Certainly, we celebrated our

---

[91] Matt 5:6.

kids' development, their choice of partners and their weddings. That they recognized our marriage as something to emulate gave us great pleasure. But becoming Nana and Pa to six grandchildren has given us more to talk about and enjoy than any other achievement. Our grandchildren, who are also flesh of our flesh, have integrated us into a complex network of life-creating-life. I am a member of a growing extended family of in-laws in which love is realized. This is a foretaste of paradise.

Imitating God

Hebrews 11 has a list of Biblical heroes to which I would like to add Don Garlits. I read the Bible as the story of God's creative exploits, interactions and relationships with his creation. But it is not just about God's great success. It also describes his disappointments and regrets. Heroes of scripture all too often have their moments of failure. Although the Bible commences with optimism and pleasure where God expresses delight in his handiwork, paradise is short-lived. Almost immediately, people created in his image, use their freedom to transgress the limits God asks them to impose on themselves. This scenario is played out many times in scripture as a warning against our presumptuousness when we make the same mistakes. Mistakes we make such as the Tower of Babel where we think we can reach up to God instead of responding to his existing offer—his reaching down to us.[92]

---

[92] Gen 11:1-9. When I read these and many other Biblical accounts of God's relationship with men and women, I am aware of his disappointment that things didn't work out as he intended. "How can this be?", I ask. Although God can control all the elements and can do with them what he will, he does not. He restrains himself. His reason for self-restraint has to do with making men and woman in his own image. He grants us freedom to choose

As the story unfolds, time and again, God's sorrow and preparedness to negotiate with humankind is recorded in scripture. We read of his dealings with Noah, Abraham, Lot, Jacob, Moses, Jonah and others with whom he desires a relationship. Finally, in a masterstroke of self-restraint, God turns to His Son, Jesus, whom he knows to be reliable because of the love they share as the triune God. The Father knows he can trust his Son to the point of death, so, in order that the world might be reconciled to God, the Son is obedient to His Father. The New Testament then takes the notion of holiness to a new level, advocating that, because are we made in his image, we should voluntarily imitate Jesus Christ[93] and to "...follow in his steps."[94] Furthermore, the apostle Paul urges us to "...become imitators of us [the apostles] and of the Lord...".[95] God has set the seemingly-impossible challenge of imitatio dei—imitating God. This indeed, is the highest possible form of mimicry and hero worship. We imitate God. We are holy as he is holy.[96] Biblical logic considers this is a perfectly reasonable idea. We should desire to return to our original state—in the image of God who made us. We are designed to voluntarily become sons and daughters of the Most High by acceptance of his grace.[97] "As I have loved you, so you must love one another.", says Jesus. "By this everyone will know that you are my disciples, if you love one another."[98] Then Jesus prays. "...Father, just as you are in me and I am in

---

for ourselves in anticipation that in the New Creation we might share his image and motivations, as does his son, Jesus.

[93] Matt 10:38; 16:24; Lk 14:27.
[94] 1 Pt 2:21.
[95] 1 Thess 1:6.
[96] 1 Pt 1:16.
[97] 2 Cor 6:18.
[98] Jn 13:34-35.

you... [may] they also be in us so that the world may believe that you have sent me."[99]

Choose Life

My soul is restless until I rest in Him. – Augustine of Hippo

If I had told you that the Don Garlits' story was a neatly packaged example of Christian rectitude, designed to show him as a hero who ticks all the religious boxes and always goes to church, prays and reads his Bible in between happy days working on dragsters, I suspect you would not have believed me. If I had told you this, you would not have read this far because the book would make you feel sick. A story that results in a trouble-free, happy and successful life of fame and prosperity is an image that my friend Paul Vander Klay, a pastor from Sacramento who interviewed me about this book on his YouTube channel calls "Bullshit Christianity." (Big Daddy Don Garlits and the Christian Life. https://www.youtube.com/watch?v=YmS4-uQ5yJ0) Nothing could be further from the truth of Don Garlits' life, or mine. The story of relationship between us and God, and each other, is by necessity, an untidy struggle. This will be fully realized when we look back after we become what we were designed to be—creatures remade in God's image to love him and enjoy him forever. We will see that our inconsistencies are an essential part of being honest about who we are and what we are supposed to be. The greatest use of our human freedom is to use it to test its boundaries, then to restrain our use of it and employ our motivations, energies and abilities in creative life-giving ways that align with God's purposes. If we

---
[99] Jn 17:21.

are honest, it is obvious by looking no further than our own lives that each of us is a sinner with the same need of a savior. *None is perfect*, says the scripture, *No, not one.*[100] Nor will we ever be perfect during our allotted place in time and space. The universal nature of human sin is the best evidence of the Bible's claims of our need to be reconciled with God for which the cross of Jesus is the only antidote available. The message on Don Garlits' dragster is to choose life because God's love makes this choice possible. If you can see that Don Garlits' enigmatic life, or someone like him, has made a difference to you, then celebrate their influence on you. But don't stop there. If you aim as high as possible, then you will allow Jesus to influence you to become like him, because what he says is true and can be authentically tested by you.

---

[100] Rom 3:10.

Sunset en route to Ocala (MILLS FAMILY COLLECTION).

Epilogue

Don Garlits' Tribute to Patricia Garlits

Dear Pat,

    I couldn't have accomplished the things that I did without the support of a loving wife, like Pat Bieger. I met her in May of 1952 during her Senior year at Hillsborough High School in Tampa Florida, I had graduated from the same school in 1950, but we had never met. A year later we were married and stayed married till she passed away in 2014, just 18 days short of 61 good years! She supported my racing from day one, when I won my first trophy at Lake Wales with my "Bone Stock" 1950 Ford Tudor Sedan, in 19.20 Seconds, and she supported me when I made my last Top Fuel run at the 2003 US Nationals, Indianapolis IN, at 310.81 mph! We raised two wonderful Daughters, the youngest, Donna Garlits is now running the Drag Racing Museum and Hall of Fame, while the eldest, GayLyn Capitano teaches piano at the College of Central Florida, plus has her own music school and she also plays for the Ocala Symphony Orchestra. Pat was a wonderful housekeeper, company comptroller and soul-mate, we did everything together for over 62 years! She was very good with money, as we were both "Depression Babies" and knew the value of a dollar, something missing with the current generation. She was the driving force behind the Rear Engine Dragster, as I had given up on the design after going out of control over 20 times at the Orlando Strip. She in no uncertain terms demanded that I return to the project, which we did, discovered the glitch and the rest is history! In 2000, she was diagnosed with Parkinson's Disease and over the years it got worse. I spent the last five years at her side, here in the home we built together in 1984, with her two Yorkshire Terriers at her side. She died in my arms with a smile on her face as we listened to Glen Miller play "Moonlight Serenade". Her two daughters were here along with

Don Garlits. The Enigmatic Hero

her sister, Sharon Keppel and GayLyn's daughter, Anna Capitano. She suffered a lot during the final days and we all prayed that God would take her, and He did. We will all join her sooner than we think! Rest in peace my beloved!

Don Garlits
September 2014.
From an email from Don Garlits to Warren Mills, September 2014.